"Too often scholars and policymakers [ ] lectual silo, divorced from a state's larger strategic behavior and grand strategy. The preeminent historian of nuclear weapons in the world today, Frank Gavin, singlehandedly corrects that mistaken approach in this masterful volume, arguing that, for the United States, its nuclear strategy is part and parcel of its grand strategy—its larger geopolitical aims and its approach to providing security for itself and the world. If you want to understand how we got here and where we might be headed, this book belongs not on your shelf, but on your desk."

—VIPIN NARANG, *associate professor of political science, Massachusetts Institute of Technology*

"As we approach the seventy-fifth anniversary of Hiroshima and Nagasaki, Gavin's essays challenge both policymakers and scholars to reexamine the conventional wisdom about what has kept the nuclear peace. His work is a cautionary and timely reminder that nuclear weapons remain one of the most consequential and dangerous features of the twenty-first century security landscape, which we neglect at our peril."

—JAMES B. STEINBERG, *professor of social science, international affairs, and law, Maxwell School of Citizenship and Public Affairs, Syracuse University*

"This important and fascinating collection of essays provides a wide-ranging, critical examination of what we do and still don't know about nuclear deterrence. Drawing on masterly archival work, Gavin illuminates our understanding of nuclear weapons, which haven't been fired in anger since 1945, yet play a major, often underappreciated, role in world politics and grand strategy. The book demonstrates that if we want to prepare for the future, we also have to grapple with the past, and it provides essential analysis for doing both."

—CAITLIN TALMADGE, *associate professor of security studies, Walsh School of Foreign Service, Georgetown University*

NUCLEAR WEAPONS
AND
AMERICAN
GRAND STRATEGY

FRANCIS J. GAVIN

BROOKINGS INSTITUTION PRESS

Washington, D.C.

Pictured on the front cover is a nearly four-hundred-year-old white pine bonsai that survived the atomic bombing of Hiroshima. It was gifted to the United States National Arboretum in 1976 for the American bicentennial by Japanese bonsai master Masaru Yamaki as a symbol of friendship between the two countries.

The Brookings Institution is a private nonprofit organization devoted to research, education, and publication on important issues of domestic and foreign policy. Its principal purpose is to bring the highest quality independent research and analysis to bear on current and emerging policy problems. Interpretations or conclusions in Brookings publications should be understood to be solely those of the authors.

Library of Congress Cataloging-in-Publication data are available.

Library of Congress Control Number: 2019953031

ISBN 978-0-8157-3791-9 (paperback : alk. paper)
ISBN 978-0-8157-3792-6 (ebook)

9 8 7 6 5 4 3 2 1

Typeset in Sabon

Composition by Elliott Beard

To Natalie, grand strategist

CONTENTS

Contents

PREFACE

Nuclear weapons haunt U.S. grand strategy like a long-rumored ghost in a large house: invisible, silent, occasionally terrifying, potentially deadly but all but forgotten on a day-to-day basis. Worries that loose fissile materials will fall into the hands of terrorists or that so-called rogue states will develop a weapons program sporadically find their way into the American political and policy consciousness. Most of the time, however, other concerns, with louder constituencies—from climate change to trade to regional instability to the return of great-power politics—overshadow the nuclear question in discussions of America's role in the world. While these are all critically important concerns, nuclear weapons could end life as we know it in an instant. Rarely is there a vigorous public debate and discussion of such a vitally important question: What role do nuclear weapons play in the United States' grand strategy?

This disparity is puzzling for several reasons.

First, the United States has spent enormous sums of money on nuclear weapons and the sprawling infrastructure that supports them and is poised to spend much more in the coming decades. Competition for government funds, both for national security and domestic priorities, is fierce. Given these costs, to say nothing of the unthinkable consequences of nuclear use, one would expect a more robust debate over what nuclear capabilities the United States purchases, for what purposes, and in service to what strategies. Second, the United States has gone to great lengths and is likely to continue to inhibit the acquisition of independent nuclear weapons by other states, a goal that shapes its nuclear posture. Third, these strategies of inhibition have been a key driver of many of the far-flung U.S. alliances and security commitments that began during the Cold War and have expanded and deepened in recent decades. At a time when many critics believe our grand strategy is overextended, or that we need to do more to counter the rising power of China and Russia, the relationship between America's alliances, inhibition, strategy, and nuclear posture demands greater understanding. Fourth, many of these inhibition-based alliances and security arrangements either explicitly or implicitly rely on the promise by the United States to do something horrific and hardly believable: threaten to and if necessary use nuclear weapons to defend its allies. What would American decisionmakers do if called on to satisfy this extraordinary pledge? This terrible prospect has haunted American grand strategy for decades, of course, but for a variety of reasons, the credibility of U.S. nuclear commitments is rarely discussed with the seriousness it merits. Fifth, to the extent that the role of nuclear weapons in American grand strategy is debated, the arguments often pull in two opposing directions: analysts either highlight what they see as the centrality of nuclear deterrence to achieving America's goals in the world or promote the need to rid the world of the scourge of the bomb. The United States, both in its rhetoric and its grand strategy, has at times managed to hold both of these seemingly mutually incompatible positions.

These issues are of fundamental importance for both the future of the international order and America's role in it. This book is an effort to place the nuclear question back where it belongs: at the center of debates over past, contemporary, and future U.S. grand strategy. It is also a meditation on the deep challenges faced in trying to ask and answer questions about nuclear weapons.

My previous book, *Nuclear Statecraft*, examines and recasts the history of America's strategies with nuclear weapons. Building on research in declassified government materials, it challenges much of our received wisdom about the nuclear past. The present analysis provides a better and more accurate understanding of the origins and evolution of U.S. nuclear strategy and thinking about the bomb. The process of researching, writing, and publishing the book, however, generated new questions and puzzles, which I set to answer in this study.

The most important question that emerged involves method, or how we, as scholars and policymakers, make and assess claims about the role of nuclear weapons in foreign policy and international relations. When I began *Nuclear Statecraft,* I was not a member of the nuclear studies field per se—my first book was a history of postwar U.S. international monetary policy—but rather a historian of American foreign policy and international relations who followed the documents where they led. My book became part of a large and growing literature on nuclear weapons, and its positive reception introduced me to different intellectual communities who went about their research in a much different way. Much of this work was smart and engaging, if sometimes perplexing.

The work in nuclear studies took varied approaches. Some scholars relied on parsimonious theories about international relations to explain the consequences of nuclear weapons. Others applied formal models or employed statistical analysis. Still others' work seemed to blend description with prescription. And regardless of the approach, authors appeared supremely confident that they were right. They also believed that their insight should be embraced and employed by the government officials responsible for overseeing nuclear weapons policy. This caused me to reflect on and analyze the different approaches to thinking about nuclear weapons, including theoretical, statistical, and historical. Much of this book reflects my efforts to make sense of nuclear weapons, to present not simply competing claims about them and their consequences but also competing methods by which to answer and arbitrate crucial questions.

I also wanted to better understand what I found to be subtle, even sub-rosa connections between grand strategy and nuclear weapons, linkages often overlooked in otherwise impressive books on both subjects. Nuclear weapons were often analyzed as a distinct subject and phenomenon, to be studied in their own right, separate from and even driving other political considerations. This way of looking at nuclear weapons seemed strange, and it was certainly not the way policymakers thought about them, as the documents revealed. Even within nuclear studies, subjects appeared unnaturally hived off from one another, as research in nuclear proliferation and nonproliferation and that in nuclear strategy rarely engaged each other. The grand strategy and foreign policy literature also suffered from the same problem, minimizing, misunderstanding, or ignoring nuclear dynamics when explaining U.S. policies and behaviors. It struck me that no meaningful discussion of the political effects of nuclear weapons could take place without understanding the larger drivers of American grand strategy. Similarly, no debate over the U.S. role in the world would be complete without consideration of the central role, both explicit and implicit, the bomb plays in how and why the United States acts as it does in the world. Bringing nuclear studies and grand strategy in conversation with each other was another driver of this book.

The chapters that follow explore the questions, challenges, and consequences surrounding how American decisionmakers have thought about nuclear weapons and integrated them into their grand strategy, often in ways that are surprising and poorly understood. They also reflect on the efforts by scholars from various methods and backgrounds to understand these issues, and they suggest ways to bridge both the gap between different disciplinary backgrounds and the academic policy divide. Five interconnected ideas are of particular importance.

First, this book challenges how much we think we know about the connections between nuclear weapons, grand strategy, and international politics. Many of the most important issues surrounding nuclear weapons are too often treated, incorrectly, as settled. Some questions, I suggest, are unanswered and should be explored further. For example, why did both the United States and the Soviet Union appear to believe that nuclear superiority, well short of an unreachable and dangerous first-strike capability, was worth enormous effort and would provide tangible geopolitical benefits? Does the United States continue to seek such superiority? What is it trying to accomplish with these capabilities, and how will its strategy affect the nuclear decisions of other states in the world? Our current stock of theories does a poor job of answering these questions.

There are other questions we thought were answered but deserve reexamination: For example, is strategic nuclear arms control always stabilizing? Can we meaningfully distinguish between compellence and deterrence when looking at America's nuclear policies in the past? What is a nuclear crisis, and what does it mean to "win" such a contest? Other important issues—such as the politics of nuclear proliferation and nonproliferation—may have suffered from the way scholars have framed and investigated the questions. Finally, other questions of fundamental importance are more difficult to answer than we have been willing to acknowledge because of the very nature of nuclear weapons and grand strategy. Truth be told, we cannot conclusively demonstrate how nuclear deterrence works, however vehement our claims to the contrary. Our analysis would be far stronger if we were to adopt the humility that recognizes the understandably speculative nature of many of our assumptions about nuclear dynamics. The relationship between nuclear weapons and American grand strategy is far more unsettled than is understood. We need to vigorously scrutinize the intellectual architecture we inherited from earlier strategists and be willing to scrap well-worn received wisdoms if they fail to fully explain the world as it is, as opposed to the world strategists expected.

This relates to the second big theme of the book: How should we assess the causal claims made by scholars and policymakers about nuclear weapons, American grand strategy, and outcomes in the world? Academics use a wide array of methods and theories to explain and predict how nuclear weapons should shape policy and world politics. In doing so, they often tell stories about what they believe to be America's nuclear history. Similarly, advocates and analysts assert a variety of arguments—often with great certainty—about topics ranging from deterrence to disarmament. These debates, in both scholarly and policy worlds, are often contentious. They also reveal, explicitly or implicitly, underlying causal assumptions about how people believe nuclear weapons shape and are shaped by politics. How should we evaluate these claims and make sense of often polarizing positions on nuclear weapons? A variety of impressive social science methodologies—from archival research to game theory to statistics to international relations theory—are used to bolster and strengthen these claims. Are these methods the right tools with which to answer these important questions, and are they being applied in the best ways? A recurring intent of the chapters that follow is to remind ourselves we are all historians of an event that never, thank God, happened: thermonuclear war. Many of the important nuclear policy debates rely on largely unproveable assumptions about why this event has not taken place, despite great fears and predictions. Understanding important events in the world is extraordinarily difficult; explaining, aggregating, generalizing, and predicting from a phenomenon that never took place is close to impossible. Given the vital importance of keeping this nonevent streak going, however, we must do our best, with the limited tools at our disposal, to understand nuclear policy and politics.

Fortunately, many smart people are trying to understand the consequences of nuclear weapons. A third theme of the book, however, is to identify where scholars are separated and intellectually stovepiped and to suggest strategies for overcoming these gaps. Advocates of deterrence, for example, rarely encounter enthusiasts for disarmament. Scholars from the United States do not engage as they should with a burgeoning global literature. Political scientists publish important work on nuclear studies that is rarely incorporated into the work of historians. Even among political scientists, there are deep methodological divisions: scholars who exploit statistical applications or formal, game theoretic approaches and those who use a more qualitative approach often ignore each other's work. Nuclear weapons involve scientific, technical, legal, and moral issues, and scholars from the physical sciences, engineering, law, and social sciences such as sociology and anthropology have made important contributions. Yet these groups rarely participate in meaningful exchanges with one another. The obvious answer is for these communities to come together, but as this book suggests, the unique issues surrounding nuclear weapons—methodological, normative, even the very language we use—makes this a daunting task.

The biggest divide, however, is that between policymakers and scholars. On any number of issues, from how worried we should be about nuclear proliferation to the benefits of nuclear superiority, the worlds of national security decisionmakers and the ivory tower are far apart. These disagreements reveal profound differences in how each group assesses risk, probabilities, and the unintended consequences of choice. Policymakers could learn much from the scholarship on nuclear weapons, but academics would do well to better understand and empathize with the world of national security officials. Decisionmakers confront difficult, consequential choices, facing an unknowable future, trapped by both domestic and international constraints, facing "51-49" problems where the odds of success are little better than the flip of a coin. This reality is all the more challenging when making choices about nuclear weapons, where the costs of being wrong are enormous at best and unthinkable at worst.

How can these gaps—between different disciplines and, most important, between scholars and policymakers—be effectively bridged? This is the fourth major theme of the book—that nuclear weapons are best understood through a lens of grand strategy. The scholar Rebecca Lissner observes that grand strategy is the "why, how, and for what purposes states employ their national power, including the crucible of military force. For policymakers, grand strategy defines a nation's international role, guides the alignment of means and ends, and serves as a lodestar for discrete foreign policy decisions." The bomb must be understood first and foremost as a tool states use to achieve their interests in the world. This may seem like a commonsense approach, but it is rarely followed, albeit for understandable reasons. Nuclear weapons have transformed international politics since 1945, although precisely how and in what ways remains a matter of debate. Furthermore, to use these weapons against another state would, by almost any measure, be a failure of grand strategy. Nuclear weapons are often studied as something apart from the tug and pull of politics, a force to be studied in isolation. According to our leading theories, the very power of the bomb takes away choice, especially on matters of war and peace, that has defined strategy and statecraft before 1945.

Nuclear weapons explicitly and implicitly shape every aspect of American grand strategy. The United States relies on nuclear weapons to deter attack, protect allies, inhibit proliferation, and coerce adversaries. Even when nuclear weapons are not explicitly engaged, their presence forms the background of America's goals and ambitions in the world. Nuclear weapons and U.S. grand strategy are inextricably interwoven in ways we sometimes forget. A policy of restraint or offshore balancing, for example, might lead to increases in the number of nuclear-equipped states in the world, with undesirable or threatening results. An overreliance on nuclear weapons, however, could have similar consequences.

This leads to the fifth and perhaps most important theme of the book. American policymakers have confronted—and will continue to face—many consequential choices about nuclear weapons, and the role of the bomb in grand strategy has by no means been obvious, predetermined, or path dependent. Looked at with fresh, open eyes, past choices made about how to incorporate the bomb into U.S. grand strategy have often been contingent and strange. Nothing was inevitable about why and how the United States made nuclear weapons the critical component to its ambitions in the world. Many of its policies, from adopting strategies that envisioned early and massive use of the bomb to its extraordinary efforts to inhibit independent nuclear weapons programs, were surprising, and outcomes were by no means certain. Understanding and assessing those choices—and evaluating, to the extent possible, alternative paths not taken—is crucial. The same should apply to other nations and their decisions with nuclear weapons, choices that have been and will continue to be made by balancing an array of variables, from the danger of the international system to the national interests and ambitions to the history and culture of the state in question. As scholars, we must balance the power of concepts and theories to help us understand a complex world with the recognition that there is no one-size-fits-all explanation for nuclear behavior.

The book can be read in order or according to chapter of interest. The first chapter identifies the key questions surrounding nuclear weapons and statecraft that are either unanswered or should be re-examined. It also highlights the stove-piped nature of the nuclear studies community. Chapter 2 assesses the debate over nuclear proliferation, focusing on the question of whether the spread of nuclear weapons is stabilizing or dangerous. Chapter 3 critiques the use of quantitative methods to understand the purpose and role of nuclear weapons. Chapter 4 chronicles the crucial and underappreciated mission in American grand strategy of inhibiting the spread of nuclear weapons. Chapter 5 connects the development of aggressive United States nuclear strategies to the unique puzzles surrounding the defense of West Germany in the early days of the Cold War. Chapter 6 provides a typology of all the complex and at times cross-cutting roles and missions nuclear weapons have performed in U.S. grand strategy since 1945. Chapter 7 explores the promise and difficulties of undertaking a history of the nuclear age. Chapter 8 looks at the rewards of capturing the benefits of both nuclear deterrence and disarmament. The final chapter lays out the deep, persistent challenges surrounding nuclear weapons and American grand strategy, while warning of new, emerging problems that will return the nuclear question to the center of debates over American grand strategy.

This book may frustrate some readers. Much of it has been published elsewhere, albeit with revisions and in such a wide array of outlets it would be hard to imagine that anyone not related to me has read all (or even half) of the essays included. I am grateful to the editors and publishers for allowing me to reuse this material. It is also written in a hard-to-define style; not quite history, not quite political science, not quite policy analysis, yet borrowing elements from all three. At times, it takes a hard approach on important scholarly contributions to nuclear questions. At other times, I ask more questions than I answer, lingering over the same questions and episodes in the hope that one more look, one different perspective can provide the elusive answer. My main hope is that these ideas, taken together, will encourage others to pursue the important questions about nuclear weapons that remain unanswered and will vigorously challenge and examine those we believe are settled. A variety of factors, from technological to moral to geopolitical, will make the nuclear question more important than at any time in recent history. Given the stakes and the difficulties of understanding nuclear weapons and American grand strategy, my hope is that, collectively, we can find better answers to these consequential questions.

ACKNOWLEDGMENTS

Soon after I finished my previous book, *Nuclear Statecraft*, I had several fortuitous interactions that made me realize how much more I needed to learn about nuclear weapons. First, Christian Ostermann and Leopoldo Nuti invited me to join the Wilson Center's Nuclear Proliferation International History Project (NPIHP), which holds an annual "Nuclear Boot Camp" in Allumiere, Italy. I have taught in several boot camps and participated in a number of NPIHP workshops since 2011, and I have learned an enormous amount from my fellow teachers and especially the smart graduate students from around the world. Second, I am grateful to the Massachusetts Institute of Technology's Security Studies Program and Liz Allison for recruiting me to become the inaugural Frank Stanton Chair in Nuclear Security at MIT, which among other things exposed me to the work of the impressive Stanton fellows during the foundation's annual conference. Third, and most important, in 2012, I began collaborating with a whip-smart Harvard graduate student, Jane Vayman, to create a program that brought together scholars from different intellectual traditions, perspectives, and generations to support exciting new work and build a network of nuclear studies scholars. Dr. Vaynam now teaches at Temple University but is still my partner in crime in the Nuclear Studies Research Initiative (NSRI), and we are grateful for the generous support that the Carnegie Corporation of New York and the John D. and Catherine T. MacArthur Foundation continue to provide.

I have benefitted enormously from the support of my wonderful colleagues at the University of Texas, MIT, and the School of Advanced International Studies at Johns Hopkins University. I am particularly grateful to the staff, scholars, and affiliates of the new Henry A. Kissinger Center for Global Affairs, which I have the distinct honor to direct. Invaluable research assistance was provided by Lena Andrews, Jessica Mahoney, Timothy McDonnell, Cecelia Panella, Reid Pauley, and Will Quinn. In addition to the ideas and scholarship from the many NPIHP, Stanton, and NSRI scholars I have learned from over the years, I want to especially thank Mark Bell, Hal Brands, Elbridge Colby, Colin Kahl, Ryan Evans, Michael Horowitz, Robert Jervis, Rebecca Lissner, Austin Long, Julia McDonald, Nick Miller, Vipin Narang, Joshua Rovner, Jim Steinberg, Marc Trachtenberg, Steve Van Evera, and Phil Zelikow.

No thinker had more influence on the writing of this book than Janne Nolan. Janne was a mensch and a mentor of unsurpassed grace, intelligence, glamour, and kindness not only to me, but also to scores of others. I miss her terribly.

Much of the work in this book appeared elsewhere in different forms, and I want to thank the Academy of Arts and Sciences, the Cato Institute, H-Diplo, *International Security,* the *Journal of Strategic Studies, Texas National Security Review,* Princeton University Press, and Yale University Press for allowing me to reproduce the work here. William Finan and his terrific team at the Brookings Institution Press have been a pleasure to work with.

I am very fortunate to find love, wisdom, and support from three extraordinary women: my daughters Olivia and Catherine and my wife Natalie. As my friends and colleagues know, Natalie is both the brains and the heart of the operation, and I could not be more thankful. It is to her that this book is dedicated.

ONE

History and the Unanswered Questions of the Nuclear Age

How much is known about nuclear weapons, foreign policy, and international relations? The bomb has been a presence on the world stage for eight decades, and an extraordinary amount of intellectual and institutional capital has been expended in an effort to understand why states do or do not seek nuclear weapons, how they deploy these weapons to achieve their aims in the world, and how and in what ways they influence war and peace. The scholarly legacy is mixed. While much has been learned, deep and often bitter divides remain, not only over the answers to key questions but also over the assumptions and methods that frame our work.

These issues are not simply a concern of the academy. Nuclear studies is an area in which policymakers and scholars have long been intertwined, sometimes enthusiastically, at other times warily, but often with great consequence. Acknowledging this relationship is especially important today, as new nuclear crises emerge and international consensus on the nuclear order dissolves. The United States, the prime driver of nuclear dynamics since 1945, currently finds itself at an important crossroads, pulled in two mutually exclusive directions, between disarmament and deterrence. Nuclear studies can and should play a role in these debates, though only after the United States acknowledges its own struggles to make sense of the bomb and its consequences.

This chapter revisits the core questions that have animated nuclear studies from the very beginning while laying out the challenges that have prevented consensus. One overarching issue, however, pervades the research on nuclear weapons: why nuclear weapons have not been used since 1945.[1] This question, the taproot of all other queries on the subject, is hard to answer with full confidence. While rarely acknowledged, the very nature of the nuclear revolution makes certainty elusive. Acknowledging this epistemological challenge, however, may help provide the humility and perspective necessary to generate insight and craft better policies.

What have been the intellectual contributions of the nuclear studies community? On the one hand, scholars and policymakers have been fortunate to be in the midst of what has been called a renaissance in nuclear studies, within both political science and international history.[2] The passage of time, the opening of new archives, and the deployment of new methods have all contributed greatly to current understanding.[3] Let me provide three important examples. First, in the last decade, scholars from around the world have exploited new sources to increase understanding of nuclear decisionmaking in a wide variety of states. The list of new states with nuclear ambitions includes Brazil, Germany, Iran, Israel, Italy, Japan, Pakistan, Romania, South Korea, and Sweden.[4] This has led to a second crucial development—a deeper, more nuanced understanding of nuclear proliferation. In the past, states were coded as either nuclear or nonnuclear.

This new scholarship, however, has called into question this binary categorization. Terms such as *recessed deterrent, threshold state, nuclear reversal, latency, hedging,* and *opacity* describe what might be thought of as a spectrum of nuclear outcomes that are historically and politically short of a full-blown survivable nuclear deterrent.[5]

The notion of who is "nuclear" and what that means is more complex than previously understood. Finally, there is a greater sense of the lengths the United States has gone to, with both foe and friend, to slow, halt, and reverse the rise of new independent weapons states.[6] This work has gone far in undermining the grand bargain conventional wisdom surrounding the nuclear nonproliferation regime by highlighting the willingness of two bitter Cold War enemies to collude in preventing proliferation.[7]

Work on these and other subjects has been impressive, and more is being produced all the time. Yet I sometimes fear that less has been learned than might have been hoped for and, in some senses, we are spinning our wheels. I see two reasons for this. The first has to do with what questions scholars are asking. Much of the research assumes the most important questions—the core issues on which its assumptions rest and on which the research is built—have already been answered, when in fact they have not.[8] Second, steep but often unrecognized methodological challenges prevent scholarship from getting good answers. This includes not only the disciplinary gaps between history and political science and the theoretical, qualitative, formal, and quantitative divides within the international relations subfield; more important, it also includes challenges in the very nature of how scholars study and think about nuclear weapons.[9]

As a scholar who interacts with both the history and international relations field, I want to use this opportunity for reflection. Frustratingly, I can offer no answers, only more questions. My goal is not to present anything new but rather to suggest that much might be gained by revisiting old questions, challenging the unstated assumptions that undergird research and scholarship, and thinking more deeply about how we, as scholars in the broader nuclear studies community, do our work.

Writing the History That Never Happened

There is a tension between historical work and the demands of both international relations theory and policy.[10] Most people study nuclear questions to understand what makes for good policy and what lessons the past can provide for the present and the future. Good historians, however, embrace uncertainty, context, and the nongeneralizable. This is, understandably, a deeply disappointing and unsatisfying answer for policymakers and many social scientists. Why study the past if it yields no direct lessons that can be applied to current, vexing policy situations? This frustration is especially acute on military issues and the grave matter of war and peace. Mistakes in this realm have the most terrible human consequences, and scholars are eager to have all the knowledge and wisdom available to avoid disaster.

Perhaps even more frustrating is that historians traffic in ironies. War and military competition are rife with dilemmas and puzzles. For example, it is understood that modern conflict is horrific. It is also understood that war can be a necessary evil. And in a terrible irony, war and military competition have played a large role in the extraordinary economic, political, social, and technological progress the Western world has achieved in the past few centuries. There is hardly a political practice, a beloved technology, or an improved norm—from the rise of finance capitalism and greater wealth, to the navigation and transportation revolution, to modern medicine, to representative democracy and efficient bureaucracy, to civil rights for African Americans and women—that cannot be traced to, if not war, then military and international political competition. This helps explain why historians are often humble, crusty, and ironic (in both their scholarship and demeanor). We hate war. But we understand that what the distinguished scholar William McNeill called "the pursuit of power" has created a remarkable, lasting legacy.[11]

The ironies and uncertainties with regard to nuclear weapons are, if anything, far greater than in other areas of conflict and military competition. Thermonuclear weapons are especially monstrous, with

4

the potential to destroy civilization. Yet people tend to think that it is the very destructiveness of the weapons that has prevented the recurrence of great-power war since 1945. Great-power land wars had been the scourge of Eurasia for thirty-one years before the United States dropped atomic weapons on Hiroshima and Nagasaki, killing tens of millions on the battlefield and tens of millions more through disease and political upheaval. Some seventy years ago, most responsible people expected a third world war to follow the first and second, with consequences far worse than those. We are all around today because that war never came, and, to misuse a title from a famous Paul Fussell essay, it has led many people to proclaim, "Thank God for the atom bomb."[12]

Have nuclear weapons prevented a third world war, and do these weapons have the intended effect of stabilizing world politics by making great-power war unthinkable? This potent notion is the foundation of what has come to be called "nuclear deterrence," and much of current thinking about nuclear weapons is centered on the concept. A large part of U.S. national security strategy has been driven for well over a half century by the idea that an attack on the United States or its allies might elicit a nuclear response, even if the aggressor had not used nuclear weapons first. This posture has been taken for granted for so long that we have long since forgotten, in the context of American history, how novel it was or what the United States had to do to implement it.

Consider that from its founding until 1950, the United States entered no permanent peacetime alliances, was almost completely demobilized during peacetime, and pursued strategies that allowed it to be hit first and mobilize slowly and massively to win wars of attrition. This strategy prioritized powerful civilian control over the military and strong legislative oversight over the executive branch in matters of war and peace while allowing the United States to remain relatively isolated from world affairs.[13] The thermonuclear revolution, and the strategies the United States adopted to deal with it, demanded permanent alliances, forward military deployments, and an often pre-emptive military strategy that left enormous discretion in the hands of battlefield commanders, permanently shifting the power to make war away from Congress to the president.[14] This represents an extraordinary break from our past.

Again, this strategy is premised on the idea that deterrence—the promise of awful retribution if attacked—kept the United States relatively safe and the world relatively stable for decades. Most important, it is widely believed that it prevented thermonuclear war.[15] But do we know this to be true? How can we be sure that thermonuclear weapons, and the deterrence that flowed from them, maintained peace and stability?

The problem is that we are trying to understand something that never happened, and we hope will never happen—a thermonuclear war. Trying to understand why something did not happen is a methodological nightmare, a situation that eludes a definitive answer from even our most powerful and sophisticated social science methods. While the idea of nuclear deterrence is intuitively compelling, there are credible alternative explanations for the relative peace and stability of world affairs after 1945.

Why does this epistemological point matter, especially to those interested in the hard realities of nuclear policy? Two crucial trends shape the nuclear world, pulling in different directions. The first is the disarmament movement, which is animated by the idea that the world should move toward eliminating nuclear weapons altogether. This aspiration was officially endorsed by President Barack Obama in his 2009 Prague speech, though presidents ranging from Harry Truman to Ronald Reagan also at times shared this goal. Yet nuclear weapons are playing an increasing role in world politics. Concerns over Iran's nuclear ambitions and the challenges generated by North Korea's burgeoning weapons program have been well publicized. Less well known is the significant expansion and modernization of the nuclear programs of Russia, China, and Pakistan. The United States is also committed to a $350 billion modernization of its nuclear program over the next decade.

One trend moves the world toward delegitimizing and eventually eliminating nuclear weapons. The other pulls in the opposite direction, highlighting the importance to states of nuclear weapons for achieving national security and foreign policy objectives. These worldviews, and the policies that flow from them, center around whether and how nuclear deterrence works and whether or not it is responsible for the absence of great-power war since 1945.

The right approach to the disarmament-versus-deterrence debate also turns on a number of other important questions from our past, questions for which answers are as elusive as they are consequential. As a historian of the nuclear age, I wrestle with a number of puzzles, but I want to focus on four of them. Debating and thinking about these questions are not only important in and of themselves but also help us assess contemporary and future nuclear dilemmas and choices. They cut to the fundamental questions surrounding nuclear weapons, deterrence, peace, and stability.

Revisiting the Core Questions

Many would protest that revisiting the core questions is a waste of time. Wouldn't it be more profitable to spend time on new issues? Think of the recent quantitative work on nuclear crisis dynamics, leadership experiences, or the forward deployment of nuclear and non-nuclear forces and their influence on extended deterrence and proliferation.[16] Other profitable areas of research are opening up all the time. For example, large global investments in civilian nuclear energy are being made around the globe.[17] Will this lead to more weaponization? It is these emerging questions and issues, it might be argued, on which scholarly efforts should be focused.

The problem is that many of the small and medium-size issues build on these larger questions that are believed, quite wrongly, to have been settled. This goes beyond the question of whether we have certain knowledge that nuclear deterrence works and of how it works and whether the nuclear revolution has prevented great-power war. Other core concepts and phenomena that are highly contestable on further examination are taken for granted: for example, that there is a universally shared definition of strategic stability (in fact, there are wide variations in how it has been understood) and that the superpowers consistently sought it (they did not); that there is a meaningful and easy distinction between deterrence and compellence; that arms control always leads to political stability and is about the weapons, not underlying political questions (the Anti-Ballistic Missile Treaty [ABM] and the Strategic Arms Limitations Treaties [SALT I and SALT II] led to deep political problems in the United States, the Soviet Union, and Western Europe that increased political tensions); that security-dilemma dynamics drove the arms race; and that the decision to go nuclear lies largely in the hands of the potential proliferator (U.S. nuclear nonproliferation efforts have been a key, if not the principal, variable). This is not to say these concepts, theories, and arguments are wrong or cannot provide great insight into nuclear dynamics; they can and do. The focus, however, should be on revisiting and challenging such claims.

Four big questions in particular warrant exploration. How dangerous have nuclear weapons made world politics? How does nuclear deterrence work, and can nuclear weapons be used to achieve other political goals? What determines a state's decision to pursue nuclear weapons? Once a state possesses these weapons, what is the ideal number to have, and what are the best strategies to employ them?

Have Nuclear Weapons Made the World More Safe?

Did nuclear weapons create the so-called Long Peace between otherwise bitter adversaries, the Soviet Union and the United States, during the Cold War?[18] The belief that they did is widely held and informs much of the contemporary understanding of nuclear deterrence. And if nuclear weapons prevented a war that would have otherwise occurred, can it be inferred that nuclear deterrence can prevent wars at other times, in other regions, and in other circumstances?

There are at least three ways to look at this. First, through the course of the whole Cold War, did nuclear weapons and the strategies the superpowers employed make great-power war and a nuclear exchange more or less likely? Second, how did nuclear weapons, and the risk of nuclear war, affect state behavior during sharp political crises? Did nuclear weapons make it easier or harder to exit crises without a risk of war? Third, how high were the risks of an unintentional nuclear launch or a nuclear accident?

On this last question, nuclear weapons clearly had contradictory effects. Writ large, the fear and horrors of thermonuclear war no doubt gave both Soviet and American leaders pause, both during stable times and in crises. That said, one could not read this history without some feeling of terror. Eric Schlosser's *Command and Control* joins the works of Scott Sagan and other scholars in highlighting the mistakes, accidents, and near misses that have plagued nuclear management.[19] Reading documents on both sides of the Cold War during the Berlin crises from 1958 to 1961, the 1962 Cuban missile crisis, or the set of challenges during 1983 and NATO's Able Archer 83 exercise is frightening.

Perhaps, more important, the most significant and dangerous crises of the Cold War were generated by the very existence of nuclear weapons. In a world without nuclear weapons, the Cuban missile crisis could not have occurred. Even the crises over West Berlin from 1958 to 1961, if they were, as is now believed, initiated by the Soviet Union to express its anger over the United States' move to arm the West German Bundeswehr with nuclear weapons, were nuclear to their core. The crises over the Euromissiles in the late 1970s, the Soviet fear of a NATO nuclear first strike—it is hard to create the counterfactual where these occur in a non-nuclear world. Could it be that in a non-nuclear Cold War, the United States and the Soviet Union, and NATO and the Warsaw Pact, would balance each other perfectly, grudgingly accept each other's sphere of influence, and avoid major crises? It is a scenario worth thinking about.

What this means is that the simple notion laid out by John Lewis Gaddis, Kenneth Waltz, Robert Jervis, and John Mearsheimer—that nuclear weapons generated stability between the superpowers—is certainly open to question. On the other hand, the bitter ideological and geopolitical rivalry did not lead to nuclear or even conventional war between the superpowers. What role did nuclear weapons play in making the world safer, or more dangerous, or both? Given that this historical experience forms the foundation of current thinking on deterrence, it would be well worth encouraging younger scholars to revisit the role of nuclear weapons during the Cold War.

Can Nuclear Weapons Compel as well as Deter?

Many argue that nuclear weapons are only good for one thing: deterrence, or preventing states from challenging the global status quo. In theory, this allows nuclear weapons to keep the peace.

The historical record reveals, however, that one man's deterrence may be another's compellence. In other words, nuclear-armed states have issued deterrent threats that most likely appeared aggressively coercive to their targets. During the dangerous crises between 1958 and 1961, was Premier Nikita Khrushchev trying to compel the Western powers to leave West Berlin or to deter the United States from supporting West Germany's nuclearization? Or both? Did the United States' threat to use its superior nuclear strength to protect West Berlin, an isolated and conventionally indefensible outpost deep within enemy territory, constitute a reasonable definition of deterrence? The distinction between deterrence, which is stabilizing, and compellence, which is not, is often in the eye of the beholder.

Nuclear deterrence is not always peace inducing. Some believe strategic nuclear deterrence allows and even encourages military conflict at lower levels. Furthermore, since the use of nuclear weapons is unimaginable in almost any circumstance, a reckless leader can take advantage of a more responsible nuclear state to make gains through nuclear threats. Furthermore, states do not always view deterrence as an unalloyed good. One imagines that China deeply resents a status quo, buttressed by American nuclear deterrence, that prevents it from exercising what it believes to be its legitimate claims to Taiwan (claims that in a non-nuclear world it may have already exercised). One reason the United States goes to such great lengths to limit nuclear proliferation is that it does not like being deterred by others. As a state with overwhelming conventional military, economic, and soft-power advantages, it has shown that it will do whatever it can to prevent its freedom of action from being limited by the nuclear deterrent efforts of others.

On the other side of the coin, if the use of nuclear weapons becomes increasingly unthinkable, is even their role as a deterrent undermined? After the Cuban missile crisis, few leaders in the Soviet Union or the United States could have imagined any political circumstance in which they would use nuclear weapons, even as both developed military strategies predicated on increasing the credibility of the threat to use them. Since the Cold War, this skepticism has only increased. While it may not rise to the level of a taboo, it is hard to dispute that there is a powerful norm against their use.[20]

Why Do States Pursue Nuclear Weapons?

Our world is far less nuclearized than predictions of fifty years ago suggested. If nuclear deterrence is so powerful, if nuclear weapons guarantee a state's sovereignty and security, it is puzzling that there are currently fewer than ten nuclear-armed states.

Many powerful explanations have been offered for this lower-than-expected number.[21] There are arguments about capacity and technology: building a weapons program was beyond the technological or organizational capabilities of the states that most wanted them, especially in an age in which sanctions and export controls were becoming more prevalent and the global supply of nuclear materials less easily accessed. There are ideational and normative arguments: nuclear weapons were increasingly seen as ineffective or immoral or both, even in the rough-and-tumble world of international politics. There are institutional arguments, as the 1968 Non-Proliferation of Nuclear Weapons treaty (NPT) added other arrangements, such as the London Nuclear Suppliers Group, and strengthened organizations such as the International Atomic Energy Agency to become an increasingly effective regime. There are arguments about a state's political system, orientation, and leadership types that would make it more prone to acquire nuclear weapons, as well as how a state positioned itself in the global economic order. Finally, there were the traditional security arguments. Some have argued that in many cases nuclear weapons were not needed to generate state security; others suggest that the vigorous nonproliferation efforts of other states, especially the United States, kept the number of nuclear weapons states low. Perhaps, one might respond, the lower numbers are not a puzzle at all, and nuclear weapons are less appealing, provide fewer benefits, and expose more vulnerabilities, or are more difficult to develop and deploy, than some of our theories expect.

In certain circles in Washington, Geneva, Vienna, and elsewhere, there is no puzzle. A relatively slow rate of nuclear proliferation has simply been a function of the effectiveness of the NPT. As such, any and all efforts should be focused on strengthening and reinforcing the regime and implementing the so-called grand bargain whereby the nuclear powers move more quickly toward their promise of disarmament.

There are several issues with that interpretation. The first is that many policymakers and analysts were skeptical that the NPT could work. Even beyond the obvious (and many thought unsustainable) hypocrisy that allowed a few states to possess nuclear weapons when others could not, when in the past had any treaty prevented the spread of powerful military technologies? Nuclear weapons possessed qualities that were bound to appeal to a government: their powerful deterrent effects practically guaranteed, for the first time in history, that a state could maintain its sovereignty, independence, and freedom from conquest. Regardless of any treaty, how reasonable was it to expect states to eschew a technology that accorded protection, power, and prestige?

There were further reasons to question the durability of the NPT. The Nixon administration was notably unenthusiastic about a treaty negotiated by the Johnson administration and did little to encourage states to sign and ratify.[22] Furthermore, the sense that the bipolar international system was giving way to a more multipolar system led observers to anticipate that middle powers (such as Italy, Japan, Sweden, Yugoslavia) would acquire the bomb. Finally, the acute energy crisis of the 1970s, marked by dramatically rising oil prices, increased the appeal of civilian nuclear energy programs. The NPT, which recognized the right of states to build a robust civilian nuclear architecture, was woefully inadequate to regulate those states that used this path to pursue nuclear weapons. Much of the 1970s saw both international efforts, such as the Nuclear Suppliers Group, and domestic policies in the United States to close the gaping loopholes between civilian and military programs left by the NPT.[23]

In fact, there were more nuclear proliferation pressures than was once thought. Australia, Italy, and Japan, it appears, may have used signing the treaty (but not ratifying it) as an opportunity to reconsider the weapons option.[24] Other countries, from Argentina and Brazil to South Korea and Taiwan, explored nuclear weapons. An intense nuclear rivalry commenced in South Asia.

Still, the prospect in 1968 that a half century later the number of nuclear weapons states would remain in the single digits would have been met with surprise and relief. Why—especially given the rough circumstances in the decade following the NPT—did so few states acquire and deploy nuclear weapons?

Again, the reasons are not fully known, and there are many opinions that demand consideration. One interesting surprise can be found in the historical record, however. The United States has expended as much effort to keep its friends and allies—countries ranging from West Germany to Australia, Italy, Japan, South Korea, Sweden, and Taiwan—non-nuclear as it has to keep its adversaries non-nuclear. And it was quite willing to work against its friends and with its major adversary, the Soviet Union, to achieve this end.

How Much Is Enough?

What are the force and strategy requirements for nuclear deterrence? Are they different from the requirements for reassuring allies? Can a state achieve meaningful nuclear superiority, and, if so, what are the benefits of achieving such primacy?

This is a complex question, but, during the Cold War, there were two leading views within the United States. Many of the academic and think tank analysts—renowned thinkers such as Bernard Brodie,

Robert Jervis, and Ken Waltz—believed that once a state possessed survivable forces—in other words, enough nuclear weapons that even after an attack it could inflict unacceptable damage on the enemy—there was really no point in building more forces.[25] Once strategic stability had been achieved, building a larger or more accurate strategic nuclear force, or spending money on missile defenses, would be a waste.

Many American decisionmakers did not seem to accept this logic. From the beginning of the atomic age and accelerating from the early 1950s to the mid-1960s, the United States actively pursued nuclear supremacy. It was once thought that by the late 1960s, U.S. decisionmakers had abandoned what many strategists saw as either a pointless or a destabilizing pursuit and accepted mutual vulnerability and strategic stability. These views appeared to be enshrined in the 1972 ABM Treaty and the 1972 SALT I and 1979 SALT II. Even here, however, there is a puzzle. Concurrent with signing these treaties limiting the numbers of strategic nuclear weapons, the United States undertook massive investments in strategic nuclear weapons and associated programs that sought (and appeared to achieve) massive qualitative superiority over the Soviet Union. Instead of seeking more and larger bombs, the United States invested in faster, more accurate, stealthier nuclear forces, a posture that most likely looked menacing and flew in the face of strategic stability. The United States developed and deployed multibillion-dollar weapons programs—the Trident D-5, the Peacekeeper, stealth bombers, cruise missiles and the Pershing II, upgrades to C3-I, missile defense, and massive investments in antisubmarine warfare and sub silencing—in what appeared to be an effort to achieve and maintain nuclear superiority. What did American decisionmakers think they were getting for this massive investment, for these counterforce systems that arguably undermined strategic stability, and did they get what they sought?

There is limited but quite revealing evidence that the Soviet side understood that the Americans were trying to acquire meaningful superiority in the 1970s and 1980s, based on capabilities that the Soviet Union possessed neither the technology nor the economic resources to match, and it worried them. It is an interesting contrast to what appears to be a much different attitude in China today, where, despite an increasingly vigorous foreign policy based on an impressive economic and technological base, its leaders seem relatively sanguine about being on the short end of the nuclear balance with the United States.

This whole story is in many ways puzzling. On the one hand, both superpowers sought to limit quantitative arms races, while also acknowledging the increasing inconceivability of any use of nuclear weapons. On the other, they pursued weapons that undermined stability and acted or reacted as if meaningful political benefit could be obtained from nuclear superiority far short of a first strike. What was going on here? Were the superpowers simply hedging? Were they purposively pursuing a form of arms racing, similar to Andrew Marshall's notion of competitive strategies, to expose the adversary's weaknesses and force it to put scarce resources into expensive weapons systems?[26] And how many of these lessons have been embraced by other nuclear powers? The People's Republic of China, for example, does not seem to have pursued similar policies. There is much that scholars do not know, and this is an area in which they should be encouraged to explore.

Framing Answers to the Core Questions

Many other big questions, and other ways of framing them, can be profitably revisited. Yet scholars and policymakers are not limited only by what questions they ask. They face barriers—often unrecognized—to developing better insight into nuclear dynamics. I count at least four: identifying the appropriate method, properly accounting for chronology, perspective, and belief, recognizing the interconnectedness between nuclear dynamics and larger political questions, and considering morality and judgment.

Method

The reasons scholars are interested in a variety of questions surrounding nuclear dynamics—especially why states do or do not acquire nuclear weapons and what factors influence that decision—derive from one great concern: how to ensure that nuclear weapons are never detonated again. A conclusive answer has proved elusive. But there are at least three competing hypotheses.

First is the well-known concept of nuclear deterrence. The argument here is simple, familiar, and powerful: nuclear weapons are horrific, and launching them, intentionally or otherwise, would be catastrophic. That very characteristic of the weapon, however, makes their use unlikely. There is no political goal worth the cost of a nuclear war. Most realists and many American strategists embrace this view and believe this explains why there have been no nuclear wars since 1945.

Second, there are those who argue that nuclear use has been avoided through sheer luck. These analysts point to the dangerous crises, the near misses, the accidents, and even the Schelling-esque competitions in risk-taking that almost led to nuclear use in the past and are bound to lead to disaster at some point in the future.[27] Nuclear weapons can create dangers even where none existed before: it is hard to imagine the dangers of a third world war over Soviet forces in Cuba or the jurisdictional status of West Berlin in a non-nuclear world. Some observers with this viewpoint challenge whether deterrence was ever as robust as advocates claim (and point out that, even if so, it would have to work 100 percent of the time forever if we were to put our confidence in it). Others see nuclear deterrence as uniquely associated with the Cold War rivalry between the Soviet Union and the United States and not as relevant to the post–Cold War world of regional conflicts, middle-size powers, so-called rogue states, and nonstate actors. Many fear that faith in the overwhelming power of nuclear deterrence lulls policymakers into false and dangerous overconfidence that makes war more, not less, likely.

Third, there are those who think factors that have nothing to do with nuclear weapons explain the absence of world war since

1945. Shifting demographic patterns, globalization, and the changing nature of power has made conquest far less appealing now than it was in the past. Land is no longer the most important source of power—states aim to be Singapore, not Kazakhstan—and ethnic and national differences make occupation far more costly now than during the imperial age. Others see norms against war and violence as playing a key role. Although the nuclear revolution may have given states pause in the first few decades of the Cold War, since at least the 1970s nuclear weapons have been largely irrelevant to explaining what matters in international politics.

What does this mean for how these questions are studied? Which framework is best? How one thinks about specific issues—one's attitudes toward disarmament, for example, or proliferation writ large, or specific cases, such as Iran's nuclear program—derives directly from these largely unprovable hypotheses about the influence of nuclear weapons on world politics. Defining (coding) nuclear crises, for example, or dealing with the selection effects inherent in any question surrounding nuclear deterrence are formidable challenges that have not been handled impressively in the international relations literature. Formal models can illuminate trade-offs and highlight strategic calculations under ideal conditions, but they forgo most context and interconnectedness.

That said, it is not clear that qualitative methods offer much more than theory and interpretations that are hard to test against the empirical record. Nuclear policy is shrouded in secrecy, and evidence is hard to come by. Even when evidence exists, there is often a gap between what policymakers say and what they do.[28] There is an even deeper issue: if the nuclear revolution did have a transformative effect on world politics, presumably there are few appropriate lessons or models from pre-1945 history that can clarify nuclear dynamics. In other words, reasoning from historical analogies may impede rather than explain what is driving the issues we care about.

Chronology, Perspectives, and Beliefs

Certain periods are marked by clear beginnings and endings. World War I began weeks after the assassination of Austria-Hungary's archduke, Franz Ferdinand, by state-supported Serbian terrorists and ended a little more than four years later, when Germany surrendered to the Entente powers in November 1918. For other events, the beginning and the end are open to debate: Did the Cold War begin in 1949, 1946, or even as early as 1917? Did it end when Mikhail Gorbachev took power, after the surprising 1986 Reykjavik conference, or when the Soviet Union collapsed?

It is far easier to assess and analyze an event or phenomenon that exists within explicit temporal bounds. We know when the nuclear age began, but we have no idea when, if ever, it will end, so we do not know where we are in the story or how it will turn out. Outcome bias can distort perception—things are much clearer in the rearview mirror of history than in the rainstorm in the night through the front windshield.

Periodization is different depending on the actor. The Cold War and nuclear dynamics were interconnected in the nuclear relationship between the Soviet Union and the United States, less so for France and Great Britain. For other actors, the Cold War was of far less significance, even if their nuclear decisionmaking took place during the Cold War. There is a move within international history to look at the 1970s, and even the 1960s, as being distinct from the Cold War, with global forces outside of the bipolar conflict driving important issues (even, according to Daniel Sargent's book, between the superpowers).[29]

Furthermore, it is likely that the influence of nuclear weapons on international relations evolves and changes over time, similar to the systems-effects process so wonderfully described by Robert Jervis.[30] The study of nuclear proliferation is a moving target: attitudes and policies about nuclear weapons have changed over the past eight decades and will continue to shift, and these changes will interact within both national and international political processes and culture to produce an ever-changing set of realities.

Finally, much of what has evolved over time are ideas and beliefs about nuclear weapons. This makes the historian's task even harder: ideational and normative factors are far more elusive than material or structural factors. How does one identify an idea, how it is generated and circulated, and when and how it matters? Ideas diverge among different groups, both within a society and between states. Epistemic communities—especially in the field of arms control—often hold ideas across national borders. How can their influence be assessed, especially as they evolve over time?

The so-called wizards of Armageddon, the RAND strategists of the early nuclear age, had powerful and important ideas about how policymakers should think about nuclear weapons. Bruce Kuklick suggests that these ideas had far less influence on policy—on what actually happened—than was once thought.[31] Even if they did matter, they emerged from a certain time and place. Thomas Schelling developed many of his ideas about nuclear dynamics during the crises over Berlin and Cuba from 1958 to 1962. In retrospect, many aspects of the history of this period were bizarre and sui generis. Should that influence how policymakers assess the theories that emerged from this experience— something David Holloway has termed "frozen theories"?

Interconnectedness of Issues

The field of nuclear studies often suffers from a certain narrowness, as if nuclear weapons can be studied as a thing alone, separate from the other great forces in politics and history. There is little doubt these weapons have profoundly altered international affairs. But nuclear weapons are still tools of statecraft and must be understood within particular national and international contexts, related to a state's goals and the realities of international relations.

In the early and middle 1950s, NATO embraced a military strategy—pushed by the Eisenhower administration—that called for the early and massive use of nuclear weapons. It was clearly a pre-emptive strategy, seeking to blunt the adversary's ability to use its nuclear weapons before a conflict began, and, as is often the case with preemptive, counterforce strategies, it produced both huge target lists and a great deal of predelegated authority to use nuclear weapons.

This was what David Rosenberg labels the "origins of overkill," and it has often been interpreted as the (especially U.S.) military's love of weapons and offensive strategies.[32] In other words, this massive buildup of nuclear weapons, combined with hair-raising plans to use them early and massively, was seen as a terrifying mix of bureaucratic and organizational politics combined with ideology.

But does that really tell the full story? It turns out that in the early and middle 1950s, NATO and especially the United States wrestled with the incredibly complicated issue of defending Western Europe while dealing with the politics of the German question. Western Europe could not really be defended without a meaningful economic and military contribution from the nascent Federal Republic of Germany. Yet rearming Germans so soon after the horrors of World War II was deeply problematic. The West Germans, for their part, had to be given something in return for embracing the Western alliance—powerful neutral instincts and incentives existed within the German political system.

The ideal outcome—a West Germany that was fully aligned with the West, contributing its ample economic and conventional military capabilities to the defense of Europe but not possessing its own nuclear weapons (an outcome that neither the Soviets nor the Western European allies would allow)—presented a difficult challenge. For their part, the West Germans would not sign on to a military strategy that saw NATO forces thrown back to France after a Soviet invasion, turning its territory into a nuclear battlefield. West Germany had to be defended at the intra-German border, or even better, within Eastern Europe and the Soviet Union, if they were to agree to contribute conventional forces but eschew their own nuclear weapons. In other words, the political realities of the German question—not strictly military preferences—demanded a preemptive nuclear strategy, which, in order to work, required predelegation.[33] As an aside, to get the French to go along with all this, the United States found itself reluctantly underwriting France's disastrous policies in Southeast Asia. The political logic driving the military strategy is often overlooked.

It makes no sense to look at NATO nuclear strategy or proliferation dynamics in a vacuum. Nuclear weapons matter, and they may push international politics to new limits. But they do not make politics irrelevant or secondary.

Morality and Judgment

Scholarship, especially in the social sciences, seeks objectivity. Historians tell themselves that they want to know why things happened in the past and what will happen in the future, without interjecting their own prejudices and hoped-for outcomes in their analysis. This is a noble but typically unreachable objective when studying war and peace and especially when exploring nuclear dynamics. At some level, scholars study nuclear dynamics because there is an outcome they desperately want to avoid. This tends to make us, as a community, passionate about our views. Passion can be a good thing, but it can also threaten objectivity. Nuclear studies often drifts into an area closer to advocacy than scholarship.

Many within nuclear studies simply assume arms control is always and everywhere a good thing. An unimpeachable belief in the strategy and arms-control community is that SALT I and SALT II were unalloyed goods, the cornerstone of strategic stability. An alternative view holds that negative reactions within the United States poisoned foreign policy debates and gave rise to neoconservatism.[34] The Soviet military was furious as well, which may have led to the deployment of SS-20 missiles.[35] The SALT agreements inspired great mistrust and dissatisfaction among many of America's European allies, and the deployment of the SS-20s generated a crisis in NATO.[36] These efforts to establish strategic stability, it could be argued, perversely helped undermine détente by the late 1970s.[37] Might the enormous political capital expended on the SALT negotiations between the Russians and Americans have been more productively spent on other issues? Long-held moral judgments prevent this kind of counterintuitive insight.

More broadly, consider the deterrence-versus-disarmament debate. Advocates on both sides share a similar hope of avoiding thermonuclear war. Each side has a tendency to ignore or disdain the views of the other. Neither—for reasons mentioned earlier—can prove its argument, yet neither has a tendency to acknowledge its own uncertainty or demonstrate the humility that is usually the product of trying to understand difficult questions. This is seen in the debates within the United States over the nuclear deal with Iran, where, with a few exceptions, opponents have laid out the issues in the most stark, binary terms, neither side acknowledging that the other may have a point. Both sides want the same thing—they share the same moral vision, a world without nuclear war—but they have strongly held, opposing views on how to get there. There are important and thoughtful efforts to find a balance between the moral horrors of nuclear use and the potential benefits of nuclear deterrence.[38] This balance, however, eludes most debates and discussion.

Conclusion

I have no answer to any of these challenges, or the others that burden efforts to address the nuclear issue. Some burdens are inherent to intellectual inquiry, especially historical work, while others are unique to nuclear studies. The plea for epistemological modesty on such critical questions can be vexing to social scientists and policymakers alike. But scholars and policymakers should confront these challenges and assumptions explicitly, undertake a rigorous stock-taking and comparison of the hypotheses they have generated, and work together to find more effective methods to produce more definitive insights into these extraordinarily consequential issues.

Why is this necessary? If for no other reason than that the important policy choices faced in Washington and abroad emerge from beliefs—often implicit and unchallenged—about these questions. Given the broad range of paths confronting policymakers—from eliminating nuclear weapons or recognizing their centrality to world politics and American national security policy—the ideas driving these options matter. There is not a more important, more consequential issue facing U.S. policymakers. Generating answers to the scholarly questions I pose would go a long way toward navigating the nuclear choices the world faces.

TWO

Fixing the Franchise:
The Ivory Tower–Policy Gap

By definition, a debate requires at least two opposing views, and there is no shortage of debates in Washington on foreign policy and national security affairs. But in a political environment in which vehement disagreement is the norm, one issue produces a powerful bipartisan consensus among American foreign policy officials: the spread of nuclear weapons is a grave challenge to U.S. national interests and must be halted, if not reversed. While there have been differences in tone and at times substance, every administration and every presidential candidate since the Cold War ended has agreed that the United States must have a robust nuclear nonproliferation policy. In a city where scores can be found to defend even the most extreme and polarizing national security positions, it would be hard to find a serving or former U.S. national security official in Washington who would champion the idea that nuclear proliferation was anything but deeply dangerous, destabilizing, and inimical to American interests.

This is one of the factors that make the widespread popularity and scholarly influence of the Sagan-Waltz "franchise" so fascinating. Kenneth Waltz, the author of *Man, the State, and War* and *Theory of International Politics*, was the world's most important theorist of international relations. Scott Sagan, a Stanford professor and former director of the prestigious Center for International Security and Cooperation, is perhaps the leading scholar of the causes, consequences, and potential remedies to nuclear proliferation. Sagan and Waltz published their first version of the debate in *The Spread of Nuclear Weapons: A Debate*, in 1995.[1] The success of the book, combined with significant changes in the world of nuclear politics—India and Pakistan's 1998 nuclear tests, the 9/11 attacks and the rise of Al Qaeda, a renewed U.S. interest in missile defense, and the increased concern over so-called rogue nuclear states such as Iraq, Iran, and North Korea—inspired a second volume, *A Debate Renewed*, published in 2002.[2] They returned again, seventeen years after they first engaged, with a revised third edition, *The Spread of Nuclear Weapons: An Enduring Debate*.[3]

The latest volume has updated the earlier editions and added new chapters on Iraq, North Korea, and Iran, and the nuclear zero movement. The authors' core positions, however, have not changed and remain simple and powerful. Waltz sees the spread of nuclear weapons as both inevitable and not to be feared. Why? The overwhelming power of nuclear deterrence—the ability of a state not to defend itself but to threaten an adversary with unacceptable damage if attacked—brings the possibility of war between nuclear-armed states close to zero. In a nuclear world, a state does not have to know how much punishment to expect from an adversary; in fact, the very uncertainty increases caution and enhances deterrence. And even if a nuclear weapon or two were used in a conflict, the horrifying consequences of further escalation would soon bring leaders to their senses and allow cooler heads to prevail. Waltz does not believe the character or regime type of the nuclear state counts for much. In fact, weak or authoritarian nuclear states have greater incentives to keep weapons under tight control and, understanding the consequences of a nuclear reprisal, are likely to be less, not more, aggressive. Waltz argues that the history of the nuclear era proves his theory: despite great tensions and geopolitical competitions, deterrence has prevented great-power war since 1945. He sees no reason why the powerful logic of nuclear deterrence would not operate in the same way among new nuclear states. Policies that ignore these realities, he suggests, are misguided and foolish.

Interestingly, Sagan's rebuttal does not directly challenge Waltz's claim about the extraordinary power of nuclear deterrence to induce fear and caution, at least in the abstract. His approach is to look inside the black box of the state and investigate who within it would build, control, deploy, and potentially use nuclear weapons. Taking an organizational approach, Sagan makes two key claims: First, "military organizations—because of common biases, inflexible routines, and parochial interests—display organizational behaviors that are likely to lead to deterrence failures and deliberate or accidental war."[4] Second, "there are strong reasons to believe that future nuclear-armed states will lack the positive mechanisms of civilian control."[5] Such a world is a place where mistakes, miscalculations, and aggressive policies may thrive.

According to Sagan, stable deterrence requires three conditions. First, there must be no preventive attack on a nascent nuclear state while it is building its forces; second, nuclear rivals must have a second-strike capability, meaning that a sufficient number of nuclear weapons can survive an attack to guarantee devastating retaliation; third, nuclear forces cannot be "prone to accidental or unauthorized use."[6] Much of their disagreement involves assessing the historical record to understand how easy or difficult it is to meet these conditions. Waltz, unsurprisingly, sees these stipulations as easily met, given the incentives a potential nuclear state has to fulfill them. Sagan, conversely, believes these three conditions are elusive and, given the likely nature and regime type of future atomic aspirants, will be even more difficult to achieve. Recent events—the U.S. war against Iraq, North Korea's and Iran's nuclear weapons programs, debates over missile defense, the conflict in South Asia, the nuclear zero movement—have not caused either scholar to shift his perspective or change his core position.

It is not hard to understand why these volumes have been so popular, especially in the classroom. Waltz's simple but compelling argument about the power of nuclear deterrence to induce caution, regardless of region, regime type, or circumstance, is a powerful corrective to the alarmist views that often shape public discussions about nuclear proliferation. There has been no first use of nuclear weapons since 1945, and common sense tells us that deterrence must have played some role in keeping the Cold War from becoming hot. Bad states with atomic bombs, Waltz reminds us, are not new; despite contemporaneous predictions to the contrary, Stalinist Russia's and Maoist China's acquisition of nuclear weapons was not a catastrophe. The challenges to a nonstate actor to acquire, assemble, deliver, and successfully detonate a nuclear device are enormous. It is highly unlikely that a state, even a bad state, would simply turn over its weapons to terrorist groups, nor is it clear that all such groups are motivated by the irrational or even suicidal inclinations often ascribed to them.

Sagan's analysis of how complex and competing organizations function (or do not) is an important alternative to the widespread acceptance of the rational, unitary state. Complicated systems can break down, humans make mistakes, and bureaucratic interests often diverge from national policy. How theory claims states should behave is not always how they act in the real world. Given how horrific any nuclear use would be, Sagan's more cautious approach appeals to common sense.

What are we to make of this book, two decades after it first appeared? Sagan and Waltz deserve extraordinary credit for constructing a sharp but respectful debate, where bold claims and counterclaims are made without sacrificing civility. This is all too rare in our intellectual discourse and should serve as a model. And while the authors' core arguments have remained constant, their exchange has shaped a generation of scholarly research and dominated the debate on the causes and consequences of nuclear proliferation within the international relations field.

Still, there is something strangely disquieting, both about the book, its claims, and its methods and about the gap between its influence within the ivory tower and its lack of influence among policymakers since it was first published. Two problems in particular stand out. The first is methodological: the occasionally selective and simplistic use of history to buttress theoretical and prescriptive claims is distressing. The new edition, *An Enduring Debate,* and Waltz's chapters in particular, proceeds without recognizing the emergence of reams of top-level, declassified documents from around the world over the past two decades that provide a view into the history of nuclear statecraft and proliferation dynamics previously unavailable.[7] While this new history pulls in different directions, it seems irresponsible not to vigorously engage the new primary materials and resulting scholarship. Rigorous history should surprise and, one hopes, cause an author (and the reader) to revisit and potentially challenge long-held assumptions; this book, and Waltz in particular, analyzes the past selectively, more to validate fiercely held positions than to break new ground.

A more serious problem, however, is the purpose and intended audience of the book. The authors emphasize that they do not see their effort merely as an academic exercise: "We believe that political scientists should try to help improve government policy."[8] Yet there is little evidence these volumes (and again, particularly Waltz's arguments) have or will influence national security officials. Waltz's argument is deeply problematic and contradictory, and it is not taken seriously by people who matter, while Sagan's broad recommendations may be seen as right by many decisionmakers but for the wrong reasons. If Sagan and Waltz's arguments fail to engage, to say nothing of find favor, among those who make government policy, what is the explanation? Are American policymakers simply blind or foolish? Or have the academics—not just Sagan and Waltz but all those who take this debate as the starting point for any discussion of proliferation—missed something crucial about the question of how nuclear proliferation affects American interests, something essential that many scholars miss but most policymakers, and the citizens they work for, understand in their bones? And if true, what does the enduring success of the Sagan-Waltz franchise say about what international relations scholarship contributes to national security policy?

Bringing Politics Back to International Relations

What does the past reveal about nuclear danger? Does the historical record demonstrate that nuclear weapons always induce caution and create stability between rivals, and does deterrence consistently work in the way Waltz and, to a lesser extent, Sagan assume?

In an important review of the second edition of *The Spread of Nuclear Weapons*, Marc Trachtenberg points out that the supposedly stabilizing qualities Waltz ascribes to nuclear weapons—characteristics Sagan does not challenge—may actually increase the chance for misperception and miscalculation between nuclear states.[9] Wars are not simply "started" by one side or another, as Waltz would have it, where one country is an obvious aggressor and the other side seeks merely to defend itself. More often, conflict emerges from a political process in which two sides interact. In that process, the so-called balance of terror can cut in different directions. Although the prospect of nuclear devastation should induce caution during a crisis, if both states understand this logic of deterrence and expect that their adversary does as well, there are powerful motivations to engage in what Thomas Schelling calls "contests in risk taking."[10] While each might be afraid of escalation, that fear could be balanced by an understanding that its rival is also afraid. If both adversaries accept the deterrence model at the heart of the Sagan-Waltz debate, each might dig in its heels, convinced the other side will back down when confronted by the danger of nuclear war. It is easy to see where a crisis between two nuclear states pursuing deterrent strategies could quickly get out of hand and even lead to war.

These kinds of competitive dynamics existed before the nuclear age, of course. But the supposedly stabilizing qualities of nuclear weapons touted by Waltz also make dangerous miscalculations more likely. Why? According to most realists, the balance of military power shapes how states behave in world politics. In the prenuclear age, a state would size up an adversary by calculating its chances of prevailing in a military conflict. In the past, if country A had 100 tanks, and country B had 300 tanks, and tanks were the weapons most likely to determine the outcome on the battlefield, country A would be highly unlikely to press its claims against country B too far and would be quick to back down lest a clash of arms leave country A defeated.

But what does the balance of military power mean in the nuclear age? As Waltz argues, nuclear weapons are the "great equalizers."[11] The overwhelming conventional military power that previously drove world politics has far less relevance in a nuclearized world. Country B's three-to-one advantage in tanks, for example, would be of little use in a crisis if country A had a survivable nuclear force. Nuclear deterrence is so robust that the fear of even a handful of nuclear weapons being used against its cities should be enough to keep B from invading, even if its advantage in every other military and economic category was overwhelming.

Waltz contends—and most so-called defensive realists agree—that such a world is more stable and peaceful. But imagine that instead of tanks, country A has 100 nuclear weapons and country B has 300. The numerical balance is largely irrelevant: both sides should be unwilling to act aggressively. But what if A exploits B's admirable risk aversion? Country B might back down in face of A's brinksmanship, to avoid a nuclear war. Invoking Schelling, Trachtenberg explains that such a world creates a perverse, potentially destabilizing incentive structure, rewarding bad behavior, even by the weak: "In the pre-nuclear world . . . the weak tended to give way to the strong. . . . But in a world of invulnerable nuclear forces, as Waltz points out, the military balance counts for little. . . . In such a world there would be a great premium on resolve, on risk-taking, and perhaps ultimately on recklessness."[12]

This is not just a theoretical argument. The history of the Cold War, the same history Waltz and many others rely on to argue for the peace-inducing qualities of nuclear deterrence, reveals examples of how a nuclearized environment can be destabilizing when subjective factors such as resolve and interest, rather than the balance of military power, come into play. Consider an easy test of Waltz's argument that nuclear deterrence stabilizes relations between states: the four-year standoff between the Soviet Union and the United States over the jurisdictional status of Berlin.* If Waltz's framework fails here, where the conditions for nuclear deterrence were ideal, we might question its applicability to other, future cases in which the factors producing stability should be harder.

Waltz's world presumes an aggressor and a defender and a clear sense of what is and is not worth the risk of a thermonuclear war. In reality these crucial issues are not always obvious. Who would have been the aggressor and who the defender in a war over Berlin? When Khrushchev told Llewellyn Thompson, U.S. ambassador to the Soviet Union, that he could not believe "we would bring on such a catastrophe" as a nuclear exchange over Berlin, the ambassador retorted that "it was he who would be taking action to change the present situation." Khrushchev disagreed, arguing, "We [the United States] would be [the] ones [who] would have to cross [the] frontier."[13] The lines between aggressor and defender were blurred throughout the crisis.

Waltz and others have argued that in a nuclearized world, which side had the greater interest and resolve would be clear and that any crisis would most likely be settled on terms favorable to that side. "States are not likely to run major risks for minor gain."[14] But to whom did the outcome of this struggle over West Berlin matter more, the Soviet Union or the United States? The latter had publicly and forcefully declared that its stakes in the city were vital and the credibility of its commitment was at stake. "If we were to accept the Soviet proposal, US commitments would be regarded as a mere scrap

---

*The Cuban missile crisis should also be an easy test, and others have revealed how nuclear weapons made it far more dangerous and unstable than it was. In fact, in a non-nuclear world, there may have been no crisis, and hence, no instability. But for a recent account using new evidence that reveals just how unstable and dangerous the crisis was, see Michael Dobbs, *One Minute to Midnight: Kennedy, Khrushchev, and Castro on the Brink of Nuclear War* (New York: Knopf, 2008).

of paper."[15] Yet West Berlin added nothing to the material strength of the United States or the Western Alliance, and its loss would have had no effect on its position in the overall balance of military power.

Both President Dwight D. Eisenhower and President John F. Kennedy understood that the Soviets had a legitimate vital interest in stabilizing the status of Berlin and the military and political status of Germany and that it could not be defended with conventional forces. Both engaged in negotiations to ease tensions and resolve the crisis.[16] Neither president was pleased with the situation. Eisenhower "expressed unhappiness that here is another instance in which our political posture requires us to assume military positions that are wholly illogical."[17] Kennedy agreed: "So we're stuck in a ridiculous situation. . . . It seems silly for us to be facing an atomic war over a treaty preserving Berlin as the future capital of a reunified Germany when all of us know that Germany will probably never be reunified."[18]

Khrushchev, like Waltz, believed the number of nuclear weapons he had did not matter in this contest of wills. " 'Missiles are not cucumbers,' he liked to say. 'One cannot eat them and one does not require more than a certain number in order to ward off an attack.' "[19] But as Frederick Taylor points out, and contrary to Waltz's position, thermonuclear weapons made Khrushchev "more, not less, bold in his foreign policy calculations."[20] This was based on his belief that "Secretary of State Dulles's threats of massive retaliation were also bluff—brinksmanship based on the fact that both sides knew where the brink was and would act accordingly."[21] But was the location of the brink clear to both sides? When Khrushchev's son, Sergi, asked his father if his ultimatum would lead to war, the Soviet premier replied, "Of course not! No one would want a war over Berlin." The Soviet leader believed that before that time came, his threat would scare the West into negotiations. When his son asked what would happen if the negotiations failed, Khrushchev, irritated, replied, "Then we'll try something else."[22]

The existence of a deterrence strategy on both sides meant that it was difficult for either side to back down. As the U.S. ambassador to the Soviet Union observed, this created the real possibility of misperception leading to nuclear war. "Both sides consider [the] other would not risk war over Berlin. Danger arises from [the] fact that if K carries out his declared intentions and we carry out ours, [the] situation [is] likely [to] get out of control and military as well as political prestige would become involved making retreat for either side even more difficult."[23] Khrushchev expected the Americans to back down before things got serious, but leaders in the United States expected the same kind of restraint from the Soviets. While the Soviet leader may have wanted to avoid a nuclear war, "the real danger is that he might risk just such a war without realizing he is doing so."[24]

This is not to say that all disagreements between nuclear-armed states always have to operate like a Schelling-esque competition in risk-taking. Consider again the situation over West Berlin, only a few years later. The jurisdictional status of the city, the supposed touchstone of the 1958–1962 crisis, had not been resolved when the Nixon administration took office in 1969. Henry Kissinger, the president's national security adviser, told Richard Nixon that, "given the city's vulnerabilities" the Soviets could "manufacture pretexts for harassment whenever they choose" and "strangle the city."[25] The United States would have had far less leverage if such a situation arose. As Nixon told the West German chancellor, owing to "disturbing developments," U.S. strategic superiority had been eliminated while Soviet conventional capabilities had been increased. "In 1962, at the time of the Cuban Missile Crisis, the US lead in strategic missiles had been so massive that no rational decision makers on the Soviet side would have risked war."[26] By 1969, the new president argued this was no longer the case.

A strange thing happened, however: despite small-scale tensions surrounding West Berlin and fears of a new crisis, the Soviet's pursued a mild, even conciliatory policy and sought to formalize the status quo with the West in a treaty. The Soviet ambassador to West Germany stated, "The Soviets respected the fact that West Berlin was occupied by US, UK, and French military forces."[27] Their ambassador to the United States, Anatoly Dobrynin, made it clear that the Soviets had no "intention of undermining the status quo in Western Europe" and did not "care about formal recognition of Eastern Germany."[28] Soviet foreign minister Andrei Gromyko assured Nixon the Soviet Union had "no intention to weaken the status of the allied powers in West Berlin."[29] Soviet leader Leonid Brezhnev even offered that any agreement on West Berlin would have to meet the "wishes of the Berlin population."[30] The Soviets offered a settlement that German chancellor Willy Brandt observed was more favorable than what "was discussed in Geneva in 1959" or what Dean Acheson's Berlin report to President Kennedy hoped to achieve in 1961, periods when the U.S. possessed nuclear superiority. A genuinely surprised Kissinger agreed: "I feel that we're doing better than, than I thought possible."[31] This success was possible, in spite of the fact that, as Brandt pointed out, "we all know the military position rather is more favorable for the Soviet Union than it was then."[32]

Why, only a few years after a dangerous and destabilizing crisis shaped by the nuclear balance and brinkmanship, was the same issue resolved in a relatively amicable manner, where nuclear weapons appeared to play no role at all? The answer is a simple but often forgotten reality, at least in the deterrence and proliferation literature, and one that is absent throughout most of the Sagan-Waltz franchise: politics intervened. The crisis over Berlin in the late 1950s and early 1960s was largely a proxy for the unresolved and contentious political issue surrounding West Germany's military status: whether the Federal Republic of Germany would have access to nuclear weapons. By the late 1960s, this problem had been resolved, and both powers were happy with the status quo: a divided, non-nuclear Germany within a divided Europe. The Soviet leadership no longer needed to threaten West Berlin, and as a consequence, nuclear weapons played little role in the negotiations that led to the Quadripartite Agreement on Berlin in September 1971.

This framework that is adopted by Sagan and Waltz—a focus on the weapons and postures, not the underlying politics—still dominates the scholarly analysis of these issues. Consider the widely divergent nuclear postures chosen by states such as China, Pakistan, and the United States. Despite few financial or technical constraints,

China has puzzled outside observers with an unsophisticated strategy that has not achieved the level of assured destruction that most U.S. strategists would have predicted.[33] Pakistan's strategy eschews assured destruction in favor of a potentially dangerous and destabilizing asymmetric escalation posture that calls for the early use of nuclear weapons in a conventional conflict with India.* The United States approaches nuclear primacy† against its former rivals, particularly Russia, alarming analysts who argue it undermines the strategic stability that leads to peace.[34] In each of these cases, international relations scholars are at pains to explain these divergences from their notion of an ideal deterrent strategy.

What seems puzzling to many security studies scholars—that states do not embrace the optimal, or most stabilizing, nuclear strategy demanded by deterrence theory—might be explained by understanding the political goals the state in question seeks. For a China exploiting its geography and interested primarily in deterring attacks on its homeland, a minimal deterrent may have sufficed for a time. Pakistan, seeking territorial adjustments against a bitter enemy with

---

* Vipin Narang, "Posturing for Peace? Pakistan's Nuclear Postures and South Asian Stability," *International Security* 34, no. 3 (2009/2010), 38–78. Narang's analysis does highlight an excellent point: arms control professionals have focused on the number and quality of nuclear weapons, when what might matter much more are the strategies, postures, and deployments of weapons. Pakistan's arsenal may be dangerous not because of its size or quality but because of how Pakistan deploys and may use it.

† Presumably, the United States possesses near-primacy against every nuclear (and non-nuclear) country in the world. Why aren't France, Israel, and Great Britain more alarmed? One might assume it is because the leaders of those states possess almost no conceivable scenario in which they can imagine the United States would use its forces against them. It might be that the passing of the intense geopolitical and ideological competition that followed the end of the Cold War has produced similar feelings in Russia. This is not to say there are not or will not be political disputes, just that it may be hard for decisionmakers to imagine them rising to the level where the use of nuclear weapons would be likely.

larger conventional capabilities, may need a more aggressive nuclear posture to secure its interests, regardless of how destabilizing it is. The United States may pursue primacy less to threaten Russia than to strengthen its vast array of nuclear umbrella commitments, to reassure and prevent proliferation by potential allies such as Germany and Japan. The existence of deep political disputes between the United States and Russia that could lead to a war would seem to be a far more important indicator of future stability or conflict than the nuclear balance.

Whether these specific assessments are correct is not the point. Rather, no policymaker would assess the consequences of proliferation or a state's nuclear strategy without trying to understand the goals, interests, situation, and character of that state. It matters if the potential proliferator in question is Sweden or Iran, less because of its regime type and more because of its external goals and interests (though those may be related). In fact, the nuclear posture may be important evidence in helping us understand the ambitions of each state in question. Which framework one chooses—whether to focus on the weapons or the underlying politics—has enormous policy consequences as well. What would be a more effective use of scarce diplomatic capital in South Asia, to seek strategic stability through arms control or to make an effort to resolve the underlying political issues driving the posture? Consider what many identify as the most important nuclear arms control effort, the strategic arms limitation negotiations in the 1970s. An unimpeachable belief in the strategy and arms control community is that SALT I and SALT II were unalloyed goods, the cornerstone of strategic stability.

There is an alternative view. Negative reactions within the United States poisoned foreign policy debates and gave rise to neoconservatism.[35] The Soviet military was furious as well, which may have led to the deployment of SS-20 missiles.[36] The SALT agreements inspired great mistrust and unhappiness among many of America's European allies, and the deployment of the SS-20s generated a crisis in NATO.[37] These efforts to establish strategic stability, it could be argued, perversely helped undermine détente by the late 1970s.[38] Might the enormous political capital expended on the SALT negotiations between the Russians and Americans have been more productively spent on other issues? Obviously, arms control and politics are not mutually exclusive focal points—they are inextricably linked—but nuclear strategies do not emerge from a political or historical vacuum, a fact often absent from the academic literature on proliferation, deterrence, and strategic stability.

This is not to say that we should discount the influence of the nuclear revolution on international politics—as the Berlin examples demonstrate, it is profound—or eschew theories and only try to explain things on a case-by-case method. Nuclear behavior since 1945, however, has eluded parsimonious explanation. The history is just emerging and pulls in many different directions. We have and will continue to get a better sense of this from the massive increase in the volume of declassified documents revealing how different states wrestled with the question of developing and deploying nuclear weapons. It is a pity these important new sources are not more fully engaged in this book, or that greater attention is not paid to the core issue in international relations: politics.

Waltz the Theorist versus Waltz the Moralist

In 1981 Waltz made a startling argument about the spread of nuclear weapons: "More may be better."[39] But whether more is better or worse may not even be the most interesting puzzle surrounding proliferation. Both Sagan and Waltz's analyses leave unanswered an important question: If nuclear weapons are so effective at preventing war and providing security, why has there been so little proliferation since 1945? In the anarchic, self-help world of Waltz (and Sagan), where security is so scarce, one should have expected far more than nine nuclear states to have emerged in the past eight decades. Certainly several dozen countries have the technology and wealth to produce their own bombs and have for some time. Intelligence assessments, policy analysts, and academic observers have, for decades, incorrectly predicted that the pace of proliferation would intensify.

Why aren't there twenty, thirty, or forty nuclear states by now, as many would have expected? Neither Waltz nor Sagan explores this question in a systematic way.

One possible answer might be that the realist description of the international system is false—that the world is not so dangerous, that for whatever reason states feel so safe and secure that nuclear weapons are extraneous. Many factors, including the increased lethality of conventional wars, emerging norms and taboos, globalization and interdependence, and the decreasing appeal of conquest, may have made large-scale, prolonged interstate wars of conquest less likely even without the nuclear revolution. Or perhaps the answer is not that the world is safe but that nuclear weapons do not provide as much security as deterrence advocates claim and may make certain states feel more vulnerable and less safe.

Perhaps the best way to understand the question is with another question: Why has the United States gone to such extraordinary lengths to slow, halt, and reverse the spread of nuclear weapons? If nuclear deterrence is as powerful and stabilizing as Waltz and most defensive realists contend, why have U.S. policymakers deployed so many tools and expended so much political capital on nuclear nonproliferation policies? Neither Waltz nor any other realist has developed a satisfying explanation for the consistent and powerful American drive to halt and reverse nuclear proliferation since 1945.[40]

In fact, this strong instinct should not be much of a surprise. As Secretary of State Dean Rusk has said, "It was almost in the nature of nuclear weapons that if someone had them, he did not want others to have them."[41] Since the nuclear age started, the United States has sought to limit nuclear acquisition by friends and foes alike, with what might be called strategies taken from a spectrum of inhibition, a range of soft to harder policies. On the softer side, the United States has tried to inhibit the spread of atomic weapons through international treaties and arms control regimes, including but certainly not limited to the Baruch and Acheson-Lilienthal plans, Atoms for Peace, the Partial Test Ban Treaties, the Nuclear Nonproliferation Treaty, the Nuclear Suppliers Group, the Additional Protocol, and the Proliferation Security Initiative. At the other end of the spectrum of inhibition are harder, more coercive measures. Coercive policies to limit proliferation are not a recent phenomenon. President George W. Bush's military efforts to eliminate Iraq's nuclear weapons were not a dramatic departure from past policies; in fact, strikingly similar preventive actions were seriously considered by the United States against the Soviets in the 1940s, China in the 1960s, and North Korea during the early 1990s. The American temptation to use force to limit nuclear spread has been a persistent feature of nuclear nonproliferation policy, regardless of administration, party affiliation, or structure of the international system.[42]

This harder, more coercive inhibition revealed itself in other policies. In the 1960s, for example, the United States put extraordinary pressure on Israel to drop its nuclear program, made it clear to West Germany that their acquisition of nuclear weapons was unthinkable even if mitigated by a multilateral framework, and contemplated pressuring the British to abandon their atomic program.[43] The idea of sabotaging French nuclear tests was discussed.[44] South Korea and Taiwan were threatened with an end to their alliance with the United States, a measure that would have exposed both countries to great peril, and, along with Pakistan, were threatened with the disruption of the sale of sensitive technology, freezes in economic aid, and promises to cut off fuel supplies if they went nuclear.[45]

America's spectrum of inhibition looks even more impressive if one expands the scope of what is included in its nuclear nonproliferation policies. Before the nuclear age, the United States had no history of making permanent alliances or providing security guarantees to far-flung nations, yet by 2010, by some estimates America covered thirty-one states with nuclear umbrellas.[46] Almost thirty years after the collapse of the Soviet Union, from whom and what exactly are we protecting these states?[47] A large part of the U.S. military commitment to Western Europe during the Cold War was motivated not only by the need to deter the Soviets but also by a pressing need to keep the Federal Republic of Germany non-nuclear. Similar dual concerns—protection and restraint—motivated U.S. security arrangements with Japan and South Korea. The benefits, from a proliferation perspective, went beyond simply keeping the target state non-nuclear. If West Germany did not have nuclear weapons, Italy, Switzerland, and Sweden, for example, might be inclined to abstain. A non-nuclear Japan, Taiwan, and South Korea most likely weakened proliferation pressures in Indonesia and Australia. Inhibiting proliferation has been a core driver of U.S. security commitments since the start of the nuclear age.

Other U.S. policies that diverge from the defensive realist notions of the ideal deterrent policies make far more sense when viewed through the spectrum of inhibition.[48] Nuclear strategies that exceeded the demands of mutual deterrence, including counterforce, escalation dominance, and an unwillingness to embrace no-first-use policies have often been explained as the product of bureaucratic politics, ideology, or misguided instincts. In fact, the need to assure states under the U.S. nuclear umbrella, and to convince them to stay non-nuclear, may have required more robust, forward-leaning, and threatening nuclear posture. Seen in this light, American policymakers' decades-long interest in missile defense may not be irrational and quixotic, as it is often portrayed, but rather serve as a tool to inhibit the effects of nuclear proliferation.

Why has the United States pursued such vigorous nuclear nonproliferation policies against both allies and adversaries? On one level, government officials, regardless of political or ideological background, vehemently disagreed with Waltz's notion that nuclear weapons were a sort of magic wand that brought stability to an otherwise unstable system. On another, they recognized its extraordinary power of nuclear deterrence to be used against the United States and, understandably, would greatly prefer that it not be applied to them. As Matthew Kroenig argues, "Power-projecting states, states with the ability to project conventional military power over a particular target, have a lot to lose when that target state acquires nuclear weapons," whether the target state is enemy or ally.[49]

There are three reasons the United States—or any leading power, regardless of regime type—would work overtime to inhibit proliferation. First, the overwhelming deterrent characteristics of nuclear weapons undercut America's broad and commanding superiority in other categories of power on issues of war and peace, and a world with more deterrence is a world in which the United States is more constrained and in many ways weaker. Furthermore, smaller states can use their nuclear weapons for catalytic purposes, to pull the United States into a conflict the latter would otherwise avoid.* Finally, feeble nuclear powers may be more willing to pursue risky brinksmanship strategies in crises with an otherwise powerful United States. As Michael Horowitz explains, a feeble state "possessing even a single nuclear weapon influences America's strategic calculations and seems to make coercive success harder."[50] This logic, right or wrong, may have driven the George W. Bush administration's effort to end Iraq's nuclear program, since proliferation "neutralizes . . . the overwhelming conventional power of the United States" and "both dampens and encourages risk-taking, rewarding states that successfully push to the brink of nuclear war, and frightening the rest into submission."[51]

It is completely rational for the United States—a state with overwhelming advantages in every other form of hard and soft power—to do whatever it can to keep these equalizers out of the hands of others, friend and foe alike. The United States has and continues to possess the world's largest and most innovative economy, overwhelming conventional military superiority, command of the air, sea, and space,

---

*There is some evidence that France, Pakistan, and possibly South Africa have thought about their nuclear forces this way. Relatedly, think how little control the United States has over how Israel deals with Iran's nuclear program; Israel's deterrent gives it independence from the United States while restricting America's own freedom of action. Far better, from a U.S. perspective, to deal with a nascent nuclear state like North Korea without the pressures and limitations that would be created by a nuclear South Korea or Japan.

favorable geography, and considerable soft power. In a world without nuclear weapons, the United States would face few constraints and would have almost complete freedom to act as it sees fit. A system in which nuclearization reduces or even cancels out many of these extraordinary advantages—and potentially rewards nuclear brinkmanship—is one that U.S. policymakers will go to great lengths to prevent. Deterrence may be more stable for some—particularly states with no ability to project other forms of power—but unappealing for a leading power whose freedom to act is seriously constrained in a nuclearized world. Richard Betts has argued that what may be good for some members of the "system"—nuclear deterrence—may not be what the United States sees as in its own best interest. "If nuclear spread enhances stability, this is not entirely good news for the United States, since it has been accustomed to attacking small countries with impunity when it felt justified and provoked."[52]

Waltz is too smart not to realize how untenable his position is. Despite sharply criticizing U.S. leaders for the divergences from the mutual vulnerability ideal throughout the book—from preventive-war thinking to missile defense to efforts to achieve nuclear primacy—he recognizes his vision for the world is not one U.S. policymakers, or any superpower, has ever embraced or ever will. He writes, "A big reason for America's resistance to the spread of nuclear weapons is that if weak countries have some they will cramp our style. Militarily punishing small countries for behavior we dislike would become much more perilous."[53] While mocking the U.S. desire for missile defense, he captures the inhibiting appeal of such a system: "In short, we want to be able to intervene militarily whenever and where we choose. Our nuclear defenses would presumably make that possible even against countries lightly armed with nuclear weapons."[54]

Waltz argues that by acting this way and inhibiting nuclear spread, U.S. leaders are the bad guys and the small states are the victims. "Our dominance presses them to find ways of blocking our interventionist moves. As ever, dominance, coupled with immoderate behavior by one country, causes others to look for ways to protect their interests."[55] Waltz even recognizes that the American interest in the Global Zero campaign is less about international law, peace, and altruism than about U.S. power:* "Transparently, it is in America's interest to get presently nuclear states to reduce or, better yet, eliminate their warheads. We are, after all, the world's dominant conventional power and have been for years."[56] But even if the goal could be achieved, it would be bad because the leading power in the system would be unrestrained. "But how can any state hope to deter a world dominant power? Conventional defense and deterrence strategies have historically proven ineffective against the United States, so, logically, nuclear weapons are the only weapons capable of dissuading the United States from working its will on other nations."[57] This is a bizarre way for the world's leading realist to look at things: In what version of realism do states seek to constrain their own power by encouraging others to acquire the means to leave them weaker?[58] Does Waltz really think the United States is primarily a bully, a revisionist state bent on war, "fond of beating up poor and weak states"?[59]

Should the United States behave this way? Waltz thinks not; in many ways, I am inclined to agree with him.[60] But this is a normative question, a matter of informed opinion and policy preference. It is not social science. I might prefer that the United States resist the powerful and persistent temptation to coerce potential nuclear powers, friend and foe alike, up to and including serious consideration of preventive military force. I might prefer that the United States consider a grand strategy of off-shore balancing and shrink America's exposure from its vast extended deterrence commitments. But that does not

---

* In such a world, not only would the other elements of the United States' preponderant non-nuclear power provide it with enormous advantages over everyone else in the system; its enormous nuclear infrastructure and technological know-how would also make it the power that could most easily reconstitute its nuclear weapons, making it a de facto nuclear power. In a sense, it could be argued this would make the United States what John Mearsheimer describes as "a hegemon, which effectively means that it has no great-power rivals with which to compete for security." John J. Mearsheimer, *The Tragedy of Great Power Politics* (New York: W. W. Norton, 2001), 128.

remove my obligation as a scholar to try to understand and explain why these things happen persistently and consistently, across decades and shifting U.S. administrations. Waltz himself says, in *Theory of International Politics,* that governments are always being told to "act for the sake of the system and not for their own narrowly defined advantage," but he notes how those urgings are pointless because states, given the kind of anarchic world they find themselves in, have no choice but to focus on their own narrow interests—how they "have to do whatever they think necessary for their own preservation." With each country "constrained to take care of itself, no one can take care of the system."[61]

Waltz revolutionized international relations theory more than sixty years ago in his classic, *Man, The State, and War: A Theoretical Analysis,* by severely criticizing realists such as Hans Morgenthau and Reinhold Niebuhr for offering informed, passionate, ad hoc opinion instead of rigorous theory. "No matter how good their intentions, policy makers must bear in mind the implications of the third image . . . : Each state pursues its own interests, however defined, in ways it judges best." A foreign policy that recognizes the anarchy of the international system "is neither moral nor immoral, but embodies merely a reasoned response to the world about us."[62] The historian Campbell Craig suggests that Waltz rose to prominence arguing that writing that "sought to advocate particular policies" was "not scholarship: it was normative policy recommendation. International politics had a logic all its own that defied the policy wishes of anguished political leaders and intellectuals. It was time, Waltz said, to study this logic analytically."[63]

Waltz reemphasizes the structural approach in *Theory of International Politics.* War and peace are determined by the structure of the system, and it is bipolarity, not nuclear weapons, that produces stability. "Nuclear weapons are not the great equalizers they were sometimes thought to be."[64] Writing in 1979 and assessing the French nuclear force, which included nuclear submarines, bombers, and land-based missiles, Waltz argues that "French officials continue to proclaim the invulnerability of their forces, as I would do if I were they. But I would not find my words credible."[65] Sounding more like Sagan than himself, Waltz contends that the "prospect of a number of states having nuclear weapons that may be ill-controlled and vulnerable is a scary one, not because proliferation would change the system, but because of what lesser powers might do to one another." Referring to the delicate balance of power, he continues, "Those dangers may plague countries having small nuclear forces, with one country tempted to fire its weapons preemptively against an adversary thought to be momentarily vulnerable."[66]

Two years later, without acknowledging it, Waltz completely reversed himself, abdicating the detached perspective of the theorist of anarchy and bipolarity and shifting to Waltz the moralist, with the publication of the first iteration of his views on proliferation, his famous 1981 *Adelphi* paper, which he expanded fourteen years later in *The Spread of Nuclear Weapons*. As Craig summarizes, "What explains international war and peace? Previously, it had been the anarchical structure of international politics, a force that human aspirations and fears were, in the end, helpless to overcome. Now, it was also the aversion to nuclear fear, a first-image phenomenon that resided in the hearts and minds of individual people."[67]

Opposing thermonuclear war is laudable, and Waltz is as welcome to express his informed opinion and policy preferences as the next pundit. As opinion and normative belief, I find some of what he says appealing. But Waltz has always been at great pains to say he is a theorist, a social scientist, above the mere ad hoc musings of punditry. What are we to make of these theories? How do Waltz's ideas on nuclear weapons fit in with his earlier idea that it was the structure of international politics—whether a system was bipolar, multipolar, unipolar—that determined war and peace, stability and instability? And what do terms like *polarity* and *power* mean in the nuclear age? If nuclear weapons equalize all other forms of powers, aren't all nuclear states, even barely functioning ones such as North Korea, poles? In his previous writings, the balance of military power mattered for quite a bit, while now, it appears to matter not at all. What is here that can help guide policy?

Fixing the Franchise

Perhaps this critique is too harsh. *The Spread of Nuclear Weapons* is, after all, a popular, respected, and much-cited work, and if the arguments are not always foolproof, so what? The problems and contradictions in this book would not be particularly noteworthy, except for two issues. First, the failure to vigorously engage and reexamine history is troubling. Second, and more important, the question of nuclear proliferation is of fundamental policy importance and the authors' explicit aim for policy relevance. The arguments must be judged on the terms they themselves laid out.

Making deductive arguments and cherry-picking from the past to justify claims discourages an effort to do serious historical work. Consider the following puzzle: Under a neorealist perspective, one might have expected a dramatic change in the international system—such as the end of the Cold War—to produce important and presumably uniform effects on the pace of nuclear proliferation. In the middle of the 1980s, Brazil, India, and South Africa had strong interests in nuclear weapons programs. By the late 1990s, however, each had gone in a completely different direction: South Africa, after building nuclear weapons, gave them up; India tested and became a nuclear weapons state; and Brazil decided to end its nuclear weapons program.[68] Nor did the United States do much to influence any of the three; each was, for the most part, immune to the American inhibition spectrum. Why the variation, when the states in question were so similar and the shift in the system presumably determinative? The only way scholars can know is to do careful historical work and reconstruct how and why these decisions were made.

The second issue is policy relevance. Decisionmakers desperately need knowledge that can help them navigate the extraordinarily complex and consequential decisions they face as they construct nuclear nonproliferation policies. Consider the hard decisions about what to do about Iran's nuclear efforts. Whatever the choices, the decisions will reverberate with important and unforeseen consequences for years. If Iran develops nuclear weapons, will the regime be deterred?

45

Will states in the region jump onto the bandwagon or balance with Iran? Will Iran's neighbors develop their own nuclear weapons? Will Israel undertake a strike, albeit a less effective and comprehensive one, pulling the United States into a conflict it never wanted? If the United States did strike, would the regime in Tehran fall, or would it become more entrenched? Would terrorism increase? What would be the wider implications for the global nonproliferation regime, the attitude of North Korea, regional stability, and relations with Europe, Russia, and China, and what would be the effect on the global economy?[69]

No one can possibly know the answers ahead of time, or how each decision, event, and outcome would interact to produce a future we could never anticipate. Yet policymakers must make decisions, choose in the face of radical uncertainty that may involve precious blood and treasure. They are correctly held accountable and can lose their careers and their reputations if they are wrong. Most would be grateful for serious help from the ivory tower, a sense of what the past might tell us, insightful and nuanced analysis that might reveal a way of understanding things that had never occurred to overstressed policymakers trying to make sense of things.[70] Instead, they open their *Foreign Affairs* to find a primer from Kenneth Waltz entitled, "Why Iran Should Have the Bomb," offering selective history, contradictory reasoning, and the pedantic tone of the wise professor chastising childlike policymakers.[71]

Does this mean Sagan wins the debate? There is no doubt that his argument is far more nuanced, interesting, and sensitive to history. But it has its own problems. Waltz is right to rein in Sagan's alarmism, particularly on the overhyped fear of nuclear terrorism. Sagan puts too much stock in the Nuclear Nonproliferation Treaty, which is only one tool in the American spectrum of inhibition, while he underplays the importance of coercive measures and even nuclear umbrellas, which require the United States to do things to extend deterrence (eschew no-first-use, explore missile defense, seek primacy) that make him uncomfortable. One would have been grateful if Sagan had examined the unusual cases; for example, Italy's outrage over the nonproliferation treaty, which incited a rancorous internal debate and exerted pressure to initiate a weapons program in the late 1960s and early 1970s.[72] Also, Sagan's focus on safety implies that the problem is less the spread of nuclear weapons than construction of safe, effective organizations and procedures to manage them. One has to ask, if the United States developed and exported a nearly perfect way to protect and store nuclear weapons, would that solve the problem of nuclear spread? In policy terms, should we spend our political capital working to ensure better safety among nuclear aspirants, despite moral hazard concerns?

The real problem, however, is that Sagan plays small ball in his debate with Waltz, conceding the big issues. Why not challenge Waltz on his core arguments about deterrence and stability? Yes, policymakers care about organizational mistakes and inadvertent escalation. But what they understand more is that nuclear weapons can transform crises into tests of will and battles of resolve that are much different from crises involving only conventional weapons. The most effective policies must try to understand the differential interests of states jockeying for power and security in ways classical realists would grasp but Waltz's one-size-fits-all approach and Sagan's organizational focus (which bypasses state interests) largely ignore.

More is at stake here than who wins an academic debate. At a time when academics, particularly those who study national and international security, are trying to find ways to more effectively bridge the gap between scholarship and policy, that the franchise is so influential within the academy and has so little impact among decision-makers is revealing. Waltz recommends policies that have no chance of being treated seriously, to say nothing of being adopted, all while chastising the policies of a country that has weathered the nuclear age by defeating its rival without using these weapons. U.S. leaders have made mistakes, to be sure, but if in 1960 you had told a serious person—Waltz included—that by 2019 the United States would have no peer military rivals; communism would be all but dead; Germany would be reunified, non-nuclear, and peaceful; Japan would be docile; the number of nuclear states would be in the single digits; and the possibility of great-power war would be lower than at any time since the creation of the Westphalian state system, they would have said you were nuts.

Waltz, the great theorist, predicted none of this, nor would these events have happened if the United States had followed the advice of Waltz the great moralist. U.S. national security figures must have been doing something right. It is no wonder his arguments are not taken seriously, which would be fine if not for the fact that he is touted to those in positions of responsibility as the father of international relations theory and the most important thinker on war and peace that political science has produced since 1945. As Sagan (but apparently not Waltz) surely knows, there is important and compelling work being done—by both political scientists and historians—in strategic studies on the nuclear question. But unless a greater effort is made to demonstrate that the field understands and empathizes with the concerns of those who make these terrible, stressful policies under extraordinary pressures, this work may be dismissed as not serious. And no one—not the scholar trying to make a difference nor the policymaker trying to make difficult decisions in an environment of complex uncertainty—would benefit from that.

THREE

What We Talk about When We Talk about Nuclear Weapons

> Susan, we need to talk. I've been doing a lot of thinking lately.
> About us. I really like you, but ever since we met in that econ
> class in college I knew there was something missing from how
> I felt: quantitative reasoning. We can say we love each other all
> we want, but I just can't trust it without the data. And after per-
> forming an in-depth cost-benefit analysis of our relationship, I
> just don't think this is working out.
>
> Please know that this decision was not rash. In fact, it was
> anything but—it was completely devoid of emotion. I just made
> a series of quantitative calculations, culled from available OECD
> data on comparable families and conservative estimates of future
> likelihoods. I then assigned weights to various "feelings" based
> on importance, as judged by the relevant scholarly literature.
> From this, it was easy to determine that given all of the options
> available, the winning decision on both cost-effectiveness and
> comparative-effectiveness grounds was to see other people. It's
> not you, it's me. Well, it's not me either: it's just common sense,
> given the nature of my utility function.[1]

In his memoirs, President Harry S. Truman claimed that he issued an
ultimatum—the first of the atomic age—that forced Stalin to remove
Russian troops from Iran in 1946. Years later, however, George V.
Allen, a former U.S. State Department official, told the political scientist Alexander George that neither he nor other high-level officials
from that period—including Averell Harriman, the U.S. ambassador

to the Soviet Union, and James Byrnes, U.S. secretary of state—knew of any explicit threat issued by the president to the Soviets during the crisis. While Allen acknowledged that sending an aircraft carrier would have sent a powerful message—"It might well have carried an atomic bomb"—he worried how scholars would portray the incident. "The 'ultimatum' story illustrates the problem of pinning down factual information in the so-called social sciences."[2]

The 1946 Azerbaijan crisis—coming less than seven months after the United States became the first and only country to ever drop nuclear weapons on another country—has both fascinated and confounded scholars. Were the Soviets compelled to leave, or deterred from violating their agreement with their wartime allies, by an ultimatum from a United States armed with atomic weapons? What exactly was communicated to the Soviets, did they understand the message as a threat, and how did it influence their policy? Or was the Soviet withdrawal unrelated to Truman's ultimatum, driven instead by what some scholars contend was their separate, successful negotiations with the new Iranian government, who granted Russia a generous split in oil revenues and promised to protect the Tudeh (communist) party in Iran?[3] More broadly, what role did U.S. atomic weapons play in the outcome, and would the crisis have played out differently in a world without the bomb? And is the ambiguity and uncertainty surrounding the 1946 crisis anomalous, or does it reflect a larger indeterminacy that marks the nuclear age?

This would not be the last time these questions would confound and perplex observers. Only weeks after the Azerbaijan crisis was resolved, the strategist Bernard Brodie published his classic work, *The Absolute Weapon*, which lays out the core challenge policymakers and strategists have wrestled with ever since the American bombings of Hiroshima and Nagasaki: "Thus far the chief purpose of our military establishment has been to win wars. From now on its chief purpose must be to avert them."[4] But how could this be done in a world in which states competed ruthlessly and where war had long been seen as a legitimate and routine policy instrument to achieve their goals? Strategists suggested that these powerful, horrific weapons might serve to prevent other states from attacking those who possessed them. But could atomic and thermonuclear weapons be used for anything more? Were there circumstances—such as possessing an overwhelming advantage in numbers of atomic weapons vis-à-vis an adversary—or strategies, including a greater willingness to risk situations in which the weapons might go off (purposively or inadvertently), in which wide space between deterrence and actual use could be exploited by a state to achieve more ambitious goals?

These are questions of fundamental importance that have been fiercely contested for years, and despite scores of articles and books, no consensus has been achieved. Furthermore, the salience of these issues goes beyond mere academic importance: where one sits in this debate influences how one feels about important policy questions. Consider discussions over Iran's nuclear ambitions. Would Iran use nuclear weapons simply to prevent its adversaries from attacking its homeland? Or might it exploit the bomb to issue threats, engage in brinkmanship, and challenge the United States and its allies in the greater Middle East? It is hard to formulate a consistent, logical position about contemporary challenges without wrestling with deeper theoretical and empirical questions surrounding nuclear dynamics. After eight decades with a nuclear sword of Damocles hanging over our heads, a period that has seen crises but no nuclear use since August 1945, what do we actually know about how nuclear weapons influence and shape world politics? And what is the best way to gain insight into these critical puzzles?

Three bright young scholars believe they have a way to answer these questions. Statistical methods, an increasingly popular and professionally rewarded approach among political scientists, are the basis for the arguments made in two papers published in the prestigious journal *International Organization* and reviewed here: "Crisis Bargaining and Nuclear Blackmail," by Todd S. Sechser and Matthew Fuhrmann, and "Nuclear Superiority and the Balance of Resolve: Explaining Nuclear Crisis Outcomes," by Matthew Kroenig.[5] How does their method work? The goal is to identify and cumulate the "universe" of like cases where important issues such as nuclear blackmail and superiority were engaged, identify and "code" the key variables, and undertake statistical analysis and draw causal inferences about what mattered and what led to certain outcomes. In these articles, coding involves clearly identifying and assigning a numerical value, often binary, to variables including which state sought to preserve the status quo and which was revisionist, what side had the greater stakes in the outcome of a crisis, which country undertook greater military mobilization to demonstrate resolve, who had more nuclear weapons, and most important, which country "won" the standoff.

Sechser and Fuhrmann want to know whether nuclear weapons give states a greater ability to compel their adversaries to change their behavior, as opposed to merely deterring them. To answer this question, they have compiled an inventory of more than 200 militarized compellent threats between 1918 and 2001. They contend that unlike previous studies, theirs explores non-nuclear as well as nuclear coercion, to generate "variation" to identify the real impact of nuclear weapons. Furthermore, they separate out crisis victories that are caused by compellence and those achieved by "brute force," pointing out that the latter are, in fact, compellence failures. Sechser and Fuhrmann conclude that compellence is likely to be effective only when a challenger credibly seeks to seize an adversary's territory and can enact a threat with few costs to itself. Neither condition is likely to hold in nuclear standoffs: the threat to use nuclear bombs to destroy the sought-after territory hardly makes sense, and few goals are worth risking the international backlash and potential military response that nuclear use would bring. Sechser and Fuhrmann's statistical analysis suggests that whatever deterrent benefits nuclear weapons may confer, they are poor tools to bring about changes in international relations.

Kroenig asks a related set of questions: What is more likely to determine the outcome of a nuclear standoff, the nuclear balance or the balance of resolve? Qualitative scholars have explored this issue through the historical analysis of a few key episodes, but Kroenig sets out to create a systematic analysis of what he considers all the relevant cases. To do so, he also constructs his own data set, made up of what he has identified as fifty-two nuclear crisis dyads, to see what factors determined the outcome. Kroenig concludes that nuclear superiority does matter, allowing the state in possession of larger numbers to "win" more often. Kroenig also finds evidence that the side with greater political stakes is more likely to prevail. Building on the work of Thomas Schelling, Kroenig argues that nuclear crises are "competitions in risk taking," or tests of nerve.[6] Possessing greater numbers of nuclear weapons allows a state to run greater risks and ultimately force the weaker adversary to back down.

These two papers are interesting for a number of reasons. Fuhrmann, Sechser, and Kroenig are part of an exciting scholarly renaissance in nuclear studies. In a field where younger scholars are increasingly incentivized to play small ball, all three deserve high praise for wresting with issues of fundamental importance; both here and elsewhere, they have taken on big questions.[7] Furthermore, both papers build on but also criticize an earlier generation of what political scientists call qualitative and case-study work on these issues.[8] Neither shy away from bold, certain claims. Sechser and Fuhrmann claim their findings carry "important theoretical implications," while Kroenig presents "a new theoretical explanation" and "the first comprehensive empirical examination of nuclear crisis outcomes."[9] The murkiness, contingency, and contention that mark many of the historical debates over specific crises (Why did Soviet Russia leave Iran in 1946? Why did the Soviet Union remove its missiles from Cuba in October 1962? How should we understand the China-Soviet crisis of 1969?) are missing here, which suggests that by quantifying and analyzing these issues scientifically, certainty can be established. Yet while both articles apply statistical analysis to many of the same issues and historical events, they arrive at different, almost opposite conclusions about nuclear dynamics and world politics. Sechser and Fuhrmann contend that nuclear weapons, while good for deterrence, are not useful to compel. Kroenig claims nuclear superiority helps states prevail during standoffs, whether their goal is to deter or compel, in part because it allows them to demonstrate more resolve.

These differences have sparked a spirited online debate among the authors and captured the attention of many younger scholars in the field.[10]

Perhaps most important, both pieces draw concrete policy lessons from the authors' research for contemporary decisionmakers. Sechser and Fuhrmann contend that, "from a practical perspective, our findings have important implications for nuclear nonproliferation policy."[11] Because nuclear weapons are not useful to compel, the United States should not be unduly worried if other states get the bomb, and certainly should not use military force to prevent countries like Iran from developing the bomb. Kroenig also argues that his "findings are highly relevant to policy debates about arms control, nuclear disarmament, and nuclear force sizing"; his conclusions can be interpreted as providing support for a more aggressive U.S. posture vis-à-vis Iran.[12] These links to contemporary policy are not surprising: all three authors have been awarded prestigious fellowships from the Stanton Foundation, which encourages scholars to produce policy-relevant work on nuclear issues, and all have published important opinion pieces in nonacademic and foreign policy venues.

In many ways, the three authors are exemplars of policy-relevant scholarship, asking big questions and seeking audiences of influence. What are we to make of their claims? Does either paper resolve the decades-long debate over these long-contested issues in nuclear dynamics, provide a methodological blueprint for how scholarship in this field should move forward in the future, and present us with much needed guidance to navigate the vexing nuclear challenges of the twenty-first century?

As a historian interested in these questions, I would assess Sechser and Fuhrmann's and Kroenig's arguments straightforwardly. I would identify the most important example where these issues are engaged, look at the primary documents, see how the authors coded crucial variables, and determine how good a job their analysis does in helping us understand both the specific crisis itself and the larger issues driving nuclear dynamics. Political scientists might describe this as running both a strong and a critical test[13]: if the authors' theories do not fully explain the outcomes and causal mechanisms in the most important and most representative case, how useful are the findings in explaining the broader issues?*

Is there such a case? In a speech on November 10, 1958, Soviet premier Nikita Khrushchev demanded that the Western powers—the United States, Great Britain, and France—remove their military forces from West Berlin within six months.[14] This ultimatum was the start of a tense, four-year period that many believe brought the world closer to thermonuclear war than any time before or since, culminating in the Cuban missile crisis of October 1962.[15] According to a leading historian of postwar international politics, "the great Berlin crisis of 1958 to 1962" was "the central episode of the Cold War."[16] And as McGeorge Bundy states, "There were more than four years of political tension over the future of Berlin. . . . Khrushchev's Berlin crisis gives us what is otherwise missing in the nuclear age: a genuine nuclear confrontation in Europe."[17]

Given the stakes and the risks, it is not unreasonable to ask that any theory of nuclear dynamics help us better understand the 1958–1962 thermonuclear standoff. I would want to know how (and why) each paper coded the key variables the way it did: who had the highest stakes in the crisis, who demonstrated the most resolve, who was the aggressor and who was the deterrer, what role did nuclear superiority play, and who emerged in a better position after the crisis? Most important, I would want to be convinced that the causal mechanisms identified by the authors did, in fact, drive the origins, development, and outcome of this crisis.

When one peruses these documents, the limitations of the coding in both the Sechser-Fuhrmann and Kroenig papers—or any effort at coding this complex crisis—becomes clear right away.[18] Available archival sources indicate that both the Soviet Union and the United

---

* The idea that there is such a thing as a crucial case is not without controversy among political scientists; some believe that while such a standard might be applicable to deterministic phenomena (such as chemical reactions), it is not appropriate to apply to nondeterministic interactions in international relations.

States saw the stakes as being higher for themselves, believed the other was the aggressor, and were dubious that their adversary was willing to risk thermonuclear war to get its way. When Khrushchev told Llewellyn Thompson, U.S. ambassador to the Soviet Union, that he could not believe the United States "would bring on such a catastrophe," the ambassador retorted that "it was he [Khrushchev] who would be taking action to change the present situation." Khrushchev disagreed, arguing, "We would be ones who would have to cross frontier."[19] To whom did the status quo in Berlin matter more? When Ambassador Thompson told Khrushchev that "U.S. prestige everywhere in the world was at stake in its commitments to Berliners," Khrushchev scoffed. "Berlin was really of little importance to either America or the Soviet Union," he replied, "so why should they get so worked up about changing the city's status?"[20]

Which state was the aggressor, and which was the status quo power during this standoff? At first glance, the answer seems obvious: the Soviets initiated the crisis and wanted to change the status of Berlin, going so far as to install medium-range nuclear missiles in Cuba to achieve their ends. Yet the Americans had long recognized that Berlin's odd occupational status was temporary and needed to be fixed. As Eisenhower put it, "We do not seek a perpetuation of the situation in Berlin; clearly, we did not contemplate 50 years in occupation there."[21] Furthermore, there are compelling reasons to believe that Khrushchev's primary goal in the period was to prevent, or deter, the Federal Republic of Germany from gaining access to nuclear weapons. The Eisenhower administration's seeming support for a nuclearized Bundeswehr would have to be coded as profoundly revisionist and deeply inimical to core Soviet interests.[22] As Khrushchev told his colleagues at the start of the crisis, "All we want to do is to secure the status quo."[23]

And for whom did the outcome matter more? In secret documents and public signaling, both portrayed their own stakes in the crisis in the highest terms.[24] The documents reveal that the Americans held what appeared to be contradictory views: they both recognized and respected Soviet interests during the crisis and complained bitterly about having to defend a city of little strategic importance, yet at the end of the day they believed that failing to defend their position could lead to a disastrous collapse of NATO and an unacceptable victory for the Soviet Union. Both Presidents Eisenhower and Kennedy, and Premier Khrushchev, were clearly willing to accept a not insubstantial risk of nuclear war to maintain their position.

Do these studies provide greater insight into what determined the outcome of the crisis, the balance of resolve, the balance of military capabilities, or some combination? There is little doubt that both sides understood the importance of demonstrating resolve: Khrushchev explicitly pursued a brinkmanship strategy, fully aware that America had nuclear superiority but believing it did not matter, while the United States pressed on despite what would seem to be greater stakes for the Soviets.[25] But is it possible to accurately code subjective factors such as interest and resolve during a nuclear crisis?*

Sechser and Fuhrmann see military mobilization as an important way of signaling intent. But during the 1958–1962 period, not everyone saw things that way: both Khrushchev and Eisenhower wanted to reduce their conventional forces in Central Europe even as the crisis was heating up. In 1961, former Secretary of State Dean Acheson recommended signaling U.S. resolve through extensive military preparations, but National Security Adviser McGeorge Bundy took the Eisenhower-Gaullist line that any conventional mobilization would undermine the "shield of nuclear deterrence."[26] In other words, calling up reserves or sending additional divisions to Europe made it seem like the West was less likely to use nuclear weapons, undermining the adversary's percep-

---

* The Americans, for their part, understood they had to demonstrate resolve but were also keenly aware that they had what they believed to be a meaningful nuclear superiority that would only last a few more years. The evidence pulls in different directions: immersing oneself in the period, one gets the sense that U.S. nuclear superiority had to matter, as a conventional defense of West Berlin by NATO was hopeless. On the other hand, American leaders took Khrushchev's threats, made from an inferior military position, very seriously, and it is quite easy to imagine much different outcomes at various points in the crisis.

tion of their resolve. Bundy and others believed that the Soviets would be deterred only if they believed any conflict would escalate almost immediately to general nuclear war, a condition that would not be affected by the call-up of reserves.[27] More important, it may not even be possible to code resolve ex ante: the crisis itself reveals that one or both sides has misread the other's resolve, which was the very reason for the crisis in the first place. In other words, it is the crisis behavior that reveals resolve, not the other way around.

How about the issues surrounding nuclear superiority—how it is measured and whether it translates into meaningful political power that affects crisis outcomes? These questions lie at the heart of Kroenig's arguments, and I find three flaws in the way he deals with this issue. First, his model does not appear to adequately address the most consequential aspect of the question, the issue that most concerned policymakers during the 1958–1962 period: whether either side believed it possessed a robust enough capability to launch a first strike and escape the ensuing response with an acceptable level of damage. While there was no consensus on the question, there is little doubt that key decisionmakers in both the Eisenhower and Kennedy administrations saw the issue of acceptable damage as the most important factor when considering the nuclear balance. In fact, the Kennedy administration worked on a sub-SIOP (single integrated operational plan) program after the failed Vienna summit that some within the administration believed could knock out the Soviet Union's ability to respond. As Carl Kaysen, who worked on the plan (and no hawk), suggested, "There are numerous reasons for believing that the assumptions are reasonable, that we have the wherewithal to execute the raid, and that, while a wide range of outcomes is possible, we have a fair probability of achieving a substantial measure of success."[28] The plan was debated and discussed throughout the fall of 1961, in language that made it clear that the key issue was not a simplistic measure of superiority but rather whether a strike could incapacitate the Soviet Union's ability to retaliate.[29]

Furthermore, many in the administration—including the president himself—were aware that this potential first-strike capability was a rapidly wasting asset, even if the United States maintained a massive numerical superiority, a fact that must have driven crisis calculations. The end of this window—and its consequences for how President Kennedy viewed future nuclear confrontations—is quite clear from a September 1963 briefing*:

> The President asked whether, even if we attack the USSR first, the loss to the U.S. would be unacceptable to political leaders. General [Leon] [Johnson] replied that it would be, i.e. even if we preempt, surviving Soviet capability is sufficient to produce an unacceptable loss in the U.S.
>
> The President asked whether then in fact we are in a period of nuclear stalemate. General Johnson replied that we are.
>
> Referring to a statement of the Air Force Association which appeared in this morning's *Washington Post*, the President asked how we could obtain nuclear superiority as recommended by the Air Force Association. General Johnson said this was a very difficult question to answer. He acknowledged that there is no way, no matter what we do, to avoid unacceptable damage in the U.S. if nuclear war breaks out. He later acknowledged that it would be impossible for us to achieve nuclear superiority.[30]

---

* Two years earlier, Kennedy had asked military officials for explicit answers to questions surrounding the mechanics and consequences of a U.S. first strike on the Soviets. "Berlin developments may confront us with a situation where we may desire to take the initiative in the escalation of conflict from the local to the general war level." Memorandum from General Maxwell Taylor to General Lemnitzer, 19 September 1961, enclosing memorandum on "Strategic Air Planning," National Archives, Record Group 218, Records of the Joint Chiefs of Staff, Records of Maxwell Taylor, Box 34, Memorandums for the President, 1961. This notion that the United States faced a closing "window of opportunity" where it could launch a first strike was not new. Secretary of State John Foster Dulles, recognizing how poor Soviet retaliatory capabilities were, lamented in 1958 that the United States had a first-strike capability that would not last forever. "We would probably not have another such chance. But probably we did not have the nerve to take advantage of the probabilities. . . . Our successors, a decade from now, might pay the price." Fursenko and Naftali, *Khrushchev's Cold War*, 177.

Obviously, there is a profound difference between numerical superiority, no matter how large, and a nuclear balance that enables a country to launch a first-strike that allows it to absorb an acceptable level of retaliatory damage.*

What about Kroenig's effort to code nuclear superiority, even in the absence of a first-strike capability? Kroenig is correct that some countries—the United States and the Soviet Union—may have wanted more strategic weapons because such an advantage "limits the expected damage that a country would incur in the event of a nuclear exchange," even in the absence of a first-strike capability.[31] It is important to note, however, that the ability to increase damage limitation capabilities has been driven as much, if not more so, by qualitative improvements as by the increase in raw numbers. SALT I and SALT II kept the strategic balance between the Soviet Union and the United States relatively stable in terms of numbers of strategic weapons and even in terms of the mix among missiles fired, submarines launched, and bombers delivered.

Yet beginning in the early 1970s under Secretary of Defense James Schlesinger and accelerating during the Ford, Carter, and Reagan administrations, the United States spent hundreds of billions of dollars on technological changes in the nuclear area that may have had a profound effect on how each side viewed the strategic balance. A wide range of initiatives to improve damage limitation capabilities,

---

*It is important to note that Kroenig mischaracterizes Trachtenberg's argument. It is clear that Trachtenberg is focusing not on simplistic numerical calculations of nuclear superiority but rather on the more meaningful notion of whether a state can go first in a crisis and suffer acceptable damage in a response. Kroenig argues that the United States was not in such a position in this period, but as the present-day perspective, it is not clear that he is correct. The September 12, 1963, briefing makes it clear that for President Kennedy, meaningful superiority meant an advantage that could be translated into better political outcomes—a first-strike capability, a capacity he may have possessed earlier but no longer had. When the Soviets, having been hit, could respond with enough force to make any U.S. nuclear attack nonsensical, the calculations changed dramatically.

including stealth technologies; cruise missiles; increased accuracy; better targeting; improved command, control, communications, and intelligence; missile defense; target hardening; submarine silencing; and antisubmarine warfare were pursued. When new platforms, such as the stealth bomber, the MX missile, and Trident D-5, replaced old ones, the overall numbers of strategic weapons did not increase—in fact, megatonnage decreased—but the damage limitation capabilities were much improved. Numerical parity in 1972 was not the same thing as numerical parity in 1985, a fact that influenced behavior on both sides.[32] The bottom line is that numerical superiority does not always convey the dynamics of damage limitation.

Finally, why, out of nine nuclear weapons states, have the Soviet Union and the United States been the most aggressive in seeking damage limitation capabilities? And why has one country—the United States—pursued damage limitation deployments far more assertively than any other nuclear country, even in the decades after its primary nuclear rival collapsed? While it may seem logical that any state would want to have more weapons than its adversaries, there is another dynamic at work: credible damage-limitation strategies were needed to reassure allies as much as, and at times more than, to deter or compel adversaries. This was not done by U.S. policymakers out of the goodness of their hearts; they knew that without the assurances provided by a robust nuclear umbrella, countries such as Germany, Japan, South Korea, and a host of others might deploy their own nuclear weapons, a development that would be inimical to America's strategic interest, for reasons Kroenig understands all too well.[33] This underlying and powerful geopolitical logic—that dampening nuclear proliferation among friends required security assurances that were much more credible when the United States pursued damage limitation—does not appear to be captured in either model. Yet the complex story of extended deterrence and nuclear nonproliferation was one of the key drivers of U.S. nuclear strategy (and at the heart of several of the key nuclear crises) throughout the postwar period.[34] Perhaps the most important question in studies concerned with outcomes is whether the papers help us better understand who won the 1958–1962 standoff and why. While most historians believe we can only understand what drove both the origins and outcomes of the crisis by seeing this period as continuous, these data sets break them down into three separate, distinct crises. What does their coding tell us? The International Crisis Behavior Project codes the 1961 construction of the Berlin Wall as a Soviet victory. But many within the Kennedy administration recognized that by walling off the eastern part of the city to stem the flow of refugees, the Soviets were more likely to allow the status quo in the western part to remain, which would make this an American victory.[35] Also, is it really clear the Soviets lost the Cuban missile crisis—as the project codes it—if Castro's regime was preserved, U.S. missiles were removed from Turkey, and, most important, West Germany remained non-nuclear? Of course, that does not mean it was a loss for the United States, as the Soviets removed the missiles from Cuba and the status quo in Berlin was maintained, and the Americans had come to recognize that perhaps German nuclearization was not in their interests either.[36] Arguably, both the United States and the Soviet Union got what they wanted, highlighting how the zero-sum win-lose approach of large-N studies is ill-suited to this case and international politics more broadly.

All of this highlights how limited any effort to code complex historical events will be. Under Sechser and Fuhrmann's own coding, compellence did work in 1962, and under Kroenig's, a vastly outgunned Soviet Union pursued nuclear brinkmanship over a long period of time—what Khrushchev called the "meniscus strategy"[37]—and may have gotten everything it really wanted. Perhaps, one might say, it is not fair to focus on the 1958–1962 superpower standoff: it might be unique, an outlier, too complex to code effectively.[38] But then what, precisely, is 1958–1962 a case of? And if these models cannot tell us anything about arguably the most important and consequential nuclear standoff in history, should I take comfort that it apparently can explain why the U.S. successfully restored Jean-Bertrand Aristide in 1994 or won in Nicaragua in 1984? Or look at the 1983 Able Archer affair, perhaps the most recent case in which the risk of thermonuclear war was possible (if highly unlikely). The crisis emerged because the Soviets were worried that a NATO war game might have been a preparation for an attack on the Soviet Union. If this fear was accurate, then what precisely was America's basic goal, if any, during this crisis? If this crisis was something one or both sides simply stumbled into by accident, with no codable goal, how is it relevant?[39] Unfortunately, these kinds of crucial subtleties are inevitably lost in the efforts to code and quantify complex events.

The problems in this approach, however, go well beyond the difficulty of coding. To make meaningful insights from statistical analysis, we need a certain number of like and comparable observations. But nuclear crises are rare precisely because they are so serious. Should every disagreement involving a country with the bomb be coded as a nuclear standoff? Why would we automatically assume that the nuclear balance is front and center when leaders of two nuclear states clash in some form? And shouldn't the model convey some sense of the level of nuclear danger and distinguish between the apocalyptic fears produced by the Cuban missile crisis and the more mundane worries generated by the 1964 Congo crisis? A commonsense approach quickly reveals that for most of the cases in both data sets there was no danger that nuclear weapons would be used.[40] While the focus in both papers is on outcomes, there really should be a fuller discussion of how we even know something is a nuclear crisis (and how much of a crisis it is) before we start compiling and comparing them.

There are other difficulties. Consider the distinction—crucial to both sets of arguments—between deterrence and compellence, a difference made famous by Thomas Schelling.[41] There are several problems here. First, deterrence is supposed to be easier and compellence harder, a proposition that has rarely been tested in either the qualitative or quantitative literature.[42] This implies that it should have been a relatively straightforward project to prevent the Soviets from taking over West Berlin but much harder to compel them to leave. But presumably the Russians would have understood that before moving in, so how could they have been deterred from taking the city in the first place? More fundamentally, as the 1958–1962 period makes clear, the definition of the status quo—and of who is the compeller and who the deterrer—is often in the eye of the beholder. Was Khrushchev trying to compel the Western powers to leave Berlin or, rather, to deter the United States from supporting West Germany's nuclearization? Or both? Did Stalin order the blockade of Berlin in 1948 to deter the creation of the Federal Republic of Germany, or was he trying to compel the West to abandon a policy—the western strategy for Germany—which it had been pursuing since 1946? Or to look at a prenuclear case: In 1914 was Austria trying to compel Serbia to abandon its policy of creating a greater Serbian state at Austrian expense (and to compel Russia to abandon its policy of supporting Serbia in that area), or was it trying to deter Serbia from challenging the status quo?

There is a more important issue. James Fearon and others have pointed out that countries select into crises like the ones studied here, meaning their preexisting beliefs about the balance of military power and resolve have already come into play in their decision to initiate and respond to a crisis.[43] To truly understand how important military balances or resolve are, one would not just analyze crisis outcomes; one would also need to include the crises that never happened, because a state calculated that either it was outgunned or did not possess the requisite resolve to prevail. In other words, the question of resolve and the military balance has already come into play before a crisis is even initiated, so studying nuclear crises does not reveal the full story of whether and how military power plays affect world politics.[44] It is hard to imagine how one could effectively control for such a thing: Who knows how many nuclear crises never happened because one side or the other was deterred from either initiating or responding to a provocation? It may very well have been the Soviet Union's sense of military inferiority or lack of resolve that caused it to stand by as the United States rearmed West Germany between 1952 and 1954, for example, a policy that was deeply threatening to Soviet Russia. It is very hard to undertake statistical analysis on nonevents. Perhaps the best we can to do is attempt to reconstruct the decision-making on both sides.[45]

The authors might respond that they are interested in the far more narrow explanation of crisis that outcomes have already been selected into. If so, then their causal explanations behind the theory must work; in other words, they cannot explain just the outcome but must also explain why the outcome happened the way it did. Even if their coding were perfect, does either theory convincingly identify the causal mechanism that drives the origin, dynamics, and outcome of the standoff? As Marc Trachtenberg reminds us, "The world at the end of 1962 was very different from the world of November 1958."[46] Do the theories or causal mechanisms identified in either paper—nuclear superiority or the taking of territory—help us understand the reasons for these important changes?

Looking at the documents, not so much. Damage limitation, the fear of unacceptable damage, and the role of territory may have played a role, pulling in different directions, but none of these factors was decisive or really tells us very much, in the same way that identifying the aggressor and the defender or coding who won the standoff provides little more than the most superficial view of these complex, consequential events. In the end, the 1958–1962 crisis was resolved through a political settlement that emerged by 1963 and that reflected the core interests of both superpowers.[47] This relates to the final point about this approach: the whole focus on military factors, divorced from their political contexts—not just in these papers but in most treatments of nuclear dynamics in security studies—can be misleading. There is little doubt that nuclear weapons have transformed world politics and that military factors played a crucial role in the 1963 settlement. But it is a state's political goals and preferences that shape its military strategies, not the other way around.

To better understand this point, think about a nuclear crisis that was expected by many but did not occur—the years leading up to the 1971 agreement on Berlin. The documents from the late 1960s make it clear that the Nixon administration feared a renewal of the Berlin crisis when it took office. None of the explicit, public issues Khrushchev demanded in 1958 had been resolved—American, British, and French troops were still in West Berlin—but the one thing that had changed was the military situation. The nuclear balance shifted from overwhelming U.S. superiority to near parity with the Soviets. Richard Nixon and National Security Advisor Henry Kissinger expected the Russians to exploit their improved military status, but to their great surprise, the Soviets were far more reasonable than anyone had anticipated, and no crisis occurred.[48] In the end, the Soviets offered a settlement that West German chancellor Willy Brandt pointed out was more favorable than what "was discussed in Geneva in 1959" or what Dean Acheson's Berlin report to President Kennedy hoped to achieve in 1961, periods when the United States possessed nuclear superiority.[49] Kissinger agreed: "I feel that we're doing better than, than I thought possible."[50] This success was achieved in spite of the fact, as Brandt pointed out, "that we all know the military position rather is more favorable for the Soviet Union than it was then."[51]

Why was there no nuclear crisis over Berlin in the late 1960s and early 1970s? One would have to look through both the Soviet and American (as well as various Western and Eastern European) documents to come up with a definitive answer, but a decent guess is that the fundamental geopolitical issue that drove the crisis in the first place—West Germany's nuclear status—had been resolved in ways pleasing to Soviet Russia's (and it turns out everyone but West Germany's) leadership. In other words, neither the nuclear balance nor the actual territory was the key variable in determining whether there was a superpower crisis. Instead, it was one of the core geopolitical issues that dominated international politics in the decades after World War II and which is not coded in either study—the nuclearization of the Federal Republic of Germany. Focusing exclusively on military factors can obscure the issues that really matter, the forces that drove the origins and outcomes of these clashes. We know this intuitively—we do not analyze the U.S. first strike advantages over Canada or Brazil, because Canada and Brazil are not enemies. But these models tell us very little about why this is so, or why Russia and China were once enemies then became, at different times, friends, and now are something in between, or why we worry more about an Iran with the bomb than a nuclear Sweden.

It turns out that this whole set of issues surrounding both nuclear dynamics and methodology is a sequel of sorts; we have seen this movie before. In 1984 Paul Huth and Bruce Russet compiled a comprehensive list of what they called "extended-immediate military deterrence situations" between 1900 and 1980 to assess when deterrence worked, when it failed, and why. Using a statistical analysis, they determined that this type of deterrence worked in only thirty-one cases (57 percent of the time) and that the keys to success were factors such as close economic and political-military ties between the defender and its protégé, higher stakes by the defender in the protégé, and local (as opposed to overall) military capabilities. Surprisingly, nuclear possession was shown to be of only marginal importance.[52] Huth and Russett updated their data set in 1988, dropping some cases and adding others and increasing the time frame to 1885–1984.[53]

These articles inspired a sharp critique from Richard Ned Lebow and Janice Gross Stein. Lebow and Stein questioned much of Huth and Russett's coding, arguing that in many cases they got the aggressor and the defender wrong, made mistakes about what was a success and what was a failure, and confused deterrence with compellence. They contended that the overwhelming majority of Huth and Russett's cases should not have even been in the data set, identifying only nine cases that met the appropriate criteria, a number too small to generate significant findings from statistical analysis. The authors went back and forth, questioning definitions, research design, scope conditions, and coding decisions.[54] Others eventually weighed in, including James Fearon, who focused less on the research design and empirical dispute and instead highlighted what he saw as "the inadequacy of rational deterrence theory," especially what he saw as the false or unhelpful distinction between general and immediate deterrence.[55] This helped popularize Fearon's important insights about selection effects.

The substantive and methodological problems that surfaced in this early debate are remarkably similar to the problems in the Sechser and Fuhrmann and Kroenig papers. This brings up a larger set of questions: because of the selection effects, the disputes over coding, the challenge of determining the unit of observation, the rarity of nuclear crises, and the difficulty of comparing across cases, is statistical analysis the most appropriate tool to understand nuclear dynamics? Both papers make claims to control for a variety of factors, such as the interdependence of cases and the survivability of strategic forces. But can even the most sophisticated statistical controls provide greater insight to these questions than other methods? These types of issues are precisely why studies of this type are so vexing to historians and policymakers.

This is the part of the review where I, the historian, should be making claims on behalf of qualitative work based on archival research to better understand nuclear dynamics. And there is a powerful case to be made. It may be that the only way to get real insight, to develop causal inferences about these kinds of critical issues, is to reconstruct the thoughts, decisions, interactions between, and reconsiderations of top decisionmakers as they wrestled with these extraordinarily important questions when trying to make policy. There is, however, another important argument in favor this kind of historical work: opportunity costs. When Huth, Russett, Lebow, and Stein first worked on these issues, archival research was much more difficult, and far fewer documents were available. Nuclear decisionmaking was a black box, and coding often involved, at best, educated guesses. Today, historians are in the midst of a declassified document revolution, with archives around the world and organizations such as the National Security Archive, the Cold War International History Project, and the Nuclear Proliferation International History Project providing access to millions of pages of previously unavailable material. The dirty secret is that with much of this material being made available online and in published volumes, international relations scholars need not leave their living room to see reams of extraordinary evidence that bear on the questions engaged in these articles, at far less effort and expense than anyone could have dreamed of when I started my Ph.D. in the early 1990s.

Let's say a scholar wanted to really understand how nuclear dynamics worked in the critical 1958–1962 period, to explore the role that deterrence, compellence, brinksmanship, and nuclear superiority played in the origins and outcomes of the standoff. What sort of evidence would be available? On the U.S. side, there are literally tens of thousands of pages of declassified documents available online about the Berlin and Cuban missile crises. A treasure trove of resources from the Foreign Relations of the United States series,[56] the National Security Archive,[57] secretly taped presidential recordings and U.S. Declassfied Documents Online can be readily accessed via the internet.[58] Great insight into the thinking of America's closest ally, Great Britain, could be gained by examining Prime Minister Harold Macmillan's papers.[59] Records on the Soviet side are not as open, but there are important materials available, including secret Presidium meetings,[60] participant recollections,[61] and secondary sources that used primary source materials.[62] Nor is pursuing this kind of work difficult or as overwhelming as it might appear for a political scientist: as Marc Trachtenberg points out, "There is a method for reaching relatively solid conclusions about major historical issues in a reasonable amount of time—say, in about three or four months of uninterrupted work. I think political scientists, or at least those studying international relations, need to know how to do historical work. They may need to know other things as well, but it is hard to see how they can hope to understand international politics if they do not know how to do historical analysis in a fairly serious way."[63] This raises an important question: should young scholars spend their time constructing a problematic data set and running regressions, or will our collective knowledge be better advanced through in-depth analyses of the truly relevant cases based on primary documents?

Of course, there are powerful disciplinary incentives that shape the research strategies of younger scholars and prevent them from making this choice. I am part of an academic discipline, history, that has largely abandoned studying important issues such as international security and nuclear weapons and is in the midst of a four-decade, slow motion act of collective suicide.[64] There simply is not, nor will there be anytime soon, a critical mass of diplomatic and military historians available to research these important questions or make use of these amazing materials. This is a national tragedy about which the field of history and our institutions of higher education should be ashamed and for which I fear that the United States will pay a price. The field of political science deserves great praise for taking up some of the slack; it is one of the few places within higher education where there is serious, sustained, collective interest and debate over crucial issues of national and international security. It is not, however, without its own pathologies. I cannot imagine that the flagship journals in the field, such as *International Organization*, the *Journal of Conflict Resolution*, or the *American Political Science Review*, would be interested in a deeply researched, multiarchival piece on the nuclear dynamics of the 1958–1962 period, though I would love to be proved wrong. From what I gather, brave—and from a career perspective, sadly, unwise—is the Ph.D. student in international relations who undertakes a dissertation that does not include formal models, data sets, and multiple regressions.

Employing quantitative tools, especially statistics, is highly rewarded within political science and often seen as being more rigorous and scientific. Whether this is a good or a bad thing for political science more broadly is not really for me to say. Statistics can be a powerful but blunt instrument.[65] Turning complex historical processes into quantifiable variables risks losing both information and even accuracy, which should affect our confidence in the findings.[66] This is especially true in the area of nuclear statecraft, where statistical analysis does not strike me as the best method for understanding complex, interactive political decisionmaking about issues of life and death where the most important Ns are 9 (states with nuclear weapons), 2 (atomic bombs detonated against other states), and 0 (thermonuclear wars).[67]

In the end, however, the real issue is not methodology per se. There are bound to be legitimate disputes about coding, just as there are arguments about historical interpretations. The authors could understandably disagree with my coding of 1958–1962 or argue that this case was exceptional and that other cases in the sample were more indicative of the underlying causal mechanisms that may operate in future cases. Their models could be refined to better deal with selection effects, more accurately handle the issue of resolve, or more effectively measure nuclear superiority. There is no shortage of problematic research designs among qualitative and formal scholars. Perhaps most important, the authors could point out that for all the availability of new primary materials, pursuing a historical strategy appears no more likely than their quantitative efforts to produce certain results.

They would have a point. In theory, access to more primary materials should provide a more accurate picture of events, but we know that policymakers can misrepresent the past, mislead, or even provide contradictory views of the same meeting in written documents.[68] Even if a deep immersion in documents produces historical accuracy, it often comes at the cost of the generalizations and policy insights about nuclear dynamics we all crave. Everywhere you look in the historical record there are puzzles, riddles, and anomalies that seem to elude our best theories. Why did the Soviets initiate the Berlin and Cuban missile crises at a time of great nuclear inferiority and prove so pliable over the same set of issues when they achieved parity? Why has China, with enormous economic resources, built rather modest nuclear forces, whereas a much poorer Pakistan seems hell-bent on deploying a massive force? Can anyone really speak with great confidence about how a nuclear Iran would behave?

Or consider the challenge of understanding Richard Nixon, a president who ratified the Nuclear Nonproliferation Treaty and negotiated the ABM and SALT treaties with the Soviet Union yet did not believe in arms control and yearned to reclaim the overwhelming, first-strike capability he believed President Kennedy had possessed.[69] "In 1962, at the time of the Cuban missile crisis, it had been 'no contest,' because we had a ten to one superiority."[70] He also regularly engaged in what he believed was nuclear brinkmanship; as he told Kissinger, "We've got to play it recklessly. That's the safest course."[71] Yet it is not clear the Soviets ever picked up, understood, or reacted to any of his nuclear threats. How can we generalize from this? How can anyone code Richard Nixon's perplexing, sophisticated, and at times frightening thinking and policies on nuclear weapons?*

Perhaps the real issue is not what methodology we use to explore these issues but rather our comfort with uncertainty, our natural reluctance to embrace epistemological modesty on questions of such great importance. For a long time, we believed that the answer surrounding nuclear dynamics was relatively simple—once the superpowers achieved secure, second-strike capabilities, the possibility of thermonuclear war dissipated, and deterrence would prevail. Some even suggested that the stabilizing features of nuclear weapons were a positive feature and that proliferation should not be seen as the end of the world.[72] While Nixon's reckless attitude may have been anomalous, as more and more documents become available we began to fully recognize how dangerous and often unstable the nuclear age has been. Top policymakers never shared the comfort felt by the strategists over mutual assured destruction. Consider Secretary of State Dean Rusk's reactions during the meeting where President Kennedy was told that the long-predicted era of mutual vulnerability had finally arrived:

> Secretary Rusk said he agreed [that nuclear war was impossible if rational men control governments], but he did not get much comfort from this fact because, if both sides believed that neither side would use nuclear weapons, one side or the other would be tempted to act in a way which would push the other side beyond its tolerance level. He added that a response to pressure might be suicidal, being prompted by a desire to get it over with. He referred to the current situation as "This God Damn poker game."[73]

---

* In the context of selection effects, it would be interesting to know how and whether the military balance affects peaceful, if coerced, bargaining. Nixon was aware of and spoke about how the nuclear balance had changed dramatically and put him in a much worse situation than Kennedy's. Does this mean that Nixon backed off more than Kennedy? I am grateful to Robert Jervis for this excellent insight.

Sechser, Fuhrmann, and Kroenig deserve credit for wrestling with these fundamental issues in a serious way. Both papers have important if obvious insights: at some intuitive level, it should not be surprising that deterrence is easier than compellence (even if it is difficult to code) or that a state may want to possess more nuclear weapons than its adversaries. But getting beyond the obvious is difficult, and in the end, both papers overstate their theoretical claims and their policy relevance and leave this historian no more confident on these questions than he was before. But can the historian provide anything more satisfying, more generalizable? While no doubt disappointing, at this point we can do little better than the assessment recently offered by Philip Zelikow, while reviewing my own work on the subject: "U.S. nuclear superiority mattered. And, at some level, it also didn't. At times both of these propositions were, at one and the same time, true. It is not easy to generalize much from this story about nuclear weapons except that they do matter, to those who have them and to those who don't."[74]

For those who would complain that such indeterminacy undermines the idea of a political "science," I would respond, guilty as charged. These two articles, it should be pointed out, are not the first occurrence of rival quantitative studies coming to starkly different conclusions about the dynamics of nuclear statecraft.[75]

The news is not all bad, of course. In the end, despite great fears, expectations, and apocalyptic predictions, we have never had a thermonuclear war, nor does it look like we will have one anytime soon. We think deterrence works. The problem is that, notwithstanding the confident claims of countless theorists, including those reviewed here, we do not really know why nuclear bombs have not been dropped since 1945, or at the very least, we cannot prove our theories and instincts. Was it good statesmanship? Was Kenneth Waltz right, and nuclear weapons really are the great stabilizers?[76] Or perhaps it was just luck? As is often said about the inadvisability of testing nuclear deterrence failures, we have never run the experiment, and we hope we never will.

This matters even more for policymakers than for scholars: while we have theories,* in the end it is close to impossible to predict how an Iran with nuclear weapons would behave, or whether it is worth the enormous consequences that would ensue from a military effort to prevent Iran's nuclearization, without trying to come to terms with these larger questions surrounding nuclear dynamics.[77] This is why the questions that both papers engage are so important, even if the papers' theories are unconvincing, their methods problematic, and the policy implications unclear. We are understandably eager to have an explanation for the most important nonevent in human history, if only to see whether there are lessons that can be applied today to keep the streak going as long as possible. It is a daunting task, far more challenging than we like to acknowledge, and many of the research questions that we do focus on are merely proxies for this larger concern. For make no mistake about it: when we talk about any number of subjects surrounding nuclear weapons, such as why states do or not build the bomb, how they behave when they get it, or how and when deterrence works, the core question animating our curiosity is a powerful desire to understand why there has never been, and, it is hoped, will never be, a thermonuclear war. Despite the limitations of these and other studies, despite the methodological difficulties and the near impossibility of being certain about our claims, it is hard to imagine a more important question, one that is worthy of the most vigorous research, discussion, and debate.

---

* Probabilistic models may be good for getting a sense of the possible trends over the next fifty or one hundred cases but are of far less use to the decisionmakers trying to craft policies for the specific, highly consequential and likely complex issues in the $n+1$ case, especially if it is unclear whether the theory/causal mechanism is correct or applicable to the case at hand.

FOUR

Strategies of Inhibition

What role has nuclear nonproliferation and counterproliferation played in U.S. grand strategy since 1945?[1] And what insights does this history provide into the sharp, contemporary debates over the past, present, and future trajectory of U.S. grand strategy?

Most accounts of postwar U.S. grand strategy focus on two broad but distinct missions: to contain great-power rivals and to open the world's economy and political systems to encourage the flow of trade, resources, and capital.[2] There has been considerable debate over the origins, continuity, and effectiveness of the containment and openness missions and of identifying when these strategies were at odds and where they overlapped.[3] U.S. nuclear nonproliferation efforts, on the other hand, have been largely subsumed under other strategies and missions, underplayed or even ignored. When it is discussed, nuclear nonproliferation is often portrayed as a post–Cold War priority, applied inconsistently and selectively, motivated more by idealistic and normative considerations than by strategic factors, and taking second billing to more important U.S. goals. Even when it has been recognized as an important policy interest, nuclear nonproliferation has rarely been understood as a core, long-standing, and driving goal of U.S. grand strategy.[4]

This is unfortunate. What Scott Sagan has labeled the "renaissance" in nuclear studies—much of it based on declassified government documents—reveals the extraordinary lengths the United States has gone to since the beginning of the nuclear age to inhibit or to slow, halt, and reverse the spread of nuclear weapons, and when unsuccessful in these efforts, to mitigate the consequences of their spread.[5] To accomplish this end, the United States has developed and implemented a wide range of tools, applied in a variety of combinations, which might be thought of as the strategies of inhibition.

These strategies to inhibit nuclear proliferation employ different policies rarely seen as connected to one another: treaties, norms, diplomacy, aid, conventional arms sales, alliances and security guarantees, export, information and technology controls, intelligence, preemptive counterforce nuclear postures, missile defense, sanctions, coercion, interdiction, sabotage, and even the threat of preventive military action. The United States has applied these measures to friend and foe alike, often regardless of political orientation, economic system, or alliance status. Although the strategies of inhibition sometimes have complemented the United States' openness and containment missions, many times they have been unrelated to or even in tension with these other strategies; in all cases, they have been motivated in large measure by inhibition's distinctive strategic logic. Collectively, these linked strategies of inhibition have been an independent and driving feature of U.S. national security policy for more than seven decades, to an extent rarely documented or fully understood in our debates over grand strategy. For better or worse, absent the United States' strategies of inhibition, we might live in a far more proliferated world.

Demonstrating the persistent and long-standing centrality of nuclear nonproliferation and counterproliferation to U.S. grand strategy is important for at least four reasons. First, the history of inhibition provides a more accurate, complex, and continuous picture of post–World War II international history than offered by standard, stylized accounts of the Cold War and post–Cold War periods. For example, inhibition often demanded that the United States cooperate with its Cold War adversary, the Soviet Union, and work against Cold War allies such as West Germany and South Korea. Second, inhibition inserts a critical and often missing variable into debates over the causes of nuclear proliferation. Scholarly treatments that focus on factors such as political leadership, regime type, norms and treaties, and the regional security environment of the potential proliferator often overlook the powerful influence the U.S. inhibition strategies have on when and why states make their decisions about nuclear weapons. Third, the strategies of inhibition challenge some of the most popular international relations theories that explain or predict how the United States should assess and react to nuclear proliferation. Defensive realism, for example, cannot explain and did not predict the long-standing, aggressive U.S. efforts to stem the spread of nuclear weapons.

Fourth, and most important, a better understanding of the strategies of inhibition recasts ongoing debates over whether the United States should continue to be deeply engaged in world affairs or, rather, should retrench. Inhibition helps explain many otherwise puzzling policies, such as post–Cold War security alliances, that analysts often ascribe to hegemonic hubris, bureaucratic politics, or ideology. The inhibition mission also helps to explain the persistence and motivation behind U.S. efforts to ensure that Iran, for example, does not develop a nuclear weapons capability. While we have a good understanding of the better known containment and openness mission, the history, logic, tools, variations, and importance of the inhibition mission have often been overlooked or misunderstood.[6]

Postwar U.S. Grand Strategy: Contain, Open, and Inhibit

Anyone trying to understand U.S. grand strategy after World War II faces two immediate challenges. First, the whole concept of grand strategy, unless properly defined, can be nebulous; as Hal Brands points out, it is "one of the most slippery and widely abused terms in the foreign policy lexicon."[7] Second, the history of postwar U.S. grand strategy can be particularly difficult to explain; it is a complex and messy subject, influenced by structural considerations, domestic and international politics, and the personality and preferences of individual presidents and their administrations. Barry Posen defines grand strategy as a "nation-state's theory about how to produce security for itself." It is "not a rule book" but a "set of concepts and arguments that need to be revisited regularly."[8] Brands explains grand strategy as "the intellectual architecture that gives form and structure to foreign policy." Decisionmakers undertaking grand strategy "are not simply reacting to events or handling them on a case-by-case basis. Rather, a grand strategy is a purposeful and coherent set of ideas about what a nation seeks to accomplish in the world, and how it should go about doing so."[9]

While the history of U.S. foreign, foreign economic, and national security policy since 1945 contains many twists and turns, discontinuities, and anomalies, scholars have identified two broad goals that have united American grand strategists and meet Brands' definition: to contain (and, if possible, defeat) great-power rivals, particularly the Soviet Union, and to open the international economic and political system. Analysts have vigorously debated the relationship between, the wisdom of, and the best ways to achieve and balance these goals, but both the containment and openness missions are recognized as pillars of postwar U.S. grand strategy.

The strategy of containment is most closely associated with the U.S. diplomat and historian George Kennan and emerged to counter what was seen as the Soviet Union's aggressive geopolitical designs on the crucial Eurasian land mass and beyond, without sparking a third world war.[10] As John Lewis Gaddis and others have highlighted, how the containment mission was implemented varied over time, as international circumstances changed and new U.S. presidential administrations appeared.* In the early 1950s and arguably the late 1970s

---

* The containment strategy had a wide spectrum of supporters, from Kennan, who emphasized economic tools and lamented the militarization of the Cold

and early 1980s, containment was more aggressive and reliant on military tools and included policies to pressure the Soviets and their client states. In other periods, containment was strictly defensive and even at times accommodating; the emergence of détente, which flourished from the mid-1960s to the mid-1970s, witnessed occasional superpower respect and cooperation. The overall goal of containment, however, was to check and over time reduce the Soviet Union's military power and geopolitical reach. Since the end of the Cold War and the collapse of the Soviet Union, U.S. grand strategists have debated whether the containment mission is relevant in a world lacking peer competitors and whether it should be applied to other emerging threats, such as Iraq, Iran, and the People's Republic of China.[11]

The openness mission in U.S. grand strategy emerged from the vigorous efforts of the United States and its allies to rebuild the world economy and encourage political liberalization after the disasters of the Great Depression and the World War II. Economically, American policymakers believed the United States had a vital interest in encouraging open trade, access to natural resources, and the easy movement of capital across borders.* The United States and its allies created international and regional organizations, regimes, and rules to encourage multilateral trade and investment. The founding of the International Monetary Fund, the Bank for Reconstruction and Development, and the General Agreement on Tariffs and Trade reflected

---

War, to more hawkish advocates who believed in employing aggressive military postures. All shared the same goal: to contain and if possible eventually reverse the Soviet Union's power without a war. For an argument that efforts to undermine the Soviet Union's control in Eastern Europe went beyond containment in the early Cold War, see Gregory Mitrovich, *Undermining the Kremlin: America's Strategy to Subvert the Soviet Bloc, 1947–1956* (Cornell University Press, 2000).

* The openness mission, similar to containment and inhibition, also evolved over time, as the international economy shifted to market-determined exchange rates and freer flows of capital and trade after the 1971 ending of the Bretton Woods system of fixed exchange rates, managed trade, and limitations on capital flows.

this desire, as did more recent initiatives such as the North American Free Trade Agreement, the World Trade Organization, and various regional and global trade negotiations.[12] These efforts often required U.S. presidential administrations to resist powerful domestic political pressures that promoted protectionism. The United States often (though not always) encouraged regimes to embrace liberal values, including the rule of law, political tolerance, independence for colonial territories, and free elections. Promoting self-determination and democracy as core elements of U.S. grand strategy had its roots in the legacy of President Woodrow Wilson but accelerated and intensified after World War II.[13]

Taken together, the openness and containment missions explain much about U.S. grand strategy since the end of World War II. Neither mission, however, can fully account for the high priority the United States has placed on slowing, reversing, and mitigating the spread of nuclear weapons. Consider five puzzles about the history of U.S. grand strategy since 1945 that neither containment nor openness can entirely explain.

Puzzle 1: Why has the United States considered preventive military action against nascent nuclear weapons states from the start of the nuclear age, even when most of those countries were far too weak to be otherwise threatening to the United States?[14] Containment, a largely defensive doctrine, is not adequate to fully illuminate debates over targeting the nuclear facilities of the Soviet Union in the late 1940s and early 1950s, the People's Republic of China in the 1960s, North Korea in the 1990s, and Iraq and potentially Iran more recently.[15] Arguments that identify hegemony or imperial ambitions as the driver fail to explain why only the adversary's nuclear programs, and not its land, markets, or economic resources, were ever coveted by the United States.

Puzzle 2: Neither the openness strategy nor the containment strategy can fully explain why the United States time and again pressured even its closest allies to eschew independent nuclear forces.[16] In some cases, the United States even threatened coercive actions, including sanctions or abandonment, against ostensible Cold War allies such as West Germany, Taiwan, South Korea, and Pakistan to prevent them from developing nuclear weapons.[17] If containment were the sole driver of U.S. grand strategy, one might imagine that the United States would want its friends to possess these powerful weapons to help maintain a balance vis-à-vis the Soviet Union or at the very least would try to avoid alienating its Cold War allies with its vigorous nonproliferation policies. The United States regularly made economic concessions to its allies, including trade and monetary discrimination against the United States, to achieve inhibition, in ways often at odds with the openness mission.[18]

Puzzle 3: Why did the United States create a vast set of alliances and security guarantees backed by implicit or explicit protection under its nuclear umbrella?[19] And why, after the Cold War ended and the Soviet Union disappeared, did it not only maintain but also expand its nuclear umbrella? The containment mission vis-à-vis the Soviet Union had been completed successfully by 1989–1991; many efforts to explain continuing and expanding alliances in the post–Cold War period are unconvincing.[20]

Puzzle 4: Why has the United States aggressively sought strategic nuclear primacy since 1945? One of the core assumptions of the scholarly literature on the nuclear revolution is that once mutual vulnerability between rivals emerges, it makes little sense to try to escape that condition by building more or better nuclear weapons systems. According to Kenneth Waltz, "Nuclear weapons eliminate strategy. . . . Nuclear weapons make strategy obsolete."[21] Yet the United States poured enormous sums of money into strategic systems that make the most sense on behalf of counterforce—damage limitation strategies to establish nuclear primacy against any potential adversary, often with little regard for stability.[22] The United States plans to spend a further $350 billion upgrading its nuclear forces over the next decade, despite possessing vast quantitative and qualitative advantages over every other current nuclear weapons state.[23]

Puzzle 5: Why did the United States cooperate during the Cold War with its sworn enemy and the target of these alliances and strategic nuclear forces, the Soviet Union, to stanch nuclear proliferation? The most famous example is the negotiations that led to the 1968 Nuclear Nonproliferation Treaty.[24] It turns out, however, that this was not an isolated example of the superpower rivals' working to inhibit proliferation. Even during the bitterest periods of the Cold War, the United States was willing to work with the Soviet Union to achieve its inhibition goals.*

These and other puzzles—which at first blush seem unrelated—can be fully explained only by understanding the crucial role the inhibition mission has played in U.S. grand strategy since 1945. The United States has been willing to pressure, coerce, and threaten nascent nuclear states, including friends, to keep them non-nuclear. It has also been willing to provide assurances of protection and make them more credible with potentially destabilizing counterforce and damage-limitation nuclear strategies and missile defense. To inhibit nuclear proliferation, the United States was even willing to work with its most threatening adversary, the Soviet Union.

The literature on U.S. grand strategy has not ignored the question of nuclear proliferation altogether.[25] When it has been discussed, however, it has generally made three problematic assumptions.[26] First, some analysts claim that nuclear nonproliferation emerged as an important U.S. goal only after the Cold War ended and focuses only on weak or so-called rogue states.[27] Second, the primary driver of U.S. nuclear proliferation policies is often identified as norms and

---

*The test-ban treaty—discussed by the superpower rivals both before and immediately after the Cuban missile crisis—was understood as an inhibition tool: "A test ban, the Soviets would be told, would mean that 'there would be no additional nuclear powers in our camp.' The Russians, for their part, would prevent their allies from building nuclear forces. And these commitments would be linked: the United States would 'take responsibility in respect to nondissemination with relation to those powers associated with it, if the Soviet Union is willing to take a corresponding obligation for the powers with which it is associated.'" See Marc Trachtenberg, *A Constructed Peace: The Making of the European Settlement, 1945–1963* (Princeton University Press, 1999), 385.

ideals, not strategic considerations.[28] Third, nuclear nonproliferation is often seen as either subsumed under other strategic goals, such as multilateralism, or only one in a long list of new global challenges.[29] These explanations do not capture the deep historical roots, the prevalence, the wide array of inhibition tools, or the driving strategic logic of the United States' strategies of inhibition.

Obviously, inhibition is not the only explanation for these and other important U.S. policies; often, the inhibition mission has intertwined with the openness and especially the containment missions. Furthermore, given the profound and unprecedented challenge presented to U.S. grand strategy by nuclear weapons, the strategy of inhibition took time to coalesce into a coherent, consistent, and effective set of strategies. Policies that were originally motivated by inhibition instincts—such as President Dwight Eisenhower's Atoms for Peace and the controversial Multilateral Force proposal—were ultimately seen as counterproductive and abandoned. The historical record makes clear, however, that inhibition has been one of the driving motivations behind U.S. grand strategy since the start of the nuclear age, pursued across presidential administrations and despite important changes in the international system.

The Strategies of Inhibition

What is the goal of inhibition, and why has it been a core feature of U.S. grand strategy since 1945? What tools does the United States use to carry it out? How should the variations in the strategies of inhibition over time be understood? And why have scholars underemphasized or even ignored the strategies of inhibition?

The objective of the U.S. strategies of inhibition was and remains simple: to prevent other states—regardless of their political affiliation or orientation—from developing or acquiring independent nuclear forces and, when this effort fails, to reverse or mitigate the consequences of proliferation. Across different administrations and changing international circumstances, the United States has shown itself willing to pay a high price to achieve this end. When it is unable to stop proliferation, it works hard to prevent the proliferator from undertaking policies—weaponization, pursuit of a missile capability, and especially nuclear testing—that would increase the pressure on other states to acquire nuclear weapons. The United States is also more willing to countenance nuclear weapons programs—such as Great Britain's—that become dependent on and coordinated with U.S. nuclear systems.[30]

Why has the United States been so interested in preventing states from possessing independent nuclear forces? Many international relations scholars argue that the spread of nuclear weapons can stabilize world politics.[31] Nuclear weapons, they contend, have little effectiveness for anything but deterrence.[32] These analysts are often perplexed, pessimistic, or critical of U.S. efforts to halt nuclear proliferation and wonder if policymakers actually understand how nuclear deterrence works. Even those analysts who do not support nuclear proliferation are puzzled by the high price of strategies the United States has employed to prevent it.

These scholars miss a fundamental point: historically, U.S. policymakers have demonstrated less enthusiasm for the supposedly stabilizing aspects of nuclear weapons for international relations. Of far greater concern has been the worry over how other countries might use nuclear weapons against the United States. The strategies of inhibition were developed to stem the power-equalizing effects of nuclear weapons and are motivated by a self-interested desire to safeguard United States security and preserve its dominant power. As U.S. Secretary of State Dean Rusk pointed out, "It was almost in the nature of nuclear weapons that if someone had them, he did not want others to have them."[33]

There are seven interrelated elements driving the United States' strategies of inhibition. They are motivated by the goal of protecting the United States from nuclear attack and the desire to maintain its freedom of action to pursue other strategic goals.

First, the United States has feared nuclear weapons being used against it, either through a deliberate nuclear attack or an accidental launch. The higher the number of states that possess nuclear weapons, the greater the risk the United States might be hit. Given the horrific consequences of an attack, decisionmakers naturally have considered it their responsibility to decrease this danger by limiting proliferation and its consequences. As U.S. secretary of state John Foster Dulles told his Soviet counterpart, Andrei Gromyko, it was "frightening to think of a world where anybody could have a bomb."[34]

Second, given the difficulty of identifying where a nuclear attack may have originated, U.S. policymakers have worried about the catalytic or "detonator" consequences of proliferation; in other words, they feared that an independent nuclear state might threaten to use or actually employ a nuclear weapon to pull the United States into a conflict in which it did not want to become involved.[35] There is evidence that Pakistan, South Africa, Israel, and possibly France pursued nuclear strategies aimed at pulling an otherwise unwilling United States into crises on their behalf.[36] A 1962 top-secret study explained this fear: the "Nth-country problem" might generate "the danger of major war being 'catalyzed,' deliberately or inadvertently, by the possessors of nuclear weapons outside the control of the major alliances."[37]

Third, the United States feared the emergence of nuclear tipping points, or dominoes, whereby one key state going nuclear might lead to four or five other states doing the same.[38] After the People's Republic of China tested a nuclear device in 1964, for example, President Lyndon Johnson's Committee on Nuclear Proliferation (also known as the Gilpatric Committee) warned: "The world is fast approaching a point of no return in the prospects of controlling the spread of nuclear weapons."[39] The committee also cautioned that "proliferation cascades" would not only increase the number of nuclear states in the world, with all the dangers that could bring, but also increase tensions and dangers in parts of the world the United States considered important. It might also drive U.S. allies—for example, Japan and South Korea—to target one another in ways that were inimical to the United States' interests.*

Fourth, U.S. policymakers fully appreciated the power of nuclear deterrence but worried that these weapons would be used to deter the United States and limit its freedom of action, both regionally and in the world at large.[40] From the beginning of the nuclear age, the United States recognized the potential for nuclear weapons to become the great equalizer, "weapons of the weak," allowing states with far inferior conventional, economic, and other forms of power to prevent the United States from doing what it wanted to do. As the Gilpatric Committee report pointed out, "As additional nations obtained nuclear weapons, our diplomatic and military influence would wane, and strong pressures would arise to retreat to isolation to avoid the risk of involvement in nuclear war."[41] As Michael Horowitz explains, a feeble state "possessing even a single nuclear weapon influences America's strategic calculations and seems to make coercive success harder."[42]

Fifth, allies who do not have their own nuclear weapons and depend on the United States for their security are easier to control. The United States has bristled at the independent policies nuclear-armed allies such as France or Israel have pursued, often against its wishes. A Germany, Taiwan, Japan, or South Korea with nuclear weapons might be more likely to challenge the regional or international status quo with threats or the use of force in ways inimical to U.S. interests. President John F. Kennedy, for example, warned that if the U.S. allies acquired nuclear weapons "they would be in a position to be entirely independent and we might be on the outside looking in."[43]

---

* "Mr. Gilpatric stated his preference for a world with a limited number of nuclear powers, finding it implausible that additional proliferation could be compartmentalized, quarantined, or regionalized and comparing the consequences for the world [to] the Sarajevo incident. He found it all the more unlikely that a nuclear conflict involving 1.5 billion Chinese, Indians and Japanese could not affect our own security." "Minutes of Discussion," January 7–8, 1965, National Security file, Committee file, Committee on Nuclear Proliferation, Minutes of Meetings, box 9, Lyndon B. Johnson Presidential Library, Austin.

Sixth, U.S. policymakers feared that otherwise weak adversaries might become emboldened to act aggressively if they acquired nuclear weapons.[44] And given the nature of nuclear weapons—where the absolute number a state possesses may be less important than its willingness to use them—small nuclear-armed states might even try to coerce the United States during a crisis.[45] Secretary of State Dulles lamented to his Soviet counterpart, "A dictator could use the bombs to blackmail the rest of the world."[46] Furthermore, containing nuclear states is far more expensive than containing non-nuclear states.[47] "Coping with the possessors of a small, extortionate deterrent force will require the mastery of some new political-military techniques."[48]

Seventh, although dozens of states could potentially build a nuclear weapon, U.S. policymakers feared that only great powers possess the economic, technological, and bureaucratic capacities to build robust command, control, communications, and intelligence capabilities and keep their weapons safe and secure.[49] This mattered for two reasons. First, small and weak nuclear states could disintegrate and lose control of their weapons, to substate actors and terrorists, among others.[50] As chairman of the U.S. Joint Chiefs of Staff, Admiral Michael Mullen said of Pakistan's nuclear program, "I worry a great deal about those weapons falling into the hands of terrorists and either being proliferated or potentially used. And so, control of those, stability, stable control of those weapons is a key concern."[51] Second, the United States might be forced to politically support—against its other interests—otherwise problematic, weak nuclear states to forestall the dangers their instability might bring. When the Cold War ended, for example, the United States decided not to encourage the breakup of the Soviet Union—the preferred geostrategic choice of the George H. W. Bush administration—because of fears over nuclear security, safety, and proliferation. As President Bush and his national security adviser, Brent Scowcroft, lamented, the Bush administration "decided they would prefer to see weapons in the hands of just one entity, which had the stability and experience to secure them."[52]

As the greatest power in the international system seeking to maintain its security and pursue its freedom of action in the world, the United States found these challenges intolerable. The strategies of inhibition were natural, if difficult, costly, and often destabilizing, responses. For all of these reasons, the purportedly peace-inducing qualities of nuclear weapons typically took a back seat to American policymakers' fears about the effect of nuclear proliferation on U.S. national interests. The United States worked hard to inhibit the spread of independent nuclear weapon programs and mitigate the consequences of proliferation when it could not be stopped.

The Spectrum of Inhibition

How would such an ambitious and historically unheard of strategy—preventing sovereign states from having independent control of the most powerful weapons the world has ever seen—be carried out? Since the birth of the nuclear age, the United States has employed different strategic tools in various ways and mixes to achieve the inhibition mission. A wide array of factors drove these variations, in particular shifting international circumstances, trade-offs with the openness and containment missions, and the changing preferences of new presidential administrations.

Looked at broadly, the strategies of inhibition fall into three categories along a broad spectrum: legal-normative, assurance, and coercive.[53] At one end, legal-normative policies involve U.S. policymakers' pursuing arms control treaties, establishing norms, and using rhetoric to dissuade states from acquiring independent nuclear capabilities. Coercive polices are at the other end of the spectrum: technology and export controls, interdiction, abandonment, sabotage, sanctions, and even the threat of preventive strikes against nascent nuclear states. Assurance policies have been the most prevalent and arguably successful tools to achieve inhibition; especially consequential has been the use of security guarantees and alliances, often backed by aggressive strategic nuclear postures, military deployments, and conventional arms sales, to extend the U.S. nuclear umbrella to limit the nuclear ambitions of potential proliferators. Taken together, these policies—

which are often seen as unrelated—reflect a powerful and consistent U.S. desire to limit the number of independent nuclear weapons states in the world, a mission that began in the earliest days of the nuclear age and continues today.

Legal-Normative Strategies

Since 1945 the United States has often employed legal-normative measures—lofty rhetoric, treaties, and regimes—to highlight the dangers of nuclear weapons and to encourage a norm against their possession and a taboo against their use.[54] Every U.S. president since 1945 has spoken eloquently about the horrors of nuclear war, lamented the nuclear arms race, and called for international efforts to limit the spread of nuclear weapons.[55] Despite controversy, the United States demonstrated a willingness to surrender nuclear weapons to international control in the 1946 Acheson-Lilienthal Report and subsequent Baruch Plan. In 1954 it proposed the creation of an international agency to control fissile materials. Although the Soviet Union rejected that proposal, it cooperated with the United States to create the International Atomic Energy Agency in 1957, the key global institution now responsible for monitoring and regulating nuclear activities around the world. In 1963, again in cooperation with the Soviet Union, President Kennedy established the Partial Test Ban Treaty.[56] Most significant, the United States partnered with the Soviet Union again to negotiate the 1968 Nuclear Nonproliferation Treaty. In the years that followed, it led numerous efforts to strengthen the treaty and broaden the global nonproliferation regime, including creating the Zangger Committee and the Nuclear Suppliers Group to better regulate civilian nuclear exports, enhancing safeguards, and supporting the permanent extension of the NPT and the approval of the 1997 Additional Protocol.

Encouraging norms against the possession of nuclear weapons and traditions or even taboos against their use provides strategic benefits to the United States. As Maria Rost Rublee has argued, "U.S. policymakers can take advantage of situations that increase the potency of norms and, in some cases, can help create those conditions."[57]

Nina Tannenwald points out that the taboo against nuclear use is in the United States' interest, because with its "overwhelming conventional superiority, only an adversary armed with nuclear weapons could truly threaten US forces on the battlefield."[58] T. V. Paul concurs, suggesting that "the preservation of the tradition" of nonuse of nuclear weapons prevents weak states from using nuclear weapons to "thwart U.S. intervention."[59]

The U.S. legal-normative inhibition policies are also open to charges of hypocrisy. Rhetorically, the United States supported arms control and even disarmament despite continuing to spend enormous sums of money, not just building more nuclear forces but building nuclear systems that were oriented toward counterforce and damage limitation.[60] Politically, it expended large sums of capital to negotiate nonproliferation treaties that often required it to work against its allies and in tandem with the Soviet Union. The United States' extensive efforts to limit the spread of nuclear knowledge, materials, and technology contradict its openness mission (and in the case of allies, containment).[61] Despite the obvious double standard, if not outright hypocrisy, of these policies, U.S.-led efforts to stigmatize the possession of nuclear weapons through treaties, international laws, and the encouragement of norms and taboos have been a critical aspect of the U.S. inhibition strategy. As Shane Maddock has argued, U.S. policymakers believed that "the arguments used to dissuade other countries from acquiring nuclear arms" did not apply to the United States.[62]

Coercive Strategies

The United States has employed various coercive measures to inhibit proliferation. These include sanctions, sabotage, threats of abandonment, and even preventive military strikes against nascent nuclear programs. Such measures have been considered from the very beginning of the nuclear age. As the Joint Chiefs of Staff declared in 1946, "If we were ruthlessly realistic, we would not permit any foreign power with which we are not firmly allied, and in which we do not have absolute confidence, to make or possess atomic weapons. If such a country started to make atomic weapons we would destroy its capacity to make them before it had progressed far enough to threaten us."[63]

Although preventive military action is rarely carried out, that it is even considered to inhibit proliferation is remarkable.[64] Preventive strikes are one of the most aggressive actions a state can undertake, one that is typically both dangerous and deeply destabilizing to the international system.[65] Yet preventive thinking was not an isolated or recent phenomenon and was displayed by both Democratic and Republican administrations and despite dramatic changes in the international system. U.S. policymakers considered preventive military action against the nascent nuclear program of the Soviet Union in the late 1940s and early 1950s, the People's Republic of China in the 1960s, North Korea in the 1990s, and Iraq and Iran more recently.[66] There is also evidence that military action may have been considered against Pakistan in the late 1970s and was mentioned by some advisers vis-à-vis France and India during the 1960s.[67] As smaller and arguably less responsible states explored the possibility of acquiring nuclear weapons, military action appeared more palatable. "A potentially important means of coping with the problem of the nuclear-armed ruffian or racketeer may be preventive sabotage."[68] One argument made on behalf of preventive action was its capacity to influence the calculations of other potential proliferator states. These plans and discussions typically focused only on the target's nuclear capabilities; there were rarely plans to conquer or destroy the state in question. Even in the case of the Soviet Union, the focus of preventive thinking was largely on its nuclear assets and not its other forms of power.

Neither the United States' openness mission nor its containment mission are able to fully explain this interest in preventive military action. Consider debate within the U.S. government over preventive military action against China. By the early 1960s it was well understood among U.S. national security officials that China was not an ally of Russia and was quickly becoming an adversary.[69] There is no doubt that the United States had concerns about China's geopolitical and ideological orientation. If containment had been the only factor shaping U.S. grand strategy, however, we might have expected the United States to accept or even exploit China's independent nuclear capability vis-à-vis the Soviet Union. Viewed solely through the containment lens, it was surprising that the United States asked Soviet leaders if they wanted to join it in a preventive strike, less than a year after the Cuban missile crisis.[70]

Perhaps even more surprising, the United States brought pressure to bear on allies who considered acquiring their own nuclear weapons. The Federal Republic of Germany, perhaps the United States' key European ally, was often treated harshly regarding its nuclear ambitions during the 1960s. Italy, Australia, and Japan were discouraged from acquiring independent nuclear weapons. Other allies, such as Israel, Taiwan, and South Korea, were threatened with sanctions and abandonment, as was Pakistan.[71] There were even high-level discussions in the 1960s about pressuring the United States' closest ally, Great Britain, to give up its nuclear weapons or at least decrease their independence.[72]

If containment alone drove U.S. grand strategy, it made very little sense to anger close friends who were part of the anti-Soviet alliance. If close Cold War allies were treated this way as part of the U.S. inhibition mission, one can imagine the calculations that took place within countries that were neutral toward or even adversaries of the United States. Any state weighing a nuclear weapons program had to consider very seriously possible reactions of the United States before moving forward.[73]

Assurance Strategies

Coercive inhibition policies, such as sanctions and threats of preventive strikes, and legal-normative inhibition policies, such as norms and treaties, often garner the most attention from scholars. It is the assurance strategies, including intelligence activities, conventional arms sales, and especially security agreements and alliances, that have been arguably the most important and consequential of the strategies of inhibition.[74]

When United States grand strategy in the postwar period is examined, two features in particular stand out. First is the deep set of sprawling military alliances and security guarantees. Second is the extraordinarily forward-leaning and, at times, preemptive nature of U.S. nuclear strategy. Neither policy has antecedents in U.S. pre-nuclear history; before 1950, the United States had always gone to great lengths to avoid entangling alliances, deploying forces abroad, or maintaining large military forces during peacetime.* Nor can the containment mission—which was often defensive—fully explain these policies.[75] Both, however, have been key elements of the strategies of inhibition.

As the Cold War confrontation with the Soviet Union emerged, the United States entered into a series of alliances and provided explicit and implicit security guarantees to a range of countries. The most famous was the North Atlantic Treaty, signed in 1949, which later developed into a full-scale, integrated military alliance.[76] There were also regional treaties such as the 1951 ANZUS agreements with Australia and New Zealand; bilateral treaties with Japan, South Korea, and Taiwan; and implicit, secret arrangements with Sweden. As time went on, a key element of these arrangements was connecting the military capabilities of the United States, particularly its nuclear forces, to the defense of these countries. This nuclear umbrella was designed to help deter and defend against the Soviet Union and was a key element of the contain strategy.

These security arrangements also served another purpose, however: to inhibit the protected state from seeking its own nuclear weapons. As Bruno Tertrais demonstrates, security guarantees "have proven to be a very effective instrument in preventing states from going nuclear."[77] Jeffrey Knopf has argued, "Security assurances are

---

*Before the nuclear age, the United States fought wars by exploiting its geographical isolation, mobilizing slowly and massively, and fighting grinding wars of attrition, postures that allowed for strong civilian control of the military and tight legislative oversight. See Russell F. Weigley, *The American Way of War: A History of United States Military Strategy and Policy* (Indiana University Press, 1960). Inhibition upended all of these traditions.

an integral part of the nuclear nonproliferation regime."[78] Countries that had the capabilities and occasionally the interest in acquiring independent nuclear forces—ranging from Australia to Sweden to Japan and West Germany—might feel reassured by the U.S. nuclear umbrella and eschew their own weapons (and they might be reminded from time to time how reassured they should feel).[79] These security arrangements continued and even expanded after the end of the Cold War.[80] Although they are no longer needed to contain the Soviet Union, these arrangements still serve to inhibit nuclear proliferation.

Writ large, these security arrangements are not like traditional alliances, which, before the nuclear age, tended to be threat specific, additive, and temporary. These arrangements in the nuclear age, with some exceptions, have been suppressive and vague and have lasted for decades, even after the original threat that spawned the alliance has disappeared. In some cases, where the inhibit aspect looms larger, it might be better to think of the United States and its clients as "frenemies" rather than traditional allies.[81]

How does the United States' nuclear strategy play into its inhibition mission? The efforts of the United States to achieve and maintain nuclear primacy during the early Cold War are well known.[82] Many nuclear strategists claimed that when the United States and the Soviet Union approached numerical parity at the middle of the 1960s, it was unwise for the United States to spend extraordinary sums on counterforce nuclear capabilities that made sense only as part of a so-called damage limitation strategy. Robert Jervis claims that the United States' damage limitation nuclear strategies "did not come to grips with fundamental characteristics of nuclear politics," were "incoherent," "conjured up unrealistic dangers," and "ignor[ed] real problems."[83] Once mutual nuclear vulnerability between adversaries is achieved, Jervis, Waltz, and others have argued, fighting and winning a nuclear war is illogical: therefore, efforts to achieve nuclear superiority are pointless.

Despite the claims of the advocates of the nuclear revolution, however, the United States continued to spend a tremendous amount of money on missile accuracy and speed, tracking Soviet nuclear submarines while improving the acoustic quieting capabilities of U.S. submarines, hardening American nuclear targets, and increasing U.S. intelligence and defensive capabilities against nuclear weapons. Keir Lieber and Daryl Press have identified how the United States vigorously pursued a "counterforce revolution" that produced far more accurate missiles and the potential for a first-strike capability.[84] Austin Long and Brendan Green demonstrate that the United States strove to overcome the two greatest challenges to the survivability of Soviet strategic nuclear forces: being able to locate and track both Soviet mobile missiles and Soviet nuclear submarines. The United States never accepted mutual vulnerability with the Soviets and worked hard to overcome it.[85] There were times in the late 1970s and the 1980s that the Soviets appeared to fear that the United States was interested in and could some day achieve a meaningful nuclear superiority.[86] Some analysts believe it has achieved nuclear primacy vis-à-vis China and Russia today.[87]

The United States' drive for nuclear primacy most likely had many causes, the most important of which was to provide coercive leverage over the Soviets in the past and perhaps over Russia and China today. Pursuing nuclear primacy has two important consequences for inhibition. First, accurate counterforce combined with better intelligence and defense could nullify the effect of small, less sophisticated nuclear forces. By setting the bar for building a meaningful nuclear force so high, the United States might also be able to dissuade potential nuclear states from building forces it could easily make obsolete. If states did build these forces, their vulnerability to a U.S. first strike removed at least some of their deterrent power vis-à-vis the United States and its allies under the U.S. nuclear umbrella. Second, by not embracing mutual vulnerability, by pursuing a counterforce (and even a preemptive) strategy, the United States made its commitment to defend its non-nuclear allies more credible. If the United States had accepted nuclear parity with the Soviet Union, few patron states would have believed its promise to defend them while risking their own nuclear annihilation. In such a case, the pressure on the nuclear state to acquire an independent deterrent would have been strong.

Which of these strategies of inhibition is the most effective? All three come at a cost. Earlier strategies that seemed wise, such as civilian nuclear assistance to potential proliferators, backfired and were soon abandoned.[88] When the United States employs legal-normative strategies, it is open to the obvious charge of hypocrisy. Coercive policies are a double-edged sword: threats of military action may not be credible. On the other hand, credible coercive threats could spur the potential proliferator to work harder, faster, or in secret—or all three—to achieve a nuclear status that might protect them against future coercion or prevention from the United States. Assurance policies have their own difficulties. Extended deterrent commitments are plagued by credibility problems, expose the United States to significant costs and risks (including entrapment), are not always popular with the American public, and allow protected states to free ride. Thus far, U.S. policymakers have discovered there is no a priori best path to achieve the inhibition mission, and U.S. policymakers have worked diligently over time to find the right mix of strategies.

Changing Expectations, Adaptation, and Mitigation

As has been the case with the openness and containment missions, the United States has not always pursued the inhibition mission consistently. More important, the strategies of inhibition have not always been successful. Although there are far fewer nuclear weapons states in the world today than anyone would have predicted in 1960, 1975, or 1990, eight countries besides the United States possess nuclear weapons.[89] What explains these inconsistencies and lack of complete success?

Enthusiasm for the inhibition mission has varied across presidential administrations, at least initially. Presidents Truman, Kennedy, Johnson, Carter, arguably Reagan, and every administration since the end of the Cold War have been very enthusiastic.[90] Presidents Eisenhower and Nixon, on the other hand, often questioned the feasibility of achieving nuclear nonproliferation. Eisenhower supported nuclear sharing with America's NATO allies.[91] Nixon told his administration to play down the importance of the Nuclear Nonproliferation Treaty when he sent it to the U.S. Senate for ratification.[92] Caveats are in order in both cases, however. Nuclear sharing was understood by many in the Eisenhower administration (if not the president himself) as an alternative to independent national nuclear forces.[93] Sharing your nuclear weapons is not the same as allowing independent national nuclear forces to emerge. And although Nixon may not have liked the Nuclear Nonproliferation Treaty he inherited from the Johnson administration, he was not interested in seeing a proliferated world.[94] By 1974, the administration's policy was unambiguous: "The non-proliferation of nuclear weapons has been a consistent and important element of U.S. policy for the entire nuclear era. Simply put, our strong, repeated, resolve in support of this objective has been predicated on our belief that the instability of the world, and the danger of nuclear war, as well as the problems of arms control would significantly increase with an unrestrained spread of nuclear weapons."[95] Nixon and especially his national security adviser, Henry Kissinger, redoubled their efforts to prevent the spread of nuclear weapons after India's "peaceful" nuclear test in 1974, focusing especially on tightening supplier controls on civilian nuclear assistance, including creating the Nuclear Suppliers Group.[96]

Despite Eisenhower and Nixon's misgivings, powerful support for the inhibition mission also emerged from other sources, from within either their own administrations or the legislative branch.[97] Remarkably, Congress—which often deferred to the executive on crucial issues on U.S. grand strategy during the postwar years—took an active and keen interest in inhibition, even when the president in question did not.[98] Since the start of the nuclear age, Congress has passed increasingly stringent laws dealing with nonproliferation—including the Atomic Energy Act of 1946, the Arms Control and Disarmament Act of 1961, the Symington and Glenn Amendments, the Nuclear Nonproliferation Act of 1978, the Pressler and Solarz Amendments, the Nuclear Proliferation Prevention Act of 1994, and a variety of laws and sanctions against Iran, Iraq, and North Korea—

that prevented the president from encouraging or even being passive about proliferation, a rare but powerful intervention in U.S. national security policy by the legislative branch.

Furthermore, the United States became more committed to the strategies of inhibition over time. Three factors drove this change. First, U.S. policymakers changed their calculations about the likelihood and pace of nuclear proliferation. Early in the nuclear age, U.S. analysts had often overestimated the time and underestimated the ease of developing independent nuclear forces. Furthermore, U.S. concern increased as states developed the means—through long-range bombers and intercontinental missiles—to penetrate and strike the United States quickly. Second, U.S. policymakers became increasingly convinced of both the importance and the plausibility of the inhibition mission over time. Although the United States wanted to prevent proliferation from the start of the nuclear age, uncertainty existed among some policymakers about whether inhibition was feasible, given the high cost and often painful policy trade-offs required of the mission. Third, the inhibition mission often competed with other U.S. grand strategic priorities. Sometimes U.S. policies were able to accommodate all three missions—containment, openness, and inhibition. At other times, these missions clashed, and choices had to be made among them. All three of these factors coalesced in the early to middle 1960s to raise inhibition's importance in U.S. grand strategy: the fear of the ease, pace, and likelihood of nuclear proliferation rose; the belief that something should and could be done to halt it increased; and the period of intense containment gave way to, if not full-fledged détente, a less aggressive Cold War competition with the Soviet Union. After 1991, inhibition trumped containment as a leading mission of U.S. grand strategy.

How do we explain the cases in which the United States failed to prevent states from acquiring nuclear weapons? It is important to remember that inhibition is a difficult goal; preventing sovereign states from acquiring weapons that might guarantee their security is beyond ambitious. That this mission would be difficult was well understood by U.S. policymakers. As George Kistiakowsky, who served as President Eisenhower's science adviser, remarked, "We must wage a campaign to keep proliferation at a minimum and be prepared to lose individual battles, but not the overall war. First, we should be prepared to impose pressures and present inducements to others."[99]

Finally, the inhibition mission does not end when a targeted state acquires nuclear weapons. Instead, the United States employs mitigation strategies, or efforts to lessen the impact of nuclearization. In the most extreme case, mitigation might include efforts at nuclear rollback.[100] Typically, however, mitigation drives the United States to go to great lengths to convince the newly nuclearized state to act in ways that would not increase the likelihood other states would follow suit. As Or Rabinowitz has demonstrated, when it became clear that the United States could not stop Israel's, South Africa's, and Pakistan's nuclear weapons programs, it adopted a second-best approach, pressuring them not to test a nuclear device. Failing to achieve "the primary goal" and to "stop or roll back existing capabilities," the United States sought the "next best thing in the hierarchy of nonproliferation goals": preventing nuclear tests.[101] This is a crucial and often misunderstood feature of the inhibit mission: The United States does not give up on inhibition when a state acquires nuclear weapons. Instead, it works to lessen the consequences and even reverse the undesired outcome, preventing testing, further proliferation, or the development of sophisticated delivery vehicles. Historical examples of the United States' being seen as unperturbed or even supportive of proliferation—such as Nixon's treatment of Israel or Reagan's of Pakistan—should be viewed in the light of U.S. decisions to mitigate the damage.[102]

Writ large, U.S. inhibition policies varied less by administration and more by period. In the earliest years of the nuclear age, U.S. policymakers hoped that limited access to nuclear materials and technology would make inhibition easy. As the Soviet Union, Great Britain, and France achieved nuclear status—and states ranging from Israel to Sweden demonstrated an active interest in nuclear weapons—many U.S. policymakers worried that inhibition was either too difficult or too costly to achieve. A dramatic shift took place in the mid-1960s, as several issues, including the fears over China's nuclearization and West Germany's interest in nuclear weapons, elevated inhibition in United States grand strategy and convinced American policymakers to pay a high price to achieve it.[103] Inhibition became even more central to U.S. grand strategy when the object of containment—the Soviet Union—collapsed and the Cold War ended.

An Often Obscure Strategy

One final question: Why, despite the enormous attention paid to both U.S. grand strategy and the nuclear revolution, have scholars and even policymakers underemphasized the strategy of inhibition since 1945? There are many reasons, but six stand out.

First, the better known containment and openness missions have deep and easily recognized roots in U.S. history and patterns in great-power politics. Grand strategists in the early post–World War II years were able to mine the past for lessons and examples of effective strategies to employ and policies to avoid. The containment mission, for example, had its roots in theories of and practice in the balance of power and geopolitics. The openness mission had been tried, off and on, by the United States since the late nineteenth century and by Great Britain even earlier. The nuclear revolution, on the other hand, presented completely new and profound challenges for U.S. policymakers. Nuclear weapons, delivering unprecedented destruction in hours and without warning by bombers and eventually minutes by long-range missiles, had no precedent in history and removed the United States' long-standing geopolitical invulnerability. The past provided few lessons, not only on how to inhibit proliferation but also on whether it was even possible or wise.[104] National security officials stumbled to articulate the inhibition mission, let alone come up with effective policies, even as they acknowledged the profound threats a nuclearized world presented to the United States.

Second, unlike traditional strategies, inhibition was aimed at a particular technology, regardless of who possessed it, rather than a particular state or regime. There were few usable examples from the past where a general capability, as opposed to a specific state adversary, was targeted. Traditional tools of statecraft, such as propaganda oriented against an enemy and its population, were less useful in efforts to inhibit proliferation in countries such as West Germany, Sweden, and Pakistan.

Third, many of the tools U.S. policymakers used to inhibit nuclear proliferation, including arms control treaties, aggressive nuclear strategies, and wide-ranging alliances, also served the containment mission (and were, in turn, served by it), often obscuring the divergent sources and ends of each.[105] Alliances and institution building also served the openness mission. In other words, many times the strategy of inhibition complemented the openness and especially the containment missions, though often it was independent and even at odds with the other missions.

Fourth, unlike the containment and openness missions, it can be difficult to accurately measure the success or failure of inhibition: Would countries such as Italy, South Korea, or Brazil, for example, be nuclear weapons states today in the absence of U.S. inhibition policies? Would more effective U.S. inhibition strategies have kept Israel or India non-nuclear? Did the threats of coercion and preventive strikes, or the promise of security guarantees and the United States nuclear umbrella, cause otherwise nuclear-capable states to opt out of weapons? Given how many fewer nuclear states there presently are than either policymakers or scholars predicted, it seems the strategies of inhibition were highly effective. Yet this claim is difficult to prove with certainty.

Fifth, because inhibition is often aimed against allies and unaligned countries as much as adversaries, U.S. policymakers have been more discrete and secretive about this critical aspect of grand strategy. The United States' strategies of inhibition lack a clear, explicit founding document, such as Kennan's "long telegram," which explained the logic of U.S. containment strategy for the emerging Cold War. Converting inhibition's strategy—of working with even the bitterest of enemies and threatening the closest of friends to prevent sovereign states from obtaining weapons they deemed crucial to

their security, because it would undermine U.S. strategic interests—
into the kind of soaring language that marked other elements of U.S.
grand strategy would challenge even the best wordsmith.

Sixth, academics often misunderstand how policymakers make
national security decisions, especially when it comes to nuclear
weapons.[106] International relations scholars often argue that global
stability has been the foremost policy goal, whereas policymakers
have often been willing to countenance international instability to
achieve national interests.[107] At the same time, policymakers are far
more sensitive to low-probability, high-consequence events, such as a
nuclear attack.[108] These factors led U.S. decisionmakers to embrace
inhibition and pay higher prices to achieve it.[109]

For all these reasons, we must often dig deeper to make the connections that demonstrate that inhibition has been as pervasive a part
of U.S. grand strategy since the middle of the twentieth century as
containing great-power rivals and opening the global economic and
political system.

Conclusion

Imagine that a cataclysmic global war has ended. In the course of
the conflict, one of the victors—the country that emerged most
powerful—has developed a weapon that can unleash unimaginable
destruction. This country decides that a key element of its postwar
grand strategy will be to undertake enormous efforts to prevent or
make it as difficult as possible for other sovereign states to independently control this weapon.

At first blush, this grand strategic goal was audacious, for at least
two reasons. Historically, states went to great lengths to develop or
acquire whatever military capabilities were necessary to protect and
advance their interests in a dangerous world. Nuclear weapons offer
extraordinary benefits to those that acquire them—they can deter
attacks on their homeland, even from far larger and more powerful
states, even those that also possess nuclear weapons. This transfor-
mational technology allows small and medium-size states to mas-

sively increase their security and power in ways unthinkable in the preatomic age, when military capabilities were directly linked to the size of a nation's economy and its population. Why would a state eschew such a powerful weapon? Joining an alliance could not substitute for this capability—historically, it is rare for a state to place its security so deeply in the hands of another if it could avoid doing so. Second, efforts to contain the spread of military technology in the past almost inevitably failed. From the armed chariot to early cannons to the Gatling gun and the Dreadnought battleship, transformative military technologies are almost always adopted quickly and widely by states that can afford them.[110]

Next, imagine that the state pursuing this unprecedented strategy possesses powerful isolationist instincts, has no history of permanent alliances, and has traditionally maintained a military far less potent than it could afford. It is a state that throughout its history preferred to remain lightly engaged in world affairs, cushioned by two weak states on its borders and protected by two vast oceans.[111] Furthermore, its domestic practices emphasized a weak executive and strong legislative oversight of national security, deliberate decisionmaking about war and peace, and strong civilian control over the military. Few states were less likely than the United States to undertake an open-ended mission that would demand sprawling global alliances, pre-emptive military strategies, and predelegated authority to use force, concentrated executive power, secrecy, nonstop diplomacy and international treaties, preventive inclinations, working with adversaries, and coercing friends.

The nuclear revolution has been with us for so long, has become so enmeshed in world politics, that we sometimes forget the profound and unprecedented challenge it presented to the safety of the United States and its freedom of action. Successive presidential administrations responded by employing new, untested, and often bold strategies to inhibit nuclear proliferation. These strategies of inhibition are one of the most underappreciated, misunderstood, and consequential aspects of postwar United States grand strategy.

Recognizing the central role that inhibition has played since 1945 has important consequences for scholars' and policymakers' understanding of history, theory, and policy. The history of the strategies of inhibition supplements the stylized picture of the Cold War period as a simple bipolar standoff. In this conventional telling, international politics was driven almost entirely by the ideological and geopolitical competition between the Soviet Union and the United States; the concerns of small and medium-size powers were not of great concern; alliances were solely additive; and the end of the Cold War completely transformed U.S. national security interests. It is now understood that, while postwar nuclear history and Cold War history overlap and are interconnected, they are not the same thing.[112] As a recent study points out, "In the afterglow of Hiroshima and Nagasaki, halting the spread of nuclear weapons became central to postwar international politics."[113]

The importance of the strategies of inhibition does not displace the centrality of the Cold War struggle between the Soviet Union and the United States. It does, however, highlight that inhibition was a distinct mission, even producing occasional cooperation with the target of containment, Soviet Russia. It also makes clear that many U.S. alliances were oriented toward balancing suppressing client states' nuclear ambitions against Soviet military power. At times, the strategies of inhibition complemented the openness and containment mission, but often they were independent drivers of U.S. grand strategy. The use of strategies of inhibition helps explain why there has been so much continuity in key U.S. national security policies despite a profound change in the international political system, the end of the Cold War.

Furthermore, inhibition provides a more convincing view of many contested questions surrounding nuclear dynamics. The question of why there has been less nuclear proliferation than expected, for example, has focused almost exclusively on the calculations of the potential proliferators. What are their capabilities to build a nuclear weapon? What are their motivations to either develop or eschew nuclear weapons? The literature on nuclear proliferation has impressively analyzed the technological, normative, security, and domestic political incentives and barriers to building a bomb.[114] Understanding the strategies of inhibition, however, reveals that a key variable determining many proliferation outcomes since 1945 may have been the grand strategy of the United States. Inhibition also bridges the divide between supply-side and demand-side explanations for the rate of nuclear proliferation, given that the United States' strategies of inhibition targeted both. Our history of the nuclear age is incomplete without a solid understanding of the lengths the United States went to to inhibit nuclearization and the way its strategies influenced decisionmaking about nuclear weapons in capitals around the world.

Kenneth Waltz claims that "in the past half-century, no country has been able to prevent other countries from going nuclear if they were determined to do so."[115] Jacques Hymans posits that "the overwhelming majority of scholarly work on nuclear proliferation argues that states do not directly respond to the international environment in making their nuclear weapons choices."[116] It seems difficult to argue, however, that nuclear decisionmaking in any number of states, from West Germany and Japan to South Korea and Taiwan to Sweden and Iraq, was not profoundly influenced by U.S. strategies of inhibition. By arresting or mitigating proliferation among key states, these strategies affected the international environment, increasing the likely costs to proliferation while decreasing the risks for states to remain non-nuclear.

The strategies of inhibition also challenge how defensive realism has explained the influence of nuclear weapons on world politics. Building on the work of strategists such as Bernard Brodie, scholars including Robert Jervis, Stephen Van Evera, and Kenneth Waltz have emphasized the peace-inducing effects of nuclear weapons and suggested that nuclear proliferation is not disastrous nor cause for dramatic policy interventions.[117] This perspective has focused on the powerful stabilizing effects of mutual vulnerability that arise when nuclear states achieve secure second-strike capabilities. Defensive realism further predicts that the United States should have been content with its own security and the security its nuclear weapons offered to other states. The inhibition mission, however, explains why a variety of U.S. nuclear strategies and nuclear nonproliferation policies have deviated so dramatically from defensive realism's predictions.

Although offensive realists have sometimes been fuzzy on the impact of nuclear weapons, their theory may better explain certain aspects of U.S. strategies of inhibition.[118] The seven drivers of the inhibition strategy all relate to the power-equalizing effects of nuclear weapons and are driven by the U.S. effort to safeguard its security, preserve its power, and maintain its freedom of action. Regardless of the stabilizing qualities nuclear weapons may have possessed, U.S. policymakers never accepted being deterred and aggressively sought to prevent the spread of nuclear weapons.

Is the inhibition mission simply an element of a larger grand strategic goal of U.S. primacy or even hegemony? It is true that the strategies of inhibition focus solely on weapons, not on territories, markets, or resources, the typical targets of imperial or hegemonic power.[119] And unlike containment, which focused on adversaries, and openness, which was applied largely to allies, the inhibition mission was applied to all states, with little regard for their economic or political orientation, geographic location, or power-political status. Furthermore, the inhibition mission required that the United States construct policies—such as semipermanent alliances backed by a highly mobilized military—that were a clear break from its long-standing history and traditions.[120] As the nuclear age unfolded, however, policymakers recognized that the "stopping power of water" no longer guaranteed the United States either safety or freedom of action.[121] The strategies of inhibition and the dramatic changes that came with them were a response to the unprecedented constraints on U.S. freedom of action and potentially devastating destruction of weapons that could be delivered on the United States by long-range bombers or missiles in hours if not minutes.[122]

Finally, inhibition provides insight into the debates about U.S. grand strategy since the end of the Cold War. Although there are a variety of schools and positions, the sharpest debate is between those who argue that the United States is dangerously overcommitted abroad and those who believe that the U.S. engagement in the world provides tangible benefits, especially economic ones. In fact, the United States' forward-leading, deep engagement in the world is driven, at least in part, by the inhibition mission, and assessing the costs and effectiveness of the U.S. grand strategy must take the strategies of inhibition into account. Furthermore, inhibition helps explain U.S. national security policies that have long puzzled students of United States grand strategy, including the interest in preventive strikes and coercion vis-à-vis emerging nuclear states; continuing and broadening Cold War alliances after the disappearance of the Soviet Union; and the persistent and expensive interest in ballistic missile defense, hard-target counterforce, and command, control, communications, and intelligence capabilities.

This inhibition logic is at work in U.S. grand strategy today. The strategies of inhibition help explain not only the persistence of U.S. efforts to keep Iran from acquiring a bomb but also the motivation to do so. Neither the ideological orientation nor geopolitical goals of the regime in Tehran—no matter how troublesome to U.S. policymakers—is the primary driver of U.S. nonproliferation efforts vis-à-vis Iran. Nor are interest-driven U.S. inhibition strategies motivated by a desire to provide public goods and global security, though these may be welcome by-products.

There is still much to learn about the strategies of inhibition. Which of the drivers and responses did the United States prioritize and why, and which strategies of inhibition did policymakers find most suitable for each particular case of potential proliferation? Even more important, how did policymakers make trade-offs between the containment, openness, and inhibition missions, and did those calculations change over time? Despite the powerful and consistent desire to inhibit nuclear proliferation, U.S. grand strategy was implemented in a dynamic, ever-changing political and technological environment and faced challenges it never had to deal with before 1945.

What is the future of inhibition? The United States is at a point where its power and ability to shape world politics is widely seen as waning, where calls for a more restrained U.S. grand strategy are more popular, yet the potential for increases in the number of states with independent nuclear forces is ever present. The inhibition mission was both more successful and more expensive and dangerous than has been recognized. Was the high price worth it, and should the United States continue to pay it going forward? What happens when the United States is no longer willing or able to be the main force for nonproliferation in the world? The debates over the future of United States grand strategy will be woefully incomplete until we come to terms with these questions.

FIVE

NATO's Radical Response to the Nuclear Revolution

In this, the eighth decade since the United States, Canada, and its Western European allies negotiated and signed a peacetime military alliance, what is its historical legacy? Broadly speaking, there are two ways to think about the North Atlantic Treaty and the institution that emerged, the North Atlantic Treaty Organization.

The first view—what I would suggest is the conventional wisdom—sees NATO as a fairly orthodox and benign organization. It emerged to deal with the looming specter of Soviet expansion that threatened a weak, disorganized, and embittered Western Europe struggling to find its bearings after World War II. Led but not dominated by the United States, NATO succeeded by creating a largely defensive strategy that deterred but did not threaten the Soviet Union. In the process, it served as a vehicle to lessen and eventually eliminate long-held intra-European tensions by focusing on cooperation and consensus. Its success in promoting European security led NATO—despite predictions to the contrary—not only to survive the end of the Cold War but to expand both its membership and its mission over the past three decades.[1]

There is much truth to this perspective. Building on and expanding the March 1948 Brussels Treaty signed by Great Britain, France, Belgium, the Netherlands, and Luxembourg, the original signatories to the 1949 treaty, while recognizing its boldness, did not see it as a revolutionary act. Few if any believed NATO was more than a political association to help pool and coordinate their collective resources while generating a mechanism to distribute military aid from the United States. No one anticipated that a fully integrated military organization would develop and last after the original threat had disappeared.

There is, in fact, a second view, that recognizes NATO developed into (and in some ways remains) a truly radical organization, unprecedented in the history of international politics. To give just a few examples: before NATO, alliances were fungible and ever shifting, constantly changing members and measured in years, not decades. NATO developed into something different altogether—once a nation gets in, it has been almost impossible (with one partial exception), for it to get out, even after the geopolitical impetus for its formation has disappeared. Furthermore, NATO became a vehicle to rehabilitate and exploit West German military power less than a decade after the horrors of Nazi Germany, a fact that alarmed not just Soviet adversaries but many members the alliance was set up to protect. At the same time, it successfully managed to restrain West German political ambitions and prevent the country from accessing the most powerful new weapons, all to reassure both NATO's enemies and its own members. When the Cold War ended, NATO was a key enabler of German reunification, despite deep reservations in Russia and throughout Europe at the prospect. In the successful aftermath of reunification, NATO expanded eastward into territories long considered part of Russia's sphere of influence. None of this was foreseen in 1949.[2]

NATO's relationship with the United States is especially puzzling and hard to square with the more conventional understanding of the organization. Looking back from our contemporary perspective, many see NATO as an instrument of American hegemony in and over Europe, reflecting the United States' imperial ambitions in the world. For more than a few American leaders, however, NATO was, from its earliest days, a resented and unloved burden. Before NATO, the United States avoided peacetime alliances and standing military deployments overseas. NATO's military strategy developed in ways completely at odds with the traditional American way of warfare, which was predicated on exploiting the United States' geographic and economic advantages to mobilize slowly but massively to fight grinding wars of attrition.[3] NATO's military plans and deployments threatened the United States' long-held beliefs in strict civilian control of the military and congressional oversight in matters of war and peace. Most important, the notion that the United States would not only permanently commit to such an entity but also forwardly deploy hundreds of thousands of troops would have been dismissed as absurd when the treaty was first considered.

What factors transformed NATO from its original, more modest ambitions in just a few years? One factor loomed above all else: nuclear weapons. The revolution in military technology—especially thermonuclear weapons, the ability to deliver them rapidly and over great distances, and the near impossibility of defensive measures—had a profound influence on geopolitics and military affairs during the postwar era, driving much of NATO's more radical orientation. In a non-nuclear world, or a world in which the United States retained its atomic monopoly, NATO might have been a conventional alliance: an agreement among sovereign states to pool resources in the face of a common enemy, an arrangement that would loosen and disappear altogether as the shared threat changed or disappeared. But the unique challenges brought on by nuclear weapons demanded dramatic responses, which shaped NATO's choices from the 1950s onward and, in ways rarely stated, continue to do so to this day.

This chapter focuses on two of these interrelated and radical strategic choices made by NATO and the challenges they presented. First, NATO adopted an extraordinarily aggressive military strategy in the early and middle 1950s. First laid out in the strategy document MC-48, NATO's strategy appeared to rely on the massive, pre-emptive use of nuclear weapons against Soviet military assets in the first hours of a war. Despite drawing in some aspects of the strategy in the 1960s and beyond, many of the aggressive features remained throughout the Cold War. The second NATO choice involved the organization's role—driven largely by U.S. preferences—as a vehicle to suppress the spread of nuclear weapons within (and outside of) the alliance. One of NATO's most important, yet unstated and largely unrecognized, missions was and remains nuclear nonproliferation.

The radical responses to the nuclear revolution lay at the heart of a series of contradictions within the alliance that were a constant source of tension. NATO's two nuclear missions were often in conflict: a military strategy that relied so heavily on threatening early and massive use of nuclear weapons intensified the desire of NATO members to possess them. These contradictions—and the difficulties spawned by the political and military policies needed to carry out NATO's radical mission—were never fully resolved, and they drove tensions and even crisis, both with those outside and those within the alliance, for decades. Ironically, these radical policies helped stabilize geopolitics in what had been the world's cauldron of war, Central Europe.

NATO Needs a Strategy

Early NATO efforts to develop a military strategy have been effectively laid out by several scholars, especially in the important work of Robert Wampler, David Rosenberg, and notably Marc Trachtenberg.[4] But the narrative is worth repeating.

The early plans to defend Western Europe, plans that preceded NATO, were rather simplistic. They recognized an essential asymmetry between the East and the West: The Soviet Union had an overwhelming superiority in conventional military power, which might allow it to overrun and dominate the European continent. The United States, however, possessed a monopoly on atomic weapons.

It did not, however, have a large number of bombs, and those it did possess were unassembled and not married to delivery capabilities. While the means to deliver the weapons and their destructive capacity were limited compared with what was to come, the United States believed—or rather, hoped—that the bomb was enough to deter a Russian attack while Western Europe recovered. Should deterrence fail and war ensue, the United States would unleash its stockpile of atomic bombs on Russia while mobilizing its industrial base to fight and win a longer war. Such a Soviet attack, however, was not expected. While there were political tensions between Russia and the United States, the former was itself recovering from the devastation of war.

The unexpected and early testing of a nuclear device by the Soviet Union in August 1949 upended those assumptions. If both superpowers had the bomb, wouldn't their weapons cancel each other out? In other words, could the United States be expected to launch an atomic assault on Russia if it would be hit by devastating attacks in return? And even if the United States were willing to take such risks, from where would it launch these attacks, and how would it return and liberate the Continent? The United States and its Western European allies faced a dire prospect: Europe quickly overrun by Soviet conventional military power, the United States held off by Soviet atomic power, and the enormous resources of the captured Continent exploited. Even without a war, this strategic reality was bound to cast a shadow over Europe, possibly leading to an unwelcome drift toward accommodation and neutrality vis-à-vis the Soviets. These disturbing scenarios seemed even more plausible after the North Korean invasion of South Korea in June 1950 and the People's Republic of China's intervention against the United States at the end of 1950. The Sino-Soviet bloc appeared united, and atomic weapons seemed to make them more aggressive. Western Europe was exposed and vulnerable, and the Communist powers appeared on the move, all while a large portion of U.S. forces were pinned down on the Korean Peninsula.

One possible response was to try to match Soviet conventional power, and early NATO goals called for just that: a force of ninety divisions, just enough, it was hoped, to keep Western Europe from being overrun. But these goals proved well out of reach for NATO members, for financial and political reasons. NATO faced a profound strategic challenge: an alliance with weak, recovering states, led by a superpower an ocean away and deeply ambivalent about any permanent military commitment to Europe. A further challenge was that the greatest reservoir of unexploited military power lay in West Germany, a divided and occupied country less than a decade removed from the end of World War II and the demise of Nazism. Any effort to build up and exploit this unused power was bound to create political difficulties of the highest order, both vis-à-vis the Soviets and within NATO.

NATO's response was a military strategy that was eventually laid out in the document MC-48 but was also deeply intertwined with complex political negotiations over the political and military status of the Federal Republic of Germany (FRG) and with the nuclear strategy of the United States.[5] The document has several components. First, West Germany's untapped military power had to be exploited if NATO was to have any chance of stopping a Soviet onslaught. But this carried enormous risks. Would the FRG's neighbors—both allies and adversaries—accept West German rearmament so soon after the war? How would rearmament affect West German behavior and ambitions? The collapse of the European Defense Community negotiations in 1954 demonstrated how complicated and volatile the German question was. The issue was not just the recent memory of the horrors of World War II and the Holocaust. Even a truly reformed, repentant FRG was not a status quo state. It was divided, and presumably one of its primary goals would be reunification. How might that square with other European powers (and Russia) that were not displeased by the status quo?

A second issue was that rearmament would require limitations and controls on German power. The FRG could not have complete freedom to pursue whatever foreign policy it wanted, nor could it have its own nuclear weapons: these restrictions were enunciated in a series of political agreements reached in 1954. But how could the

FRG's limited political and especially military status be maintained? The rest of NATO would demand a strong American presence to keep a lid on German ambitions. Would West Germany accept such discrimination, given the resentment such restrictions produced in interwar Germany? Would the United States—long resistant to such commitments—be willing to commit forces to the continent in large enough numbers, and over a long enough term, to make its European allies (and again, the Russians) comfortable with a semi-sovereign West German state and a revived army? And how might the Soviets— emboldened by their acquisition of atomic power—react to this new arrangement? None of these questions could be answered with great confidence as the strategy was developed and implemented.

The military challenges for NATO were as daunting as the political issues. There were two big issues here. First, NATO still confronted considerable Soviet conventional superiority it was not likely to match. Despite the loss of the nuclear monopoly, atomic weapons were bound to be part of any military strategy. How would they be employed? Second, to ensure West German participation, the FRG would have to be defended as well as possible at the intra-German border; West Germany was unlikely to participate in a plan that ceded its territory in the first days of the conflict. Better still, from the German perspective, would be to attack Warsaw Pact military assets before they even reached the border with the FRG.

The military strategy that ensued—both from MC-48 and the U.S. efforts (including President Dwight D. Eisenhower's Project Solarium exercise to explore different possible strategies) that embodied the administration's New Look policy or produced massive retaliation—was truly radical. It contained both pre-emptive and counterforce elements. To defeat a Soviet attack, nuclear weapons would have to be used early—even, it was hinted, when it was clear that the Soviets were invading but before any actual shots had been fired. The key, however, would be to incapacitate, or blunt, the Soviet ability to respond with its own nuclear weapons. This meant that Soviet nuclear assets would have to be targeted.[6] The United States would not simply react, slowly, as the war developed, biding its time and slowly mobilizing for a war of attrition. Instead, it would react as soon as possible, perhaps as soon as war was clearly imminent.

It is important to keep in mind what NATO's military strategy was not: it was not passive or reactive, and it not did rely on the concept of mutual assured destruction. Instead, it was a strategy that planned on massive and early use of nuclear weapons against specific Soviet military targets at the start of a war. The number of weapons, the sophistication of the delivery systems, and the intelligence capabilities needed to implement such a strategy were extraordinary, far, far beyond what would be required if NATO had adopted a less far-reaching strategy or if the United States was only defending itself. More worrisome, this strategy, and the forces designed to carry them out, would look highly threatening to the Soviets; it could even be interpreted as a first-strike, pre-emptive, force.

The strategy was possible only because the United States implemented a massive military buildup, as called for in the April 1950 document NSC-68 but applied in the years after China's intervention in the Korean conflict. The U.S. defense budget was almost quadrupled, and most of the funds went to building nuclear weapons and the ability to deliver them. In 1952 the United States successfully tested thermonuclear weapons, leading to massive increases in the destructive capacity of the American stockpile. This military shield, it was hoped, would deter the Soviets while NATO developed and implemented its sweeping transformation. The strategy also required a complex set of political trade-offs and compromises developed in 1954, a significant American military commitment to allow West German rearmament to take place despite significant limitations on the political and military independence of the Federal Republic of Germany. The vision behind Lord Hastings Ismay's oft-cited observation—the goal of NATO was to keep the Americans in, the Russians out, and the Germans down—was to be realized, though at considerable risk and cost.

Massive retaliation was, by all measures, successful. Western Europe recovered, politically, economically, and militarily, the Soviets were deterred, and the danger of war appeared to recede. By the middle and late 1950s, stability and confidence began to replace panic in Central Europe. The military strategy, however, had within it the seeds of its own demise. What would happen if and when the United States grew tired of its expensive military commitment to Western Europe? What if the West Germans resisted the political and military restrictions placed on them? The most pressing short-term concern was the Soviets' reaction to NATO's strategy: What if they responded with their own military buildup, developing their own ability to strike quick and hard with nuclear weapons, not just against Western Europe but also against the continental United States? The launch of the Sputnik satellite, and the ensuing fears of both bomber and missile gaps, highlighted the worrying fact that the pre-emptive nuclear strategy that was at the military and political heart of the NATO strategy would last only as long as the United States and its Strategic Air Command could credibly threaten a first strike.

Thus the conventional wisdom, while acknowledging the aggressive nature of the MC-48's massive retaliation policy, argues that it was a short-lived strategy. Even by the end of the Eisenhower administration, and certainly by the Kennedy-Johnson period, this aggressive strategy fell out of favor. Building on the work of many of the critics in the strategy community, NATO adopted a more nuanced, fine-tuned strategy that came to be called "flexible response." This strategy—first laid out by U.S. secretary of defense Robert McNamara to the NATO defense ministers in a secret speech in Athens, Greece, in the spring of 1962 and formally embraced as NATO strategy in the document MC-14/3 in January 1968—was supposed to be a dramatic break with the past. The United States' promise to defend Western Europe with its strategic nuclear weapons was seen as problematic. The crisis over the status of West Berlin revealed scenarios in which employing military forces at a far lower level of the escalatory ladder might be appropriate. Flexible response was supposed to be a strategy that relied far more on conventional forces, that paused before using nuclear weapons, and that resisted rapid escalation. Furthermore, as the 1960s and 1970s progressed, there seemed to be at least a public embrace in certain strategic and policy circles of the idea of "mutual vulnerability," a condition of mutual assured destruction between the superpowers.[7]

There is evidence that the differences between the older NATO strategy and the new one were overdrawn.[8] Judging by the strategic nuclear plans of the United States, the backbone of any NATO military strategy against the Soviet Union, it still appeared to contain pre-emptive and counterforce elements. Despite lots of pressure, NATO never came close to embracing a no-first-use doctrine. Nor did the United States ever permanently forgo its efforts to achieve the nuclear primacy needed to make NATO's radical nuclear strategy plausible. For example, the United States spent hundreds of billions of dollars on nuclear forces, delivery capabilities, and targeting intelligence in the later years of the Cold War, well after quantitative parity had been achieved. These enormous resources were not spent to increase the sheer numbers or destructive capabilities of the weapons—both of which were restricted by the Strategic Arms Limitations Treaties. Instead, the money went into making U.S. forces more survivable, faster, more accurate, and better able to locate, target, and destroy Soviet nuclear forces—that is, Pershing II, Trident D-5, B-1, the MX, cruise missiles, C-3-I (command, control, communication, and intelligence)—and developing the ability to locate and seek Soviet subs with nuclear weapons (antisubmarine warfare).

These forces, it appears, were the backbone of a counterforce strategy, one whose emphasis on intelligence, accuracy, speed, and hard-target capabilities seemed to indicate it retained its pre-emptive qualities.[9] A strategy based on mutual assured destruction—which assumed that NATO and the United States would respond against enemy civilian targets after absorbing a first strike—would not demand such technologically advanced, sophisticated, and expensive systems. Why build these forces, at such financial and political cost, if one's strategy was based on mutual vulnerability?

The point to be made here is that this strategy and these deployments were not produced solely by aggressive or imperial instincts on the part of the United States: top American decisionmakers often resented and tried to lessen or end the commitment. Nor were they the result of bureaucratic, organizational, or ideological instincts alone. They were not, to cite one of our foremost scholars of nuclear strategy, illogical.[10] Instead, they were driven by the same political and military puzzles that were present at the start of the thermonuclear age and persisted for decades—namely, how to deter and defend Western Europe, relying on West German economic and military power, without allowing it to develop its own nuclear weapons. If the strategy accepted nuclear parity, or mutual assured destruction as a fact, there was little reason for the FRG to take seriously NATO's promise to defend it. If the FRG were to pursue the logical next step—acquire its own nuclear weapons—the consequences might be grave indeed.

What Is Good for Me Is Not Good for You

If NATO retained elements of an aggressive, nuclear-intensive counterforce, pre-emptive strategy, why then did the rhetoric of the alliance change in the 1960s and beyond? Why did both the United States and NATO try to distance themselves from the ideas embraced during the 1950s?

There is no doubt that some of the more aggressive elements of the early NATO strategy were reined in. Part of the issue, however, surrounded the influence such a forward-leaning nuclear strategy had on nuclear proliferation. There were several aspects to this question.

First, NATO's strategy prioritized nuclear weapons, making it clear that they—and not other types of armaments—were what mattered in the modern world. Having tanks, planes, and divisions were fine, but they were not the assets that were decisive in conflict. States that did not possess nuclear weapons would be placed, almost by definition, in a position of second-rate status. The centrality of nuclear weapons in NATO's plans made it hard to argue—as many advocates of nuclear nonproliferation were to contend—that nuclear weapons were ugly, immoral, or irrelevant.

The second issue was the nature of the strategy itself: if nuclear weapons were to be used very early in any conflict, almost preemptively, then the decision of when and how to use them would have to be predelegated from the highest political levels down to commanders on the battlefield. There would be very little time for national legislatures to meet and debate whether to go to war. Decisions would have to be made in hours, not days or weeks, and national leaders would have to rely on military officials in place on the ground. And NATO, as an integrated military organization, might find high-ranking military officials from any number of states—including West Germany—involved in these decisions.[11]

We now know that West German officials consciously sought to resist closing off an atomic option for themselves and to pressure the United States to have some say over nuclear decisionmaking within NATO and even access and control of the weapons themselves. This desire—and President Eisenhower's personal sympathy to the desire—generated grave tensions with the Soviet Union and great concern within the alliance itself. Even those who did not share Eisenhower's view that a nuclearized Bundeswehr was both inevitable and not disastrous recognized that the question had to be handled carefully. There was a widespread fear of the consequences of blatantly treating West Germany and its nuclear ambitions differently from those of, say, France and Great Britain.

As the 1960s progressed, broader concerns over the consequences of unchecked nuclear proliferation grew.[12] West Germany's potential nuclearization was, because of its history and geopolitical situation, in a category by itself. By the late 1950s, the Soviet Union made it quite clear that it would not accept a West Germany with the bomb—this was the driving issue behind the great crisis period of 1958–1962—and by 1963, the United States agreed. But the possibility that other nations, either within the NATO alliance (say, Italy) or outside (say, India, China, Japan, Sweden, or Australia), might acquire the bomb was a cause for concern. Other nations with nuclear weapons would make the restrictions against the FRG seem especially discriminatory, which was always a concern. How could West Germany remain non-nuclear if less important states such as Sweden or Israel had atomic weapons? There was also a fear of what are often called nuclear "tipping points," or dominoes, whereby one key state's acquiring the bomb would lead several others to do so as well.[13] This would, potentially, not only make the world more dangerous: the United States, in particular, was worried that nuclear weapons would be used to deter its own defense efforts. Nuclear nonproliferation became a far higher U.S. strategic interest, and its policies in this area became more vigorous. By the end of the 1960s, after remarkable cooperation with its adversary, the Soviet Union, the Nuclear Non-proliferation Treaty was signed.

The United States' nuclear nonproliferation policy, and NATO's forward-leaning nuclear strategy, were in some tension with each other.[14] NATO's military strategy emphasized the primacy of nuclear weapons: they would be used first and against other nuclear targets. Yet the United States also vowed to prevent other sovereign states, including its close alliance partner, West Germany, from getting their hands on these weapons. Various efforts were made to bridge this gap, such as the ill-fated Multilateral Force initiative and the Nuclear Planning Group. The strategy of flexible response, with its stated emphasis on the need for centralized control of nuclear decisionmaking, was also an effort to ease proliferation pressures within the alliance. There is no doubt the Kennedy and Johnson administrations were alarmed by the rather loose controls and predelegation orders they inherited in NATO's nuclear plans. But it was not lost on European observers, such as the French and even the British, that requiring centralized control was an argument against independent nuclear programs.

On the other hand, NATO's radical military strategy served a nonproliferation purpose. If West Germany and other non-nuclear NATO states were to eschew the bomb, they would have to be convinced that the strategy would deter an attack and protect them should war come. The credibility of American's nuclear umbrella, its extended deterrent guarantee, would be (and was) doubted in an age of nuclear parity, especially if the Soviet Union retained a significant edge in conventional capabilities.[15] To a certain extent, this was a situation that simply had to be accepted. But a strategy could be devised and forces developed that at least made a military defense of Europe against a Soviet invasion plausible. If the United States had hundreds of thousands of conventional forces on the front lines of any battle, disentangling from any conflict would be hard. And if it continued to build a force that made a counterforce, pre-emptive nuclear strike plausible—not to say wise—if all other options failed, this could enhance deterrence. West Germany, first and foremost, but others inside and outside the NATO alliance, might make the calculation that U.S. security guarantees were, if not as effective a deterrent as their own nuclear weapons, good enough and would come without all the complications, costs, and controversies a national nuclear weapons program would bring.

To a certain extent, this narrative—both the continuing elements of NATO's radical strategy through the end of the Cold War and the linkage between this strategy and nuclear non-proliferation—is more speculative than we would like. We do not have the quality or quantity of documents for the 1970s and 1980s that we do for earlier periods, and most documents involving both nuclear weapons and the German question are likely to remain classified for the foreseeable future. Furthermore, the deep sensitivity surrounding these questions—the treatment by the United States of its closest allies— often produced a euphemistic language to avoid hurt feelings (for example, the phrase "European stability" often became a cover for the German question). The argument for this later period is less supported by historical evidence than a certain appreciation of the logic of nuclear weapons and their profound influence on international affairs. But the documents may well tell a different story.

Constant Crisis to Generate Stability

Efforts were undertaken to make NATO's military plans more flexible and less frightening. The 1967 Harmel Report and ensuing MC-14/3 document officially enshrined aspects of flexible response into NATO's war planning, though again, the degree of change has often been overstated. In some ways, however, the narrow specifics of the strategy are less important than the overall logic. Relying on the nuclear umbrella of the United States, NATO's embrace of extended deterrence was guaranteed to generate continual crisis, both within the alliance and with the Soviets.[16] This took place on several dimensions—between the United States and its European NATO partners, among NATO's European powers, between NATO and the Warsaw Pact, and within the United States itself.

What drove this sense of perpetual crisis? It was in the DNA of NATO's radical strategy itself. Consider the position of the Federal Republic of Germany within the alliance. The West Germans would feel resentment that they were being discriminated against in the nuclear field, especially as Great Britain and France over time developed their own weapons. Why should they be singled out, especially when the strategy emphasized nuclear weapons? American policymakers were keenly aware that the failure of military restrictions on West Germany during the interwar period played some role in the rise of the Third Reich. Nevertheless, any efforts by NATO or the United States to reassure the FRG on this point—by giving them access to nuclear weapons—brought complaints by the Russians and other European countries. To generate the reassurance necessary to keep West Germany content, the United States had to deploy large numbers of conventional forces.

NATO's strategy also generated a sense of tension within U.S. policymaking circles. The expense of these conventional forces—both in budgetary and balance-of-payments terms—provoked constant complaints from U.S. policymakers. Keeping several hundred thousand U.S. troops and their families in West Germany, while the Vietnam War and other conflicts raged and America's economic woes pressured budgets and currency reserves, tested the political capabilities of several administrations.[17] The whole NATO strategy of extended deterrence was predicated on meaningful U.S. nuclear superiority and a willingness to use nuclear weapons, if not first, at least early in a conflict. Such an aggressive and potentially dangerous strategy was alarming both to the Soviet Union and to many in the United States.

Many of the crises in NATO's history had one or more of these dynamics as their taproot. Consider the whole period from the late

1950s onward. In the late 1950s, NATO moved toward allowing West Germany greater access and control of nuclear weapons. The Soviets responded by initiating the Berlin crises of 1958 and 1961, in part, to indicate their great displeasure. By 1963, the United States recognized that NATO could not allow nuclear weapons to fall into the hands of the Federal Republic and, through the mechanism of the partial test ban treaty negotiations in the summer of 1963, came to an agreement on this point with the Soviets. As a result, the West German government was deeply upset; the United States tried to meet this concern with a promise to permanently keep United States troops in the country. The costs of these troops, however, were onerous, and throughout the 1960s the United States made efforts to pull them out, to the anger of West Germany.[18]

The story of crisis in the 1970s turned around these issues and the Soviet achievement of strategic nuclear parity with the United States. How could the United States' extended deterrent, its willingness to use nuclear weapons if Western Europe was attacked, be carried out if the promise to trade Chicago for Hamburg was not credible? And as the Soviets continued to upgrade their strategic nuclear forces, medium-range missiles, and conventional forces, this sense of crisis deepened. The so-called Euromissile crisis—generated by the Soviet deployment of massive, rapid SS-20s targeted at Western Europe—caused deep anxiety, as did NATO's response—deployment of Pershing II missiles.[19]

Tellingly, NATO's perpetual sense of crisis abated but did not completely disappear once the Cold War ended and the supposed target of NATO's military strategy, the Soviet Union, disappeared. At least one part of NATO's radical strategy, nuclear nonproliferation, presumably remained. Consider the controversial subject of NATO expansion. From its earliest days, the policy was justified by the need to spread stability and democracy to the former Eastern bloc. But consider another (though complementary) logic. Given what we know about the extraordinary power of nuclear weapons to deter conventional invasions, such weapons must have been extraordinarily appealing to a newly independent Poland. Poland's history was, of course, scarred by brutal invasions and land grabs by both Germany and Russia, and the prospect of forever ending such a nightmare must have been appealing. But a Poland with nuclear weapons, no matter how justified and understandable it would have been given its history and interests, would have upset the nuclear nonproliferation regime. More to the point, it would have opened up the awkward question of nuclear weapons in Central Europe, and in particular, a newly unified Germany. Could Germany long remain non-nuclear with nuclear-armed countries both to the East and West? Perhaps, but would anyone really want to risk finding out? Expanding NATO, and a credible U.S. nuclear umbrella, to Poland and others would arguably resolve, at least partially, these concerns.

The irony of NATO's radical military strategy during the Cold War is that while it created constant crisis and tension within and across alliances, it was ultimately stabilizing. Consider the alternative strategies NATO might have chosen. NATO could have attempted to match Soviet conventional capabilities, with potentially ruinous economic and political consequences. Or the United States could have left Western Europe to its own devices, to organize its own defense. As long as nuclear weapons existed, however, and as long as the Soviet Union possessed and demonstrated a willingness to use them, the temptation for Western Europe, and particularly the Federal Republic of Germany, to acquire them would have been enormous. A divided Germany—a division welcomed by all in the East and West but West Germany itself and a few Americans—with nuclear weapons would have been unacceptable not only to the Soviet Union but Great Britain and France, as well. A Western alliance would have been difficult if not impossible to create under those circumstances. Eschewing the nuclear route, however, the FRG would have feared domination by the Russians. The drift toward neutrality may have been unavoidable, with all the geopolitical dangers that would bring. In the absence of NATO's radical nuclear strategy, where West Germany was both credibly protected and constrained by American power, the options were not appealing.

The constant crisis and tension, both within the NATO alliance and with the Soviet Union and the Warsaw Pact, was a high price, but one most likely necessary to remedy the difficult and potentially explosive issues surrounding the German problem in a nuclear world.

Conclusion

To argue that NATO's nuclear strategy during the Cold War was radical is not necessarily to condemn it. On the one hand, a counterforce, pre-emptive strategy involved serious risks and dangers. A strategy focused on the utility of nuclear weapons made the bomb more appealing and efforts to promote nuclear nonproliferation less convincing. In a crisis, NATO's strategy made the dangers of miscalculation or an accident far higher. Furthermore, any effort to establish credibility in a nuclear crisis could lead to dangerous brinkmanship and an unthinkable disaster. Even absent such a cataclysm, NATO's radical nuclear strategy demanded extraordinary expenditures to develop qualitative improvements in targeting, speed, accuracy, survivability, and intelligence. This fueled an expensive, contentious qualitative arms race, ironically at the very time SALT I and II successfully limited the quantitative competition in strategic nuclear arms between the superpowers. NATO's strategy was expensive, both economically and politically, and risky.

The obvious answer, however, is that the strategy appeared to work. Historians are sensitive to the fact that correlation is not always (or even often) causation, but the Cold War ended on terms favorable to NATO. Germany did not acquire nuclear weapons, and there are far fewer nuclear weapons states around the world today than anyone would have predicted or hoped for fifty years ago. Most important, nuclear weapons have never been used by or against NATO, or anyone else for that matter, since 1945. Would a less radical strategy—one based solely on conventional defense, or one that acknowledged and accepted mutual nuclear vulnerability—have produced similar results? We cannot know, of course. But it does highlight how remarkable NATO's history has been.

SIX

Beyond Deterrence

Nuclear deterrence theory is widely viewed as a powerful intellectual tool, developed by a unique intellectual community whose work shaped not only how we think about war and peace but, more important, how policymakers, especially in the United States, crafted their own strategies.[1] How well did this intellectual tool capture both U.S. nuclear statecraft and the global nuclear dynamics? And how useful is this tool in understanding our contemporary and future nuclear world?

The primary concept underlying nuclear deterrence theory is simple but powerful: states that possess survivable nuclear weapons are unlikely to be conquered, because no adversary would pay the potential price of its own annihilation to attempt (or even threaten) to acquire the state's territory.[2] During the period of intense Soviet-U.S. rivalry, some questioned whether the benefits of nuclear deterrence were worth the risk that nuclear weapons could be launched, either intentionally or by accident. On balance, however, the recent memory of a catastrophic great-power war within an international system marked by a bitter ideological clash, deep mistrust, and intense security competition made the possibility that nuclear deterrence could provide stability and decrease if not eliminate the prospect of total war appealing. Much of the Cold War debate surrounding nuclear deterrence was less over what it was and whether it worked than over how many nuclear weapons, what kinds, and within what strategies nuclear weapons should be deployed to best realize the greatest stabilizing benefits at the lowest cost and danger.[3] Does this picture of nuclear deterrence, however, capture the complex motives and strategies that drove U.S. nuclear statecraft, both during the Cold War and after?

Imagine that the United States unilaterally decommissioned all of its strategic nuclear forces tomorrow. Surrounded by two oceans, facing weak countries on its borders, and possessing command of the commons and overwhelming conventional, economic, and soft-power superiority, would the odds of the American homeland being invaded increase at all? It is not clear whom, in this scenario, nuclear deterrence is keeping at bay. The unlikeliness of an invasion or conquest is not simply a product of the post–Cold War world. Fifty years ago, a similar decision by the United States was unlikely to make the Soviet Union or any other potential adversary more inclined to invade and conquer the United States. In fact, by removing the need to target alerted U.S. nuclear forces, a case could be made that the overall danger to the American homeland would have decreased.

This revealing if unanswerable counterfactual is not presented to make a case for or against deterrence or disarmament. Nor is it to avoid the obvious point that the United States had and has interests and ambitions that go far beyond protecting its homeland. Rather, this hypothetical presents us with a puzzle to be explored. Few countries have had less need for the most important benefit nuclear deterrence provides: protection from invasion and conquest. Yet no other state has been as determined to build large numbers of weapons married to the most sophisticated delivery systems, and employed in comparatively aggressive strategies, while working hard to deny independent nuclear weapons capabilities to others. Furthermore, the most dangerous nuclear crises involving the United States—the Korean War, the Berlin crisis,* and the Cuban missile crisis—engaged political issues that were far from existential and arguably would have been handled differently in a world without nuclear weapons, if they had happened at all.[4] Nuclear deterrence theories struggle to explain important parts of this international history.

How are we to explain these apparent puzzles and this tension between theories of nuclear deterrence and the history of American nuclear statecraft? If the United States has little fear of invasion, to what purpose does it put its nuclear weapons? Why does the United States threaten to use nuclear weapons, or to unleash a process that might lead to catastrophic nuclear use, over conflicts that are not remotely existential—such as the political status of a city deep in enemy territory six decades ago? Does that threat—explicit or implicit—remain for similarly nonexistential scenarios, such as the defense of a Baltic country or man-made islands in the South China Sea today?[5] And what do these strategies tell us about the power and limitations of nuclear weapons? Are these insights applicable to other countries? There is very little in the classic literature on nuclear deterrence that provides satisfactory answers to these questions.

This chapter examines the concept of nuclear deterrence through the lens of the history and the grand strategic goals of the United States. Strategists may have missed important elements of U.S. nuclear statecraft, both its history and the theoretical underpinnings, and underplayed deep continuities between the Cold War and the

---

* Both President Eisenhower and President Kennedy recognized that West Berlin, deep in enemy territory, could not be defended by conventional forces alone and that the threat of nuclear use by the United States was its primary tool to keep the Soviet Union and Soviet premier Khrushchev from implementing his threats against the city. Furthermore, losing West Berlin would not alter the conventional military balance of power but would damage U.S. credibility, the latter recognized as far more important in a nuclear than a non-nuclear world. Given the limited options and their own views of the Berlin situation, it is hard to imagine either Eisenhower or Kennedy going to great lengths—such as fighting a massive conventional war—to protect West Berlin in a non-nuclear world.

post–Cold War worlds. My point is not to criticize earlier strategists, who built impressive deductive tools and developed keen insights into nuclear deterrence, but rather to emphasize how complex and often obscure nuclear dynamics can be and how difficult it is to correctly identify those elements of international relations that are shaped by nuclear weapons and those that are not. There are immense challenges to the task of making sense of nuclear politics and statecraft since 1945.

The analysis offered here is an admittedly basic framework to better understand American nuclear statecraft in order to capture its complex and often crosscutting strategies and goals. This framework—labeled "multiple and interactive deterrence, assurance, and reassurance" (MIDAR)—attempts to capture the complex, wide-ranging missions that the United States tries to implement through its nuclear weapons strategy. The strategy of MIDAR is aimed at allies, adversaries, and neutrals alike, often involving basic and extended deterrence, at other times assurances, and sometimes even compellence and coercion. Various parts of the mission have been emphasized at different times, based both on geopolitical realities and the preferences of shifting presidential administrations. Some of the missions—simultaneously deterring and assuring allies while deterring and assuring adversaries—find themselves in deep tension. The main point of the framework is to reveal that the way the United States incorporates nuclear weapons into its overall grand strategy goes well beyond the basic ideas of deterrence against invasion and conquest highlighted by early strategists and embraced by most nuclear weapons states. Much work is still left to be done on topics once long thought settled: how and why the United States uses nuclear weapons and what influence these decisions have on international relations.

Challenges

The consensus on the core ideas surrounding nuclear deterrence and what has been called the "nuclear revolution" is that a full-scale nuclear war is not winnable, especially after a state achieves what is called "second-strike survivability," or the ability to unleash unacceptable destruction on an adversary even after absorbing a nuclear first strike.[6] Under such circumstances, deterrence by denial is unobtainable. In other words, developing nuclear weapons, delivery systems, and strategies aimed toward prevailing in a nuclear conflict is pointless, expensive, and dangerous.[7] Furthermore, according to nuclear revolution advocates, nuclear deterrence, including extended deterrence, is relatively robust. Since there is both uncertainty and risk in any nuclear crisis, and the consequences of getting it wrong are so horrific, both sides have powerful incentives to act responsibly. Conquest and invasion are too costly in such a world to even contemplate.

Deterrence theorists developed other concepts as well, including the framework for strategic arms control. If mutual vulnerability was the goal between nuclear pairs, then negotiated treaties might prevent other external factors from undermining the desired goal of strategic stability. Arms control would stem the action-reaction cycle of the arms race and restrain the domestic and organizational forces keen on building more nuclear weapons. Deterrence theory and the nuclear revolution also had consequences for thinking about the spread of independent nuclear weapons programs. If nuclear weapons prevent conquest and guarantee security, then one would have expected every economically and technologically advanced state to seek them. Nor should other states, especially self-proclaimed status quo powers such the United States, be unduly alarmed by nuclear proliferation, since by limiting interstate war they increased global stability.[8]

How well did deterrence theory and its natural offshoots do in predicting nuclear statecraft? It certainly got its major claim or prediction correct: great-power wars of conquest have largely disappeared from the global landscape. There were dangerous crises and the risk of war between the Soviet Union and the United States, but the Cold War ended peacefully. While dangers abound, interstate relations are certainly more stable today than they were in, for example, 1930, 1870, or 1790. It is, of course, hard to prove that the nuclear revolution is responsible for decreasing large-scale interstate war; a variety of other alternative explanations, from increased globalization to norms against nuclear use and even possession to the increased costs of conventional war and conquest, have been offered.[9] It is hard to imagine, however, that nuclear deterrence has not played the central role.

On other aspects of nuclear history, deterrence theory's expectations were not met, especially in the case of the United States. While American leaders did pursue strategic arms control, they simultaneously sought expensive and potentially destabilizing counterforce nuclear systems that went well beyond what was required for strategic stability.[10] American leaders often appeared to act as if nuclear primacy might have conveyed important and worthwhile political leverage in international relations. Relatedly, the United States was quite or fairly active in its extensive efforts to prevent other countries from acquiring independent nuclear weapons. It applied a variety of measures, from alliances to norms to threats, addressing friend and foe alike, in its nonproliferation efforts.[11] This unexpectedly aggressive nonproliferation effort by the United States helps explain another aspect of nuclear dynamics—the present existence of fewer than ten nuclear weapons states in the world—despite its powerful appeal and its being within the technological and economic reach of scores of countries.

How do we reconcile the clear, powerful, and parsimonious predictions of nuclear deterrence theory with the complex, messy, and often obscure history of nuclear statecraft? There are at least two challenges. First, there are the methodological challenges to fully understanding nuclear dynamics and statecraft. Second is the need to recognize and attempt to integrate the competing, parallel, and at times contradictory narratives and perspectives of the nuclear age. This is a massive and multifaceted undertaking, and the most one can do here is to highlight profitable paths for future scholarship.

Methodological Challenges

In an earlier study, I highlighted the methodological challenges to generating a clear and comprehensive understanding of nuclear dynamics and statecraft.[12] The obstacles are many. First, nuclear decisionmaking is one of any government's most secret activities. While accessing declassified documents from around the world has become easier, it is still a monumental task to piece together the various national and international histories of nuclear statecraft. Even when nuclear weapons are discussed, the language employed often is sanitized and drained of meaning, the horrors of thermonuclear use replaced by colorless euphemisms through a process Reid Pauly has aptly described as "rhetorical evaporation."[13]

Second, what is it we are actually studying when assessing and analyzing nuclear deterrence? Nuclear statecraft is primarily concerned with what has not happened since the Hiroshima and Nagasaki bombings in August 1945—namely, a nuclear war. Nuclear deterrence is difficult to confirm or measure; it aims to prevent from happening something that would have otherwise occurred in the absence of the deterrent. What this means is that it is unobservable and hard to generalize on. Scholars have often tried analyzing a variety of proxy phenomena, from signaling to crises to deployments, to understand the underlying causal mechanisms behind deterrence; but it is unclear whether these proxies actually tell us much about how deterrence does or does not work.

Third, it is hard to disentangle the development of nuclear weapons and arms races from the Cold War rivalry between the superpowers and other important historical drivers of the post-1945 world. The fourth challenge involves separating the history of how knowledge and thought about nuclear weapons was developed—that is, the intellectual history of the deterrence theorists—from the actual history of how states made decisions about nuclear weapons. In the past, the powerful allure of these deductive theories, which were meant to describe what scholars thought should happen, were inserted as explanations for what did happen.

There are other challenges, as well. Nuclear studies, more than many areas of inquiry, is often marked by gaps, or distinct, often stove-piped communities that rarely interact. Think tank scholars often do not engage with nuclear engineers, who rarely talk with nuclear historians, who often have few interactions with policymakers. Within the field of international relations, divisions exist between those who use qualitative, formal, and quantitative methods as well as with those who take constructivist approaches. Genuine and productive interactions across fields and disciplines do not happen nearly enough. Given the complexity and importance of the subject, these disconnects between scholarly communities is inefficient and disconcerting.

Finally, nuclear weapons engage deep moral considerations. Being prepared to use such weapons, even under extreme circumstances, is at the heart of deterrence. The use of these horrific weapons against people, however, is unthinkable. While the goal of guaranteeing that these weapons are never used is universally shared, there is great disagreement on how to achieve that goal. Advocates of disarmament contend that these are immoral weapons, and the overriding goal of policymakers should be to permanently rid the planet of them. Deterrence advocates, while acknowledging the catastrophic prospects of use, point out that nuclear deterrence, by preventing great-power war, may have saved countless millions of lives since 1945. To their minds, the disarmament position is naïve: Even if it could be accomplished, how could you prevent states from cheating? Hard as scholars try, it is quite likely impossible to avoid engaging normative and value judgment, which is, in a way, at odds with how most scientific analysis works. This can make conversations and policy debates about nuclear deterrence difficult.

Which History?

To better understand U.S. policy and nuclear deterrence, we need to explore at least three distinct histories: the history of nuclear weapons development and nuclear weapons policies, the intellectual history of thinking about nuclear weapons and nuclear strategy, and the geopolitical history of international relations since 1945. These distinct histories are often mistakenly conflated, and while they are interwoven and interconnected, it is important to disentangle them as much as possible. In other words, the history of nuclear thought, which includes deterrence theory, is not the same as the history of nuclear policy and strategy. Nor is the history of the nuclear age the same as the history of the Cold War, and the history of the Cold War does not comprise all or even most of the history of international politics since 1945.

These distinct strands are often told as the same history, however. A simplified version might go like this: For more than forty years, postwar international relations were shaped by the geopolitical and ideological struggle between the Soviet Union and the United States. This conflict was, in large measure, driven and defined by an intense nuclear arms race. These political and military dynamics were interlocked, and it was sometimes unclear whether geopolitical and ideological competition drove the arms race, whether the nuclear arms race drove the rivalry, or whether some toxic yet inseparable mix of the two were to blame. The Cold War was viewed through a nuclear lens, and nuclear weapons were framed by the Cold War, including such key events as the development of thermonuclear weapons, the Soviet launch of the Sputnik satellite, the development of intercontinental missiles, and the Berlin and Cuban missile crises. According to this stylized narrative, strategic arms control—namely, the 1972 ABM and SALT I treaties—arrested the vicious arms race that fueled the rivalry and laid the foundation for détente, or mutual understanding, between the superpowers. Since arms control was the intellectual product of the nuclear strategists, three histories—of nuclear weapons, nuclear thinking and analysis, and international politics—merged nicely into one seamless narrative.

Except, of course, that they did not. The Cold War rivalry was always driven by underlying geopolitical issues (sharpened, of course, by ideology), and the conflict heightened when these issues were contested and lessened when they were resolved.[14] Détente preceded and had deeper roots than arms control. Nor could arms control prevent the reemergence of superpower hostility in the late 1970s and early 1980s. As both states continued their arms buildups, neither conformed precisely to the theories laid out by the strategists of the nuclear revolution. And the most interesting developments in nuclear statecraft in the 1960s, 1970s, and 1980s were the decisions of various states to develop nuclear weapons while others eschewed such efforts. Few of those cases were motivated solely by Cold War dynamics, except in that their decisions were shaped by the unusual and unexpected efforts by the two superpower rivals to work together to staunch nuclear proliferation. The twin thrusts of decolonization and globalization, for example, were as important in shaping the global political and nuclear environments as the Cold War in the decades following World War II.

Decades later, according to standard accounts, the stylized narrative shifts again. The Cold War ends, and with it, presumably, the superpower arms race. According to most analysts, we move to a "second nuclear age" after 1989–1991.[15] For some, this post–Cold War nuclear environment is far more unpredictable and unstable, if not more dangerous. So-called rogue states, with little regard for international law or norms, together with nonstate actors such as terrorist groups, cannot be counted on to understand or follow the logic of deterrence, at least in the way the superpowers did. Long-submerged regional rivalries are expected to reappear and develop a nuclear dynamic. Both the policy and intellectual efforts shift away from the dyadic superpower arms race to the fears of horizontal proliferation or of new actors getting nuclear weapons. Many argue for disarmament, either because of these dangers or because of the decreasing utility or relevance of nuclear deterrence or both.

Most historians recognize this stylized, monocausal history as deeply misleading. Several powerful trends and currents marked postwar international relations. Although these histories were intertwined and interconnected, the processes of decolonization, civil war, and state building following the collapse of the great European empires affected far more people, for both good and bad, than the rivalry between the Soviet Union and the United States. Even the process of European integration, with clear Cold War connections, had its own powerful non–Cold War drivers.[16] The intensifying period of globalization that marks our own contemporary world, with massive movements of trade, money, ideas, technology, culture, and people, had its beginnings long before the Cold War ended.[17] Each of these histories has a nuclear component: Does the Cold War really provide a better lens into the nuclear statecraft of Great Britain, France, Israel, or India than seismic shifts in the international system unleashed by decolonization? Did countries ranging from Brazil to Sweden to South Korea turn away from their earlier nuclear weapons programs to participate better in the globalized, open order that was emerging well before the Cold War ended? This is not to dismiss the centrality of Soviet-U.S. rivalry to the postwar nuclear story but to suggest that the politics of nuclear weapons often went well beyond a simplified and stylized narrative of the Cold War.

And what of the history of the nuclear weapons themselves and how they shaped international relations? In the past, nuclear history often has consisted of two simple stories: first, the Cold War nuclear statecraft of the superpowers, and second (and very secondary in conventional histories), the decisionmaking of the other seven states with nuclear weapons at the time. Because of the extraordinary increase in declassified documents available to scholars, we have a better sense of how many other states made decisions to acquire or not to acquire nuclear weapons and how they used their nuclear status in their statecraft. For example, we now understand that the simple binary distinction between states being nuclear and nonnuclear fails to capture key elements of the story. States can pursue a range of postures, such as nuclear latency or hedging, that may generate beneficial political outcomes while still being far short of fully deployed weapons. Countries like Brazil and Japan, for example, are key parts of this nuclear history, yet we have often overlooked or misunderstood their nuclear statecraft. What is clear is that all this history, unlike nuclear deterrence theory, is messy. It blurs received historical narratives, both in terms of causes (Cold War? globalization? nationalism?) and chronology. There is but one nuclear age, which persists today, and it both drives and is shaped by the larger international forces that mark our complex world.

Finally, part of the challenge in understanding nuclear statecraft is recognizing that the same history can look different from two distinct perspectives. This is true of all political subjects, but nuclear dynamics present at least two challenges that are somewhat unique. History allows us to see things through distinct lenses. Let me provide an example.

Deterrence theory often assumes a static world in which there is a recognized status quo and a potential challenger. In any multiplayer interaction, however, does everyone agree on who and what are being deterred and why? We have long associated the deterrer with the state that seeks to prevent an adversary from compelling a change to the status quo. Strategists have spent much time assessing whether nuclear weapons can be used to compel or bring about change, or whether they are good only for deterrence. But consider the most perilous period of nuclear peril in world history, the four-year period from Soviet premier Nikita Khrushchev's November 1958 ultimatum to the West to pull out of West Berlin until the end of the Cuban missile crisis in October 1962.

We now have a good sense that this four-year crisis centered on a complex set of issues surrounding the political status of Germany and the role of nuclear weapons in its defense. The Soviets feared the United States was changing the status quo by allowing West Germany access to nuclear weapons and launched a crisis over West Berlin's status to deter this from happening. Presidents Eisenhower and Kennedy did not believe the status quo in West Berlin was sustainable or wise over the long term. Putting missiles in Cuba also was a way of highlighting Soviet concerns about West Germany, in addition to deterring a possible American attack on Cuba and emphasizing what the Russians saw as dangerous nuclear missiles in Turkey. Throughout the period, identifying who was attempting to change the status quo—the compeller—and who was trying to maintain the status quo—the deterrer—was open to interpretation. Furthermore, the deterrence perspective lends an implicit moral superiority to those keeping the status quo, a position at odds with the ebb and flow of international relations before 1945.

Equally important, however, is trying to identify the appropriate frame or lens through which to analyze nuclear statecraft and dynamics. This is the question of perspective: Are nuclear weapons and their consequences a structural, global variable that shapes state behavior, or are they best understood as tools of national state decisionmaking? In the language of political science and the international relations theorist Kenneth Waltz, are nuclear weapons best understood as a second or third image factor in conflict? From which vantage point or "level of analysis" are they best studied?

The answer is, of course, that nuclear weapons must be viewed as both a national and global issue, a factor decided by particular states that shape, and are shaped by, the structure of the international environment. Nuclear weapons transformed international politics in profound, if at times obscure, ways. Most international behavior is shaped, sometimes explicitly but more often implicitly, by the long shadow cast by the nuclear revolution. Great-power wars of conquest, which dominated modern political history until 1945, no longer make sense. The specter of nuclear use concerns the whole world: like epidemics, financial contagion, or climate change, the consequences of nuclear war cannot be limited to the adversaries in conflict. On the other hand, nuclear weapons are a tool of national strategy. Their development, deployment, and possible use are best viewed through the decisionmaking of the nuclear states in question. States vary dramatically in their interests and vulnerabilities, technological and economic capabilities, and political institutions and cultures. Understanding the global effects of nuclear weapons tells us only so much about why France or India developed nuclear weapons while Sweden and Egypt did not. Nor can it tell us why the United States exploits nuclear weapons within its grand strategies in ways that are quite at odds with any other nuclear power.

Multiple and Interactive Deterrence, Assurance, and Reassurance

Is there any way to overcome these obstacles and have a better understanding of nuclear statecraft? For example, can we generate better frameworks to understand how and why the United States has made policies about nuclear weapons and incorporated them into its grand strategies since 1945?

We know the deductive models from nuclear strategists explain some things better than others. Traditional nuclear deterrence theory identifies the power to prevent another state from invading and conquering one's homeland as the most powerful and appealing characteristic of possessing nuclear weapons, especially if these weapons are designed and deployed in such a way as to avoid being eliminated in a preemptive attack. Avoiding invasion and conquest, however, has not been a real fear of the United States since at least the American Civil War, if not before. Why then has the United States made nuclear weapons such an integral part of its grand strategy? And why has it pursued nuclear weapons in numbers and delivery configurations, and often employed them in aggressive strategies, that go well beyond what is needed to deter any potential adversary crazy enough to threaten the American homeland?

Ironically, what is often missed in the strategic studies literature dominated by American thinkers is that the United States has sought to achieve far more ambitious goals than simply deterrence with its nuclear weapons. These vast goals include a complex mix of often crosscutting objectives oriented at deterring, assuring, reassuring, and competing with adversaries, allies, and neutral countries. Eight missions in particular are crucial drivers of MIDAR:

Deter adversaries from attacks on the homeland but also deter attacks by adversaries against an ally, even in geographically distant regions: The United States extends deterrence with security guarantee to dozens of countries. This policy promises that the United States will protect those states under its nuclear umbrella by responding with force if the state in question is attacked, even if it means the United States has to use its own nuclear weapons and expose itself to nuclear attack from another state.

Deter allies from acquiring their own independent nuclear forces: The United States has threatened allies with a number of measures, from abandonment to sanctions, if they develop their own independent nuclear capability. This mission is rarely discussed in public, given the sensitivity involved in suppressing the ambitions of otherwise allied countries.

Deter neutral and independent countries from acquiring their own nuclear forces: The United States would greatly prefer that no state other than itself have nuclear weapons, as ambitious or perhaps unrealistic as that goal may be. It has far less leverage over states that are neither adversaries, whom it can target, or allies, whom it can coerce or assure, than independent states. Still, the United States makes it clear that it will impose costs on any state that seeks nuclear weapons.

Assure allies that the United States will neither abandon them nor pull them into a conflict they do not want: Many U.S. allies, especially in Western Europe and East Asia, faced grave dangers during the Cold War; new dangers have arisen in both regions in recent years. The United States deploys its nuclear weapons to assure its allies that it will protect them against threats but not act so belligerently or aggressively as to provoke a conflict in which they would be on the front lines.

Assure independent and neutral countries that the United States will strive to create an international environment that decreases the perceived need and appeal of independent nuclear weapons: Nuclear weapons can provide extraordinary benefits to states that acquire them. How do you best assure a state that, either by its own or U.S. preference, is not protected by the United States to forego nuclear weapons? Assurance is guaranteed by both avoiding threatening that state with conquest or invasion and supporting international norms, practices, and institutions that discourage interstate war.

Reassure adversaries that the United States will deter or restrain its allies: The United States, alone or at times in collusion with its adversary, has sought to keep its allies non-nuclear. Some of these allies had been aggressors in earlier wars or had reason to challenge the territorial status quo; the United States, through its security guarantees, seeks to implicitly signal to the adversary that it would restrain these countries.

Reassure adversaries and neutrals that the capabilities the United States seeks for deterring adversaries and assuring allies are not oriented toward first-strike capabilities, even as it seeks nuclear primacy: The United States could not accomplish the ambitious goals of extended deterrence, inhibition, and assurance by simply accepting parity with its adversary. It would not be credible to assure allies they were secure and deter them from acquiring their own nuclear weapons if the United States blithely accepted vulnerability to a nuclear attack from the adversary. On the other hand, the United States wants to avoid the destabilizing conditions of a full-out effort to achieve a meaningful first-strike capability and strategy, even as it seeks some form of nuclear primacy.

Compete with and potentially defeat an adversary without recourse to war: The United States wants to avoid a nuclear exchange or a conventional conflict that could escalate into a nuclear war with its adversaries. It also recognizes the costs and potential dangers of the nuclear arms race. At various times, however, it has believed it possessed technological and economic advantages that allowed it to pursue sophisticated nuclear weapons and delivery systems to pressure its adversary, even when doing so threatened strategic stability. The United States also appeared to believe there were meaningful coercive benefits to conditions of nuclear superiority short of a first-strike capability.

A few important observations about this complex mission are in order. First, MIDAR should be understood as a heuristic framework. It is a rough and incomplete cut at the way we might think about why and how the United States pursued the nuclear statecraft that it did. Like any heuristic, it does not fully capture the nuance and context of the history of U.S. nuclear statecraft. It is easy to think of many U.S. behaviors or policies that are not explained by or that even contradict this analysis. Nor does it capture the fundamental importance of various bureaucratic, organizational, and domestic political forces that shaped nuclear decisionmaking over the past eight decades. Finally, this framework is not especially sensitive to the shifting preferences of different presidential administrations or changes in the international system. It may, however, provide insight into why U.S. nuclear statecraft seems at odds with the predictions of much of nuclear deterrence theory.

Second, many of the goals enumerated above are in tension if not at outright odds with one another. This means that American nuclear statecraft required and continues to require careful and constant calibration to achieve what might be thought of as a complex deterrence-assurance-reassurance equilibrium. Too great an emphasis on reassurance to an adversary, for example, can weaken deterrence toward the same and undermine assurance to allies. Assure allies too much, however, and their freedom of action might undermine reassurance of the adversary and fail to deter one's ally. There are, obviously, many combinations and policy strands that have to be delicately balanced. One of the advantages of this framework, however, is that it captures the deep but often hidden connection between the United States' nuclear strategy and its nuclear nonproliferation goals. Much of the writing on nuclear strategy has focused on U.S. competition with its adversary, the Soviet Union. Containing, deterring, and, for some, bankrupting the Soviet Union was, of course, a most important goal of America's nuclear strategy. The United States also employed nuclear statecraft as part of its grand strategic goal of limiting the proliferation of independent nuclear weapons states, a goal that was missed by many early nuclear strategists. It is also a goal that continued and was even elevated after the Cold War ended, explaining why there was far more continuity in U.S. nuclear statecraft after the demise of the Soviet Union than most scholars anticipated.

Third, this appears to be a uniquely American story. Every other nuclear weapons state save one appears to have acquired nuclear weapons largely if not solely because of its ability to prevent invasion and conquest. Even the Soviet Union, with nuclear forces at times as large, sophisticated, and within equally destabilizing postures as Western weapons, seemed primarily concerned with avoiding invasion and more often than not appeared to mimic U.S. decisions rather than develop unique strategies. Ironically, the main insights of nuclear deterrence theory, which were developed by American strategists, explain the nuclear statecraft of other states far better than that of the United States.

Fourth, this framework captures some of the more puzzling aspects of the history of U.S. nuclear statecraft. For example, the MIDAR strategy helps explain why the United States worked at various times during the Cold War with its greatest adversary, the target of its nuclear forces, to limit the spread of nuclear weapons to other countries, even America's allies.[18] It also provides insight into the puzzling question of why the United States began a massive investment in counterforce weapons soon after signing SALT I and the ABM Treaties. Through SALT and ABM, American policymakers seemed to accept mutual vulnerability with the Soviet Union and to acknowledge that seeking nuclear primacy was wasteful and potentially destabilizing. The United States spent hundreds of billions of dollars on nuclear weapons, delivery systems, and auxiliary capabilities that focused on speed, accuracy, and stealth—qualities unlikely to be prioritized if the goal was to possess enough nuclear firepower to cause unacceptable damage to an adversary even after it had launched a nuclear attack.

Conclusion

In the 1950s and 1960s, American strategists created a powerful intellectual architecture to explain how nuclear weapons influence international relations and what strategies and policies could be enacted to take full advantage of the benefits of nuclear deterrence while minimizing the risks. Scholars in the decades since have built on this legacy to understand nuclear strategy, proliferation, and nonproliferation.

This framework, based largely on deductive reasoning, offered important insights into how to think about nuclear weapons. But it also missed many of the complexities of nuclear statecraft. This is not surprising: understanding nuclear policy is a challenge. But as we think about future research, it is important to highlight some of the shortcomings of the original deterrence framework.

Disentangling nuclear history from other important drivers of world politics, while difficult, is crucial. One implication is the need to disconnect the notion of a distinct nuclear age that coincided with the Cold War and disappeared when the Soviet Union collapsed, giving birth to a second nuclear age. There have been continuities and discontinuities in nuclear history since 1945, but it may be more useful to talk about one nuclear age, which we are still in.

Analysts have separated the study of nuclear strategy (what states do with their nuclear weapons) from issues of nuclear proliferation (why states do or do not acquire nuclear weapons) and nuclear nonproliferation (how and by whom states are constrained in their nuclear ambitions). The history of nuclear statecraft clearly demonstrates that these three separate issues are interrelated and cannot be fully understood in isolation from one another.

There is the question of perspective, or the lens we use to understand nuclear dynamics. Nuclear weapons are primarily one of the tools states use to accomplish their goals in the world. In other words, nuclear weapons policy can only be understood as a part of a particular state's grand strategy, what a state wants to achieve in the world and how. On the other hand, nuclear weapons and their consequences cast a shadow that spills over national borders. The use of these weapons, or even their threatened use, has global consequences, and the whole structure of international relations since 1945 has been transformed by the nuclear revolution. When studying nuclear statecraft, how do we reconcile profoundly different national perspectives with the universal experience of living under a nuclear sword of Damocles?

Finally, we need to reassess how the United States has thought about and deployed nuclear weapons. On one level, this is problematic: an overly American perspective in nuclear studies and deterrence may have obscured much of the complexity behind the nuclear statecraft of other countries. American scholars have also dominated our discussions of nuclear dynamics, often generalizing from U.S. experiences that are hardly applicable to other countries. That said, the United States has been and will remain the eight-hundred-pound gorilla on nuclear issues. And its own behavior and policies are puzzling, at least from the perspective of the American school of deterrence. From the earliest days of the nuclear age, the United States, unlike other states, sought to do far more with nuclear weapons than merely exploit their power to deter invasion and conquest. Over time, it developed a complex mix of deterrence and assurance toward allies, adversaries, and neutrals. More research needs to be done to better understand this mix and to what grand strategic purpose it aims.

SEVEN

The History of What Did Not Happen

How does one explain something that never happened? How can a historical lens and sensibility help us understand why there has never been a thermonuclear war? At first glance, such an effort would seem challenging. It is hard enough to make sense of things that have actually occurred. Despite the labors of countless scholars from around the world assessing millions of pages of documents, for example, no one agrees on what caused World War I.[1] The same can be said about the origins, course, and consequences of any number of geopolitical events critical to shaping the world we live in.

Fortunately, despite great fears and apocalyptic predictions, we have never had a thermonuclear war. Notwithstanding the confident claims of countless theorists, however, we do not really know why or, at the very least, cannot prove our theories and instincts. We are understandably eager to have an explanation for the most important nonevent in human history, if only to see whether there are lessons that can be applied today to keep the streak going as long as possible. It is a daunting task, far more challenging than is acknowledged, and many of the research questions focused on are merely proxies for this larger concern. For make no mistake about it: when we talk about any number of subjects surrounding nuclear weapons, such as why states do or not build the bomb, how they behave when they get it, or how and when deterrence works, the primary question animating our curiosity is a powerful desire to understand why there has never been a thermonuclear war.

This chapter is an effort to lay out, in an admittedly incomplete and rather unsystematic way, the benefits of a historical approach to these issues, especially to understanding how we have avoided thermonuclear war. I would like to suggest three overarching "meta" points about the historical approach, oriented toward scholars' thinking on nuclear issues. All three relate to how historians can contribute in a meaningful way to how we understand the consequences of the thermonuclear revolution and contribute to effective policies.

The first point is an obvious but important one about method: all historical work involves an intense dialogue between the empirical and the conceptual. The evidence we find informs our theories of the world, as the world informs our theories, back and forth in an interactive fashion.[2] All good historians know this, but many outside the guild, including important policymakers and international relations experts, have a different view of how we operate. We are often thought of as either storytellers or collectors of data. They see Michael Beschloss or Doris Kearns Goodwin on television, read Robert Caro's magisterial biographies of Lyndon Johnson or, on the nuclear question, Richard Rhodes, and think of the historian as a sort of bard, weaving tales. There is also the image of the less famous, academic historian, working away in a dusty archive, collecting reams of documents that might be fed into the models and regressions of social scientists. While outsiders cannot help but be impressed by the elegant prose and the carefully crafted narratives, there is little sense that important, serious arguments are being made or that there is an explicit conceptual framework or theory for understanding the world.[3]

Why does correcting these caricatures—even while acknowledging there is some truth to them—matter? This question involves the second point: Any historian working in the nuclear policy area immediately confronts an enormous and often intimidating conceptual hegemon, the strategic studies literature on nuclear weapons and their influence on world politics. A powerful corpus of ideas, based almost entirely on deductive reasoning, began to emerge almost as soon as the first atomic bomb was dropped, when Bernard Brodie declared, "Thus far the chief purpose of our military establishment has been to win wars. From now on its chief purpose must be to avert them."[4]

For eight decades, strategists trained in the natural sciences, mathematicians, and economists and, most prominently, political scientists have been working to develop theories surrounding nuclear dynamics and statecraft. Several generations of this work have shaped the conventional wisdom, established the issues for debate, and provided us with the framework with which to investigate these questions.[5] While there is some reason to question whether the strategists were as influential with policymakers as is often claimed, from an intellectual history perspective this body of work is extraordinary, both in its sophistication and its influence on public discussion.[6] It is a literature, however, almost bereft of a historical sensibility and the skepticism, comfort with uncertainty, and humility the study of the past brings with it. I have had more than one important scholar in this field tell me we know all need to know about how nuclear deterrence works and, by extension, why we have never had a thermonuclear war. The power and certainty of this theoretical literature acts as its own deterrent to young scholars mining archives to make sense of how states have made decisions about nuclear weapons over the decades.

This leads to a third issue: the question of policy relevance, or what I call "public mindedness." Historians have mixed feelings about whether and how our scholarship might contribute to decisionmaking. As a discipline, we have long been wary of power, both how it corrupts those scholars who try to court it and how those in power misuse the past for less than noble purposes. The standard reply of even the most policy-sympathetic historian when asked what the past tells us about a contemporary issue is, "It's complicated," which in the end is not a very helpful answer. When people talk about policy-relevant work, what they typically mean is scholarship that provides accurate forecasts about the future and, if not theories, at least generalizable rules of thumb that are parsimonious. All of these demands cut deeply against the instinct and practice of the historian, who emphasizes historical context, unintended consequences, and the complex interaction of multiple forces. This poor fit, one would think, would provide powerful incentives for the historian to stay as far away from policy as possible.

Avoiding policy relevance in nuclear history, however, is not only not the right answer: it may be impossible. Elsewhere, I have laid out what I think historians can contribute to policymaking: there are a whole set of insights and, perhaps more important, a sensibility that comes from studying the past that is bound to improve decisionmaking.[7] The contributions that can be made by historical work stack up quite nicely when compared with the efforts of other disciplines, such as economics and political science. But these arguments resonate even more strongly on this particular subject. Any effort to come to terms with why we have not had a thermonuclear war is bound to be of great and understandable interest to people in positions of great responsibility, whether or not individual historians want their work used in this way. Scholars mining archives around the world to understand how nuclear states made decisions about nuclear weapons, and how the thermonuclear revolution affects statecraft, national, and international security, are bound to intrigue, if not help, decisionmakers. Such knowledge can usefully supplement, if not at times replace, the dominating, deductive views of the strategy world.

One of the virtues of historical work is something I call "horizontal history," a relating of the connections between issues over space as opposed to time. Social science scholars often focus like a laser on one particular issue, say, nuclear strategy or America's relations with China, and see how it develops over time. But at the top levels of policy, all sorts of seemingly separate issues turn out to be interconnected in a surprising way. The story of how I stumbled into nuclear history, quite by accident, reveals both the persistence of horizontal history and the benefits of following the documents wherever they might lead. It all began with research on postwar international monetary relations.[8]

In the late 1950s, the United States developed a balance-of-payments deficit. In other words, an excess of dollars ended up in the hands of overseas central banks and, given the rules of the system at the time, these surplus dollars could be exchanged for gold held by the United States. There was great concern that if large deficits continued unabated, eventually the American stock of gold would be run down, with potentially calamitous consequences for both the domestic and international economy. Both the U.S. balance-of-payments deficit and the outflow of dollars and gold made four successive presidential administrations (Eisenhower, Kennedy, Johnson, and Nixon) feel quite vulnerable, and all four strove to find ways to end the deficit and ameliorate its effects.

When a country runs such a deficit or is worried about the strength of its currency, decisionmakers possess certain macroeconomic tools to improve the situation. Interest rates could be raised or the domestic monetary supply restricted to attract capital from abroad and dampen inflationary pressures at home. Trade restrictions and capital controls could be installed. Failing that, a nation could devalue its currency or even remove it from the strictures of a gold-exchange standard and simply allow the market to determine its value (which has been the case ever since the Bretton Woods system collapsed in the early 1970s). None of these options were attractive to U.S. officials. In the first instance, these measures would slow or even deflate the domestic economy, which was certain to be unpopular. The more dramatic option of devaluation and ending the linkage between the dollar and gold was anathema to most American policymakers. This was largely because government officials in the 1950s and 1960s operated with certain historical memories and beliefs. In the collective mind of the time, decisionmakers believed that that the steep downturn in the U.S. economy in the late 1920s and early 1930s turned into the Great Depression because of beggar-thy-neighbor policies that included restrictions and competitive currency devaluations. They also believed (not entirely correctly) that the economic collapse led to the rise of authoritarianism, aggression, and World War II.

Not eager to pursue harsh macroeconomic measures, policymakers looked for ways to dramatically reduce the number of dollars spent abroad. By far the largest account they could control was the cost of sending U.S. troops and their families overseas. Most of these troops were part of America's commitment to NATO to defend Western Europe. Not coincidentally, the countries with the largest balance-of-payments surpluses—the countries holding dollars and asking for gold—were the most obvious beneficiaries of America's expensive military protection, West Germany and France. Reducing the United States' conventional force posture abroad was, from a domestic political and economic perspective, an ideal solution.

What does all this have to do with nuclear dynamics and nuclear statecraft? The clear evidence in the documents reveals that Presidents Eisenhower, Kennedy, and Johnson and many of their closest advisers were not only willing but at times eager to pull American troops from Western Europe. Plans to undertake withdrawals were debated and discussed and in some cases implemented. This story, however, contradicted the narrative that was laid out and repeated in the strategic studies literature. In an age of mutual vulnerability, where the credibility of America's pledge to defend Europe would be under great scrutiny, nuclear deterrence demanded more conventional forces in Europe, not fewer. The oft-repeated story was always the same: the "massive retaliation" strategy laid out by Eisenhower's secretary of state, John Foster Dulles, was no longer credible or wise by the late 1950s. According to the strategic studies community at RAND and elsewhere, a policy that demanded massive and preemptive nuclear attack to the slightest provocation had to be replaced with something more nuanced and appropriate.

This same intellectual community claimed that its views—which included increased American conventional forces and more nimble nuclear packages (and controlled escalation capabilities)—were embraced by the Kennedy administration and became the basis for the strategy of what was known as "flexible response." They certainly had reason to believe this was so, as Defense Secretary Robert Mc-Namara laid out this strategy, incorporating many of the views of the strategy community, in a secret speech to NATO and in a public version in Ann Arbor, Michigan, in the spring of 1962. Yet, as I looked through the documents detailing the events leading up to and following both speeches, the rhetoric seemed hollow. No one really seemed to buy the core logic of the strategy, and McNamara himself was one of the leading advocates throughout the 1960s for steep U.S. troop withdrawals.

I was struck by the contradiction—embracing a strategy that required more conventional forces while actively seeking to bring U.S. troops back from Europe. How was this to be explained? And were there other contradictions in the flexible-response strategy? As it turns out, judging from my further archival work, there were. U.S. policy on tactical nuclear weapons, for example, pulled in all sorts of different directions and was never really resolved at the highest political levels. The SIOP did not really become all that more flexible, and as far as I could tell, our nuclear strategy was still largely based on the massive, pre-emptive strike articulated by Dulles a decade earlier. Phrases were thrown about in both the strategy literature and public policy utterances—second-strike counterforce, the "pause," mutual assured destruction—that found little corollary to what was found in the documents. The man responsible for implementing strategy in Europe, NATO's supreme allied commander in Europe, General Lyman Lemnitzer, went so far as to "forbid the use of the term . . . ['flexible response'] . . . throughout [Supreme Headquarters Allied Powers Europe] and Allied Command Europe." Lemnitzer complained that "many of my people didn't really know what flexible response meant."[9]

The official history of America's nuclear command and control effort contends that "to the extent it amounted to a doctrine, it was open to different interpretations, and it is not easy (if at all possible) to find a single coherent, clear statement of it, even among authoritative pronouncements of the President and the Secretary of Defense."[10] When Nixon's secretary of defense, James Schlesinger, examined the war plans, he and his team were stunned to see the rigid, massive SIOP everyone thought had been discarded by the Kennedy administration.

I will not go into all the complicated details of what I call the "myth of flexible response," the specifics of which I have explored elsewhere.[11] The main point I want to make is that what I found in the documents was not at all like the received wisdom I found in the largely deductive strategy literature. The literature described a policy process that was clean, crisp, and driven by a powerful logic. But the historical record revealed that the policies themselves were messy and pulled in different directions. What explained this gap, these contradictions? Was this simply a product of how bureaucracies and organizations work? There was certainly a strain within the strategy literature—beginning with the great Andy Marshall—that said bureaucratic politics was the way to explain suboptimal strategy outcomes.[12] Perhaps the SIOP remained large and inflexible because the Strategic Air Command wanted it that way. Perhaps the battle over conventional forces in Europe was a typical struggle between domestic political actors—in this case, the more economically minded folks from the Treasury versus the strategists in the Defense Department.

I am somewhat skeptical of bureaucratic political explanations for something as important as nuclear policy.[13] Being immersed in the documents and reconstructing U.S. national security policy, one gets a sense that on the questions that truly matter—and issues of war and peace, especially nuclear war, certainly qualify—what the president decides is almost always carried out. And one might see that the kind of bureaucratic messiness over, say, where to put a military base or at what level to set a farm subsidy simply disappears on these critical issues. My sense was that something else was going on here, that there was a fundamental and important political and strategic logic that must have been driving things that the analysts simply missed.

And, in fact, there was an underlying logic. It turns out the flexible-response doctrine was as much about nuclear nonproliferation vis-à-vis America's allies as about nuclear strategy against our adversary. The great geopolitical struggle at the time was what to do about West

Germany's atomic ambitions. Why was this an issue? Early in the Cold War, America's close European allies—first Great Britain and then France—developed their own nuclear capability. It was only natural that West Germany, under greater threat and with a more vibrant economy, would be interested in these weapons as well. It was also natural that any West German move to acquire its own weapons, only a generation or two after the Nazi calamity, would be deeply unsettling, not just to the Soviets but to the rest of Europe as well. Even without Germany's terrible history, a nuclearized Bundeswehr was a threat to peace and stability. The Federal Republic was also, by definition, not a status quo power. Divided by the wartime allies, West Germany was separated from its eastern territories and was committed to eventually reunifying with them.[14]

The strategy of flexible response accomplished a few things on the nuclear nonproliferation front. By emphasizing an array of nuclear and non-nuclear options and demanding dominance on all levels of the escalation chain, it increased the credibility of the strategy. Emphasis on U.S. conventional forces helped strengthen the American security guarantee and nuclear umbrella; the more U.S. forces engaged in defending Western Europe from a Soviet onslaught, the more likely the United States would be to use strategic nuclear weapons. Finally, such a complex, nuanced strategy would require stricter command and control. To make flexible response work, one could not have a bunch of independent forces operating on their own. American strategists claimed the strategy made these independent forces not only redundant but even dangerous. In sum, by strengthening extended deterrence and marginalizing non-American nuclear forces, the flexible-response strategy was aimed at reassuring the West Germans and lessening their desire for their own nuclear forces. It also allowed a nonproliferation policy that, under the cover of an alliance strategy, did not overtly discriminate against the key target, the Federal Republic of Germany. This, as much as anything the Soviets were doing, was the driving logic of the strategy.

Again, this highlights the value of archival work. Remember, I waded into this subject because the documents led me in this direction. I was trying to explain U.S. international monetary policy and came to discover the enormous gap between the rhetoric and reality of U.S. military strategy in Europe. Methodologically, this exposed the difficulties of relying on only public government statements for one's findings and highlighted the weaknesses of the purely deductive approach used by the strategists. Still, while I had several puzzles, I did not have a full answer to what was going on, and the documents forced me to reexamine my conceptual framework. This research generated three big questions: First, did the United States care far more about stemming the spread of nuclear weapons than the strategic literature had recognized? Relatedly, was its focus simply on particular complexities surrounding nuclear weapons and West Germany (as I originally believed), or was there a broader concern with nuclear proliferation writ large? Finally, could U.S. nuclear strategy be seen both as a tool of nuclear nonproliferation and as an effort to deter the Soviet Union? I went back to the archives to test these claims.

As every historian undertaking archival research knows, sometimes it is better to be lucky than good. During a visit to the John F. Kennedy Presidential Library, I was looking through the personal papers of Roswell Gilpatric when I came on a veritable treasure trove of good fortune. As McNamara's deputy, Gilpatric was involved in both the deliberations over balance-of-payments-inspired troop withdrawals and the status and strength of U.S. nuclear forces. After he left office, President Lyndon B. Johnson asked him to chair a committee charged with determining how the United States should respond to China's detonation of an atomic device in October 1964. Top policymakers were worried about how to respond: China's nuclear status was deeply disconcerting, and they wondered both how to react to China and what the effect of the test would be on nuclear proliferation more generally. There was no agreement within the administration over what to do—some were advocating preventive attacks, others suggested negotiating with China—so the president reached out to an external blue-ribbon group for answers.[15]

Outside government commissions are rarely important or influential, but the documents associated with their deliberations make clear that this one was different. First, the Gilpatric Committee went beyond the question of how to respond to China, looking to the whole issue of how the United States should think about and deal with nuclear proliferation. Up to this point, the general attitude of most U.S. policymakers was that while the spread of atomic weapons was regrettable, there was little the United States could do to stop it. The American experience with France had been decisive here: all the United States had received in return for its efforts to halt France's nuclear program had been mistrust and enmity. There were some—including Secretary of State Dean Rusk—who suggested that since proliferation was inevitable, the United States should get ahead of the curve and provide nuclear weapons to friendly aspirants such as India and Japan. In the end, few people thought much could be done.

The Gilpatric Committee helped transform this attitude. First, the committee looked at a variety of different worlds—an early version of the type of scenario planning that is so in vogue now—to explore the consequences of a proliferated world and the costs of preventing it. In even greater detail and with more sophistication than had been expended on the vaunted Solarium exercise of the Eisenhower period, the committee analyzed options ranging from the aggressive rollback of nuclear states (including preventive action against allies) to a fully proliferated world (aided by the United States). They investigated difficult political issues: Should China be attacked or appeased? What would happen to American power in a proliferated world? How could West Germany be kept non-nuclear? Should the French and even British be coerced out of the nuclear business? Was it necessary to escalate military activities in Southeast Asia to demonstrate to allies such as Japan and Australia that the United States would stand up to nuclear-armed bullies like China?

Another important part of my luck was that, somehow, government officials had forgotten to classify or redact any of the sensitive information in these documents, which were included in Gilpatric's donated, personal papers. This was fortunate for two reasons: first, because information that is always classified (coercive policies, controversial discussions about allies, and the like) were out in the open.

The second piece of good fortune was that the same set of documents was available in the Lyndon B. Johnson Presidential Library, albeit heavily classified and redacted. Comparing the redacted with the unredacted version provided a key for understanding what is typically kept classified and what is not. This allowed me to make educated guesses about what was in documents that still had words, sentences, or whole paragraphs blacked out.

Starting with this unbelievably fortunate archival find, I started to piece together the story of a fairly dramatic, and by no means inevitable, shift in global U.S. nuclear nonproliferation policy. The Gilpatric Committee had recommended that the United States make nuclear nonproliferation a far higher policy and use every policy short of preventive action to achieve the goal. The report was not popular within every part of the government—the old hands in the State and Defense Departments did not like paying the political costs associated with the new policy. And the costs were not insignificant: to make this robust new nonproliferation work would require a new attitude toward America's Cold War enemy, the Soviet Union. In short, the United States had to work with its bitter adversary at the expense of its friends. President Johnson personally intervened to make this policy shift happen—a fact that has been missed by almost everyone but the perceptive historian Hal Brands. And the policy laid the groundwork for the 1968 Nuclear Nonproliferation Treaty, which remains the bulwark of nonproliferation efforts to this day.[16]

Once again, the historical details, while important, are not the point. What I want to emphasize here is that historical work uncovered a completely different narrative from the one found in the strategy literature. The politics of the German question, the worries over the spread of nuclear weapons, and the policies needed to assure allies were as important as the strategic nuclear rivalry with the Soviets during the 1960s and 1970s and, at times, more important. This not only put the nuclear question in a different light, it also made me look at the Cold War differently. In my reading of the strategy literature, the history of the Cold War was often the same thing as the history of the nuclear rivalry between the superpowers: any change in strategy, whether it was the New Look or flexible response or mutual assured destruction or SALT, reflected a change in Cold War realities.

Obviously, these two histories—that of nuclear weapons and that of the geopolitical rivalry between the superpowers—overlapped and interacted and were hard to separate. But there were other, powerful forces at work that were driving nuclear dynamics. To provide an obvious example: Most of the nuclear aspirants of the postwar period—be they France or Great Britain, India or Pakistan, China or Japan, Israel or Egypt, South Africa or Brazil—were motivated less by Cold War dynamics than their own regional security or desire for prestige, or the other fundamental political driving of world politics, imperialism and decolonization. Furthermore, the United States and the Soviet Union had powerful incentives to work together to limit the spread of nuclear weapons, regardless of their other conflicts. The main picture of nuclear nonproliferation from the mid-1960s onward is that of Russians and Americans working together to keep allies and ideological fellow travelers like West Germany, Japan, China, and Yugoslavia from going nuclear. This was not the story the strategists told, and clearly, to paraphrase the Oldsmobile ad, this was not my father's Cold War.

Many people with whom I shared these findings pushed me to make connections to current nuclear policy. Was the dramatic shift in nuclear nonproliferation policy during the 1960s the correct choice? And were there lessons for contemporary policy? At this point, I was torn, and not simply because I was wary of facile historical comparisons separated by four decades. The issue was still my conceptual framework for understanding how nuclear weapons affect international relations. I was still influenced by the strategy literature, namely, the defensive realist position on nuclear weapons. For theorists influenced by Kenneth Waltz, nuclear proliferation was not to be feared. Few went as far as Waltz to actually welcome or encourage the spread of nuclear weapons, but there was a general consensus that the spread was not the end of the world. Nuclear weapons, it was argued, had powerful deterrent effects. Few political goals were worth a nuclear war, and while states might push their claims to a certain point, they would back off far short of nuclear war. The logic of this position was compelling. Wasn't nuclear deterrence stabilizing?[17]

I was undertaking this research soon after the United States appeared to go through a rather dramatic shift in its nuclear nonproliferation. The 9/11 attacks on the United States and the focus on access to weapons of mass destruction by so-called rogue regimes, highlighted in the 2002 U.S. National Security Strategy Report, seemed to push American policy toward an even more aggressive, almost preventive nonproliferation strategy. The threat of a rogue nuclear state and the acquisition of a weapon by a nonstate actor were seen as not simply dangerous possibilities but as likely. The war against Iraq, and threats against Iran, appeared to be driven in large measure by a fear that the post–Cold War world faced new and more dangerous types of threats than any the Russians and Americans had faced.

My first response was to be dismissive of this view. The U.S.-Soviet nuclear rivalry had been extraordinarily dangerous, and whatever the dangers of nuclear use today, I judged them to be far less than during the height of the Cold War. Nor would the unlikely use of one or two crude fission bombs, no matter how horrific, compare with the threat of a full-scale thermonuclear exchange between the superpowers, a nightmare that seemed at times in the late 1950s and early 1960s to be not at all implausible. And wasn't Mao's China the ultimate rogue regime? The People's Republic of China had fought U.S. forces in Korea, supplied the Viet Cong, threatened Taiwan and its other neighbors, and attacked democratic India. It had undergone domestic upheaval that led to millions of deaths, and Mao himself had used highly irresponsible rhetoric about prevailing in a nuclear war. If there was ever a state that was resistant to deterrence, it was not Saddam Hussein's Iraq or the Iran of the mullahs but Mao's China. Yet the United States had not overreacted, had not launched preventive attacks, and instead had learned to live with a nuclear China while dramatically strengthening its global efforts to limit proliferation. Its reward was not the feared tipping point of nuclear weapons in Japan, Australia, Indonesia, and elsewhere but rather an adversary that not only remained deterred but in short order became a de facto ally.

Did this mean the Bush administration's policy was both folly and a radical break from the past? That was certainly my first inclination. But my judgment went beyond the administration, to a certain nonpartisan alarmism I detected from a variety of circles.[18] Nuclear weapons were terrifying, to be sure, and should be at the top of the policy agenda for any U.S. president. But did policymakers overstate the threat posed by rogue and nonstate actors, at least compared with far more dangerous and realistic nuclear challenges from decades earlier? And by overstating or misrepresenting both the past and the present, was there not a danger the medicine could be worse than the cure?

As I looked at what could be gleaned from public policy discussions about both Iraq and Iran—always a dangerous undertaking, as my flexible-response undertaking had made clear—I wondered whether this preventive instinct, this desire to inhibit nuclear proliferation, was, in fact, new. American policymakers had seriously considered preventive action under three administrations led by Democrats, and the debate about whether to hit the Soviets in the 1940s, the Chinese in the 1960s, and the North Koreans in the 1990s went beyond simply idle chatter.[19] What was going on here? I was deeply influenced on these questions by Mira Rapp-Hopper, an international relations scholar whose empirical and conceptual research convincingly demonstrated deep similarities between these "preventive inclinations" over time, administrations, and even structural shifts in the international system. And as we examined this issue in greater detail, it became clear to us that the United States was willing to brandish coercive measures short of military action to prevent proliferation, even against its own allies.[20] From France in the 1950s to Pakistan, South Korea, and Taiwan in the 1970s, the United States went to great lengths to do what it could to limit the spread of nuclear weapons.

The defensive realists and nuclear strategists did not have compelling answers to explain a consistent and persistent American inclination to go to great lengths to limit proliferation, in the same way they did not understand why the United States continued and in some cases expanded its security assurances and nuclear umbrella after the Cold War had ended and the Soviet Union had collapsed. Once again, I went to the documents to reevaluate my earlier assessments. Did the United States simply not understand the compelling and stabilizing logic of nuclear deterrence? Did they not see that nuclear possession prevented wars and interventions and favored the status quo?

Or could it be that since the dawn of the nuclear age, American policymakers fully understood the power of nuclear deterrence and recognized, first as a superpower and then as a global hegemon, that deterrence could be oriented against the United States? As the world's strongest state, with overwhelming superiority in every conceivable form of power, from economic to soft to conventional, the United States did not especially prize stability or the status quo. What it wanted was the freedom to act in the world as it saw fit, even if it meant using military force or intervening in the internal affairs of other countries. But nuclear weapons, even in the hands of otherwise impotent states, deterred the United States from doing things it wanted. The United States had a deep strategic reason to limit nuclear proliferation—not for moral reasons, not even because of the fear of nuclear war, but because nuclear deterrence limits U.S. freedom to act as it sees fit in the world.

The strategy literature had fundamentally missed America's strategies of inhibition or its efforts to limit if not completely eliminate nuclear weapons from the planet. Sometimes these efforts were coercive (threatening preventive military action or sanctions), sometimes they were more normative or legal (arms control treaties), and other times they involved tools like alliances or nuclear strategy. Sometimes these inhibition strategies, like flexible response, went hand in hand with other goals, such as deterring the Soviet Union. At other times, such as cooperating with the Soviet Union to negotiate the Nuclear Nonproliferation Treaty, the inhibition strategy seemed at odds with the grand strategy of containment. It was clear, however, that something important had been missed.

This new conceptual understanding helped explain things that had made little sense before. Why did the United States continue preemptive counterforce strategies, even after the Soviet Union achieved secure second-strike forces? Why did the United States pursue missile defense, refuse to eschew no-first-use restrictions, and spend hundreds of billions of dollars on command, control, communication, and intelligence of nuclear forces, postures that puzzled most strategists after the superpowers achieved parity? Why did the United States obsess about the nuclear forces of otherwise weak states such as North Korea, Iraq, and Iran? Why did the United States not only not abandon its security commitments and alliances after the Cold War but actually expand and strengthen them? The new conceptual lens suggested that these strategic tools were adopted in large measure to dampen proliferation, either through coercion or assurance. The requirements for such a strategy are much different from, and much more difficult than, a strategy of simply deterring nuclear use by an adversary. This conceptual framework, combined with new evidence, allowed me to see a critical aspect of American grand strategy in a new light.

All of this points to the importance of historians' developing their own conceptual framework and testing it by working through the evidence. My experience has caused me to think that many other aspects of the dominating conceptual frameworks have not only missed important aspects of nuclear history but also provided misleading categories and theories for thinking about these issues. This is both a challenge and an opportunity for the young scholar of nuclear history.

Two examples suggest where deep historical work might challenge the conventional wisdom. First, every graduate student from the strategy community is taught that a fundamental cornerstone of nuclear dynamics is the clear and important distinction, first laid out by Thomas Schelling, between deterrence and compellence.[21] Deterrence, according to the common view, is easier and compellence harder; furthermore, deterrence is the policy of the status quo power and compellence that of the aggressor. Most of the stylized history of the nuclear age is arranged neatly into these categories: the parties in crisis are sorted into an aggressor trying to compel and a status quo state trying to deter. The Soviet Union, for example, is coded as the aggressor using compellence during the Berlin and Cuban missile crises, whereas the United States is the status quo deterrer.

How helpful is this framework in understanding how nuclear statecraft actually works? I was strongly influenced by my mentor, Marc Trachtenberg, on this question. As I looked over the documents on the U.S.-Soviet crises over Berlin in the late 1950s and early 1960s, I began to wonder how meaningful these distinctions were.[22] If deterrence was easier, it should have been relatively straightforward to prevent the Soviets from taking over West Berlin but much harder to compel them to leave. But since presumably the Russians would understand that before moving in, how could they be deterred from taking the city in the first place? What is more, as the 1958–1962 period makes clear, it was obvious that the status quo—and who is the compeller and who is the deterrer—is often in the eye of the beholder. The Soviets were trying to change the status of a city that even the Americans recognized was completely untenable in the long run. And the Soviets were doing it largely to deter the Americans from policies that were leading to the nuclearization of the Bundeswehr, which would have been deeply unsettling to the status quo.[23]

Consider other examples: Did Stalin order the blockade of Berlin in 1948 to deter the creation of the Federal Republic of Germany, or was he trying to compel the West to abandon a policy—the "western strategy" for Germany—which it had been pursuing since 1946? To look at a prenuclear case, in 1914 was Austria trying to compel Serbia to abandon its policy of creating a greater Serbian state at Austrian expense (and to compel Russia to abandon its policy of supporting Serbia in that area), or was Austria trying to deter Serbia from challenging the status quo? In the end, how useful is this core idea of the strategy literature, once one gets into the documents and reconstructs how policy was actually made?

Or consider another fundamental conceptual cornerstone of the strategy world: the need to have nuclear arms control to calm the so-called security dilemma that drives nuclear arms races and can lead to unintended nuclear war. One of the unimpeachable truths of the strategy and arms control community is that the SALT Treaties between the Soviet Union and the United States were unalloyed goods, the cornerstone of strategic stability. But a historian, working through documents in several countries, might come to an alternative view. The vehemently negative reaction to the negotiations within certain domestic circles within the United States, which gave rise to neoconservatism, is well known.[24] There is evidence that the Soviet military was furious as well, which may have led to the deployment of SS-20 missiles.[25] The SALT agreements inspired great mistrust and unhappiness among many of America's European allies, worried as they were about the credibility of America's extended deterrence, and the deployment of the SS-20s generated a crisis in NATO.[26]

These efforts to establish strategic stability, it could be argued, perversely helped undermine détente by the late 1970s.[27] It would be useful for a historian to explore the relevant archives in the United States, Europe, and Russia to see what really drove arms control and assess whether it was as valorous as many strategists claim. Policy is all about choices and trade-offs; historical work might suggest that the enormous political capital expended on the SALT negotiations between the Russians and Americans could have been more productively spent on other issues. The nitty-gritty of trade-offs, difficult choices, and unintended consequences that historians are comfortable with is often missing from the academic literature on proliferation, deterrence, and strategic stability. This is where good historical work—going back and forth between the evidence and testing and erecting new conceptual frameworks—might provide us real insight into how the nuclear policy process works. As I cautioned in the beginning, however, the yield may be meager, as we are ultimately trying to understand why something truly horrible has never happened.

Almost seventy years ago, an American B-29, the *Enola Gay*, dropped a gun-fission weapon made with U-235 on the city of Hiroshima, Japan, killing more than 100,000 people. Three days later, a plutonium device was dropped on the city of Nagasaki that may have killed as many as 80,000 people. That these two detonations transformed the world of politics and international affairs forever is universally accepted. The precise meaning and consequence of this legacy, however, is deeply contested. Policymakers and scholars would like to understand why these terrible weapons have not been used since 1945 and what might be done to ensure at least another eight decades without a nuclear attack.

What does the historical approach I have suggested contribute to understanding this issue? Unfortunately, those looking to history to resolve these questions will come away disappointed, as they often are when the past is mined for direct and relevant lessons. On the one hand, most people are understandably repulsed by the existence of weapons whose use in large numbers could literally end human civilization. As we know, some experts contend that we have avoided a catastrophe by sheer luck that is unlikely to continue, and that restraining, reducing, and eventually eliminating these weapons from the planet is the international community's most important priority. One can look to the past to make this argument. Others argue that nuclear weapons have served as a sort of necessary evil, preventing the kind of murderous, global conflagrations that plagued the first half of the twentieth century. Advocates of nuclear deterrence contend that millions of people and their descendants may be alive today because of the caution these weapons induce in even the most aggressive and tyrannical governments. There is certainly evidence for this view in the archives.

These larger views, of course, frame many of the contentious discussions surrounding contemporary challenges; consider the furious debate over what to do about Iran's nuclear program. Iran's aggressive behavior in the Middle East, its disturbing rhetoric about Israel, and its relationship with terrorist organizations convince many that the United States must do all it can to protect against its hostility, including using or supporting force to keep Iran non-nuclear. Others are equally convinced that a nuclear Iran can be easily contained and deterred and that using force would be a disaster. Kenneth Waltz once suggested in the lead essay in *Foreign Affairs* that a nuclear Iran would actually stabilize the Middle East and generate peace.[28]

Who is right? Do nuclear weapons make the world safer or more dangerous? It is hard to imagine a more important question. Can a deeper understanding of the past, a great reliance on historical work as opposed to the strategy literature, provide more usable insight that can be translated into better policies? I would certainly like to think so. The uncomfortable truth, however, is that despite bold assertions from scholars, advocates, and policymakers, we simply do not know the answers with complete confidence, and deeper history is as likely to cloud as to sharpen our views.

The historian can, however, provide needed skepticism and humility about broader claims. What is rarely commented on in the voluminous and often shrill debate over contemporary nuclear dynamics is how consistently abysmal our record of explaining and predicting nuclear politics has been since the start of the atomic age. Once the Soviet Union replaced the defeated Imperial Japan and Nazi Germany as America's main foe, as early as 1947 a third world war involving nuclear weapons was considered all but inevitable. Once fears of a thermonuclear war between the superpowers abated (somewhat), concerns turned from cascades of proliferation to the behavior of dozens of smaller, less responsible states that were unlikely to imitate the superpowers' restraint. In time, nonstate actors, including terrorist groups, would get their hands on these weapons, and some of our leading experts saw a detonation on American soil as a near certainty.

None of these terrible scenarios came to pass. Does this mean that the advocates of nuclear deterrence are correct? Not necessarily. Having pored through the declassified documents, I have no doubt that Cold War nuclear crises were often far more unstable and dangerous than we had thought, and the temptations to attempt nuclear blackmail hard to resist. The Berlin and Cuban missile crises would have been unlikely in a world without nuclear weapons. The superpowers experienced terrifying nuclear accidents and false alarms. Saddam Hussein's captured documents and recordings reveal he wanted the bomb both to deter and to coerce.

I end where I began: it is difficult to explain precisely why something did not happen. Correlation does not equal causation, and the absence of conflict does not necessarily mean that deterrence worked. After decades of global bloodletting, a clash of arms between a war-devastated Soviet Union and a United States uninterested in territorial gain would have been by no means inevitable in a non-nuclear world. In theory, nuclear weapons are best for preventing invasion from other states, but in more recent times, the prospect of great-power conquest has largely disappeared for reasons that appear to have little to do with deterrence. Given aging populations, massive increases in agricultural productivity, economic interdependence, technology, norms against violence, and, as we have learned in Iraq and Afghanistan, the high costs of occupation and the power of nationalism, conquest rarely pays. A visit to Singapore, Dubai, or the Netherlands illustrates that land is no longer power.

Where should this leave us in thinking about our nuclear future, and what role can the historian play in thinking about these things? More than anything, we should be humble in the face of these terrible weapons and recognize that despite what we might read in blogs or hear on the campaign trail, we understand very little about nuclear statecraft. More than seven decades later, we still do not even know if the bombing of Japan was the cause of its surrender.

My best guess, based on more than a decade of archival research on the question, is relatively modest and unsophisticated. Fewer nuclear weapons in the world is probably a good thing, but using force or coercion to achieve that goal is probably not. Perhaps the most useful advice we can give to policymakers facing the awesome responsibility of nuclear stewardship comes from a famous military historian, John Keegan, in his classic, *Mask of Command*: "Indeed, what is asked first of a leader in the nuclear world is that he should not act, in any traditionally heroic sense, at all."[29]

EIGHT

Deterring while Disarming

It is easy to forget we live in a world in which nine states possess thousands of nuclear and thermonuclear weapons of unimaginable destructive capacity.[1] A tour of the Hiroshima Peace museum, however, dramatically reminds visitors of the potential horrors.

Like many Japanese cities, Hiroshima is in a valley surrounded by mountains, the population concentrated in a dense and easily targeted urban setting. On August 6, 1945, the military was busy building defenses in the center of town; despite the protests of teachers and families, many children were drafted into this work and were working outdoors near where the atomic bomb detonated. As many as 20,000 slave laborers from Korea were also killed, as well as more than 90 percent of the city's medical personnel. All death during war is horrible, but the death unleashed by the bomb that day was especially horrific. The most fortunate were immediately incinerated by the tremendous impact of the blast. Others, still alive but with their skin melting off, lived for excruciating hours or days in inconceivable pain. Shards of glass and metal from shattered buildings penetrated scores of victims. Within minutes of the blast, a yellow rain began to fall, bringing intense radiation sickness over the next weeks that killed thousands who had survived the blast, fire, and collapsing infrastructure. Many lucky enough to survive the horrors of that day and the weeks that followed had their lives cut short by an array of cancers. While the final death toll is disputed, at least 80,000 people and perhaps as many as 140,000 died as a consequence of one bomb detonation. Three days later the city of Nagasaki suffered the same fate, with as many as 80,000 dead within two months of the bombing.

In retrospect, perhaps the most frightening aspect of the Hiroshima and Nagasaki atomic bombings is how small these detonations were compared with the capabilities that were to come. As the United States and the Soviet Union both developed and tested the so-called super or thermonuclear weapon in the 1950s, bomb yields increased to orders of magnitude beyond those used in August 1945. The infamous fifty-megaton Tsar Bomba, tested by the Soviet Union on October 30, 1961, had a destructive capability equal to 3,800 Hiroshima-style atomic bombs and would have killed at least 7 million people had it been dropped over New York City. Both sides developed plans to use these weapons during war, massively and early, that could have killed tens if not hundreds of millions of civilians and caused catastrophic damage to the earth's environment. In that same year of 1961, American planners estimated that implementing their nuclear war plan, called the SIOP-62, would have in a matter of hours killed approximately 108 million people in the Soviet Union, well over half of the population, as well as 104 million Chinese and 2.6 million Poles.[2] In all likelihood, fatalities would have vastly exceeded those figures, considering the number who would perish of radiation poisoning, to say nothing of the massive environmental damage, famine, and disease that would follow the collapse of the targeted state.

During the Cold War, there was a greater shared awareness of the dangers of a nuclear catastrophe. The United States tested a thermonuclear weapon on March 1, 1954, that obliterated Bikini Atoll. Radioactive coral rained down on a Japanese fishing boat almost five miles away from the blast site, killing one of the fisherman and sparking an international outcry. Crises throughout the first two decades of the Cold War, culminating in the eyeball-to-eyeball nuclear confrontation between the superpowers in October 1962, reminded the world of the constant and pressing dangers of nuclear war. American president John F. Kennedy estimated the odds of a nuclear war during this Cuban missile crisis as "between 1 in 3 and even."[3] The threat of nuclear catastrophe was ubiquitous in popular culture as well, as seen from comic books to popular movies such as *On the Beach, Fail Safe,* and *Dr. Strangelove.* In the 1970s and 1980s, focus waned but did not disappear, as the superpower nuclear rivalry reintensified and political clashes over Euromissiles and the neutron bomb combined with movies such as *Wargames* and the widely watched ABC television drama *The Day After,* each from 1983, to remind people of the horrors of thermonuclear use. President Ronald Reagan called the Soviet Union an "evil empire," international tensions increased when the Russians shot down South Korean Airliner, and grassroots protests against the nuclear arms race grew both in the United States and abroad.

The end of the Cold War rivalry early in the next decade dramatically reduced the dangers of nuclear war. Arms control treaties and mutual reductions cut the numbers of nuclear weapons stockpiles significantly. Concern over nuclear weapons and the fear of nuclear war has faded considerably in the past quarter of a century. The public consciousness of and debate about these weapons has decreased, and references in popular culture have almost disappeared. Yet thousands of nuclear weapons remain. As the investigative journalist Eric Schlosser hauntingly reminds us, "Right now thousands of missiles are hidden away, literally out of sight, topped with warheads and ready to go, awaiting the right electrical signal. They are a collective death wish, barely suppressed. Every one of them is an accident waiting to happen, a potential act of mass murder. They are out there, waiting, soulless and mechanical, sustained by our denial—and they work."[4]

New dangers have emerged as well in the twenty-first century. Many in positions of responsibility fear nuclear terrorism. The new states that have developed nuclear weapons since the Cold War, such as North Korea and Pakistan, do not inspire confidence that they fully understand the dangers these weapons represent or that their warheads can remain in safe hands. Russia again appears to be emerging as a nuclear rival to the United States, as does China. Former secretary of defense William Perry recently claimed that the combination of increased U.S.-Russian rivalry, tensions in South Asia, cyber attacks, and North Korea's nuclear program means that the "probability of a nuclear calamity is higher today, I believe, than it was during the Cold War."[5]

The post–Cold War era and the decades of the twenty-first century still to come invite a critical question: Can we limit, even eliminate, the nuclear threat while retaining the benefits to U.S. interests and world peace that many believe nuclear deterrence conveys? The answer to these concerns centers on a series of difficult questions Woodrow Wilson and his contemporaries wrestled with as a result of the horrors of World War I, questions that remain largely unanswered today. The continuing dangers of nuclear weapons make resolving these issues more important than ever.

Arms Races and War

Is war an inescapable part of human life? And if so, can it be restrained, or will every available means be used to win? Scholars and policymakers have long debated these questions. More than 100 years ago, President Woodrow Wilson revealed at least part of his answer to the question in his Fourteen Points speech to Congress in 1918. Article IV states that "adequate guarantees [must be] given and taken that national armaments will be reduced to the lowest point consistent with domestic safety."[6]

Behind this statement lay a contested theory of conflict that has been debated ever since, centered on whether arms races, separate from the political intentions of states, lead to war. In other words, is the production and deployment of weapons and military capabilities an independent cause of war, and can enforceable regimes or treaties negotiated among states and international institutions successfully reduce armaments and make peace more likely? Or are arms control and disarmament a chimera, more likely to expose a state to danger, an unacceptable risk to a nation in a dangerous world?

President Barack Obama began his administration by committing during a 2009 speech in Prague, Czech Republic, to working toward the eventual elimination of nuclear weapons from the planet. "Now, let me describe to you the trajectory we need to be on. First, the United States will take concrete steps towards a world without nuclear weapons. To put an end to Cold War thinking, we will reduce the role of nuclear weapons in our national security strategy, and urge others to do the same."[7]

When he completed his two terms in office, however, the United States was little closer to the goal of ridding the world of nuclear weapons. In fact, during the years that followed the president's hopeful statement, the Obama administration committed to spending $1 trillion over the next three decades to modernize and improve American strategic nuclear forces. Rather than eliminating the country's nuclear arsenal, in other words, he committed to ensuring its effectiveness and existence for generations to come. Efforts to reduce the role that nuclear weapons play in U.S. grand strategy have had only had limited success. "It's pretty clear the Prague agenda has stalled," comments Joseph Cirincione, the president of the Ploughshares Fund.[8]

These same contending, conflicting forces between nuclear deterrence and disarmament can be seen at work on the global stage. Dozens of states around the world have been advocating for nuclear disarmament with great passion, with a recent focus on the humanitarian consequences and illegality of nuclear weapons use. In October 2016, over the protests of the nuclear weapons states, the United Nations General Assembly voted overwhelmingly to begin negotiating a treaty to permanently ban nuclear weapons.[9] At the same time, many of the current nuclear powers—Russia, China, and Pakistan— are pursing their own expensive modernization plans. North Korea continues to test nuclear weapons and missiles while making nuclear threats. The United States and its allies also face increasingly bold

Chinese and Russian leaders in some regions and over issues that make nuclear escalation, inadvertent or purposeful, a terrifying if (for now) remote possibility. In fact, only one issue brings all these rival states together. "For all the divisions among world powers, one concern unites Russia and the U.S., India and Pakistan, North Korea and Israel at the United Nations: keeping their nuclear weapons."[10]

How should we think about the role nuclear weapons have played and will continue to play in world politics in the years and decades to come? Do they make war more or less likely? It is a pressing question with no clear answer. On the one hand, any intentional use of nuclear weapons is repugnant and unthinkable. Few if any causes could justify the instantaneous and wanton destruction of thousands of lives and livelihoods that would be ended by even one nuclear bomb. On the other, many skeptics believe disarmament an impossible and foolish dream. Historically, states do not typically give up weapons they believe protect their security and advance their interests. Even if they did, few states would trust others to faithfully disarm. Furthermore, some of these same people believe that the massive decrease in deaths caused by interstate wars over the past eight decades is related to the power of nuclear deterrence. No political end is worth risking nuclear devastation, nor can employing nuclear weapons conquer (as opposed to irradiate) territory. In other words, many believe nuclear weapons serve a crucial role in reducing war and saving lives. Nagasaki and Hiroshima were terrible; but since witnessing that horror, global war has been avoided.

The great challenge facing policymakers is this: Is there a way to capture what many see as the benefits of the thermonuclear revolution—the elimination of the destructive great-power, total wars of conquest that plagued the first half of the twentieth century—while minimizing or eliminating any possibility that nuclear weapons might be used, intentionally or inadvertently? Is there a way to capture the benefits of nuclear deterrence, which relies on the credible threat that nuclear weapons would be used in extremis, while ensuring they are never used? Can this tension and dilemma be reconciled to the benefit of global peace and stability? To resolve these tensions we must first acknowledge the compelling logic behind both the nuclear disarmament and deterrence positions while exploring ways to reconcile them to achieve global peace and stability and advance American interests in the world.

President Wilson and many of his contemporaries believed that World War I was caused, in large measure, by unrestrained arms races, on land and especially at sea, between the major European powers. England and Germany raced to increase both the number and power of their capital ships, while the continental powers continued to increase the strength of their land armies. At its most extreme, the arms race theory holds that the quantity and quality of weapons production can be independent sources of conflict, whereas a more limited point of view sees arms races as generating conditions of volatility and uncertainty that can cause states to misperceive the intentions of other states and stumble into war. It was hard to argue in the war's aftermath that the large increases in the quality and quantity of the implements of military power did not play some role in the nightmare that began in August 1914. Could this disaster have been prevented? More to the point, how could future world wars be avoided? For many, the solution to this problem was obvious: negotiate agreements to limit certain weapons—arms control—and in the case of especially dangerous weapons, ban them altogether—disarmament. Once the weapons were removed and, more important, the race between states to acquire more and better weapons ended, states could resolve their disagreements far freer of suspicion and fear. As Walter Lippmann, one of the twentieth century's great journalists and political commentators, argued after his days advising Wilson on such matters, "Big warships meant big wars. Smaller warships meant smaller wars. No warships might eventually mean no wars."[11]

Not everyone shared Wilson's view of arms races and arms limitations. The most expensive and longest arms race in the century before World War I, critics pointed out, was the naval race between future allies France and Great Britain. Arms races did not lead inevitably to war, and to focus simply on the weapons was to miss the larger, more important story. To some, acquiring and deploying military armaments reflects political decisions: a state and its leaders assess the security threats and opportunities it faces and build military forces that they perceive as the most appropriate to pursuing the state's national interests. If a state builds armaments or increases the size of its military, it is because it feels threatened or has interests it wants to pursue. As the historian Marc Trachtenberg observes,

> If states understand that hostile behavior will provoke a military buildup on the part of their adversary, whereas conciliatory behavior will be rewarded with a relaxation of the military pressures directed against them, they will all have a great interest in avoiding conflict and in improving relations with each other. This, then, is a world in which the possibility of military competition, not as a self-propelled phenomenon, but as an instrument of and outlet for political competition is not dysfunctional, but rather has an important, and indeed stabilizing, political role to play.[12]

In other words, armaments are not an independent cause of war; states start wars, not guns.

Under this view, arms control or disarmament may be, at best, a symbolic gesture, reflecting temporary political goodwill between potential adversaries. At worst, however, it can be dangerous. Skeptics doubted how successful arms control could ever be in calming the tectonic forces driving states to conflict. Inspection and verification are difficult. An adversary might cheat, and a state could be left exposed, without effective means to defend itself. At a more basic level, building armaments and increasing defense expenditures can be an effective way a state can use to signal to an adversary that it is unhappy and wants an issue resolved. By limiting a powerful tool to communicate its feelings to adversaries, a state may increase the likelihood of misperception and unwanted conflict. A state's resources might be poured into new, even more dangerous weaponry that is not yet covered by international agreement.

President Wilson's theories were put to the test during the interwar period, with at best mixed results. The German military was limited in terms of size and quality by the Treaty of Versailles, restrictions the Weimar Republic found ways to elude in collusion with the Soviet Union and then outright ignore once Adolf Hitler rose to power. The League of Nations included a pledge to seek disarmament and created several committees and initiatives to realize this goal, though its efforts failed. Attempts to ban submarines and poison gas were also unsuccessful. The 1922 Washington Naval Conference established strict ratios on capital ships between the major sea powers, which were adhered to for some time, albeit with different degrees of faithfulness by signatories. Even in the absence of major treaties, many Western powers restricted their military expenditures, both to avoid arms races and to devote resources to important domestic efforts. The resurgence of global war in the late 1930s destroyed further efforts to limit armaments, though the idea would resurface again after World War II.

Do arms races inevitably lead to war? And can limitations on weapons—and outright disarming in some cases—make conflict less likely? The literature on arms races—written largely after Wilson's Fourteen Points—is vast and contains no consensus. Ironically, both idealists and realists saw reasons to embrace at least parts of the view. Idealists clearly saw weapons and militaries as the source of war. Many realist theorists, however, argued that in a world without a world government or enforceable international law, nations lived in a state of fear and mistrust. A state might build weapons solely for the purpose of defending itself, but an adversary—not knowing or trusting the state's intentions—might see that move as a threat to itself and build its own weapons for its own defensive purposes. This cycle of mistrust and misperception—labeled the "security dilemma" by international relations theorists—could lead to an expensive and potentially dangerous arms race that could increase the chances of war. As the distinguished international relations theorist Robert Jervis has pointed out,

> The lack of an international sovereign not only permits wars to occur, but also makes it difficult for states that are satisfied with

the status quo to arrive at goals that they recognize as being in their common interest. Because there are no institutions or authorities that can make and enforce international laws, the policies of mutual co-operation that will bring mutual rewards if others cooperate may bring disaster if they do not. Because states are aware of this, anarchy encourages behavior that leaves all concerned worse off than they could be, even in the extreme case in which all states would like to freeze the status quo.[13]

For many, the anarchical nature of the international system made the idea of banning certain types of weapons not only impossible but also dangerously naïve. While the kinds of mistrust that spurred arms races made disarmament impossible, there was some hope that potential adversaries could successfully negotiate limits on the types and numbers of weapons they built. Perhaps arms control could at least limit the extent of dangerous misperception.

Arms Races and Disarmament in the Nuclear Age

The issue of the role arms races played in war and peace took an increased urgency after the bombing of Hiroshima and Nagasaki in August 1945. Atomic weapons—and especially thermonuclear weapons developed several years later—were armaments of a completely different order. Further use of such potentially civilization-ending weapons had to be avoided at all costs. If the arms race theories were true, the outcome of a nuclear arms race could be cataclysmic. Previous wars had been horrific. The next war, pundits feared, could be extinguishing. Adversaries would acquire larger numbers of increasingly devastating weapons, and more states in the world would strive to get the bomb. The unique characteristics of nuclear weapons— while no use was far and away the best outcome, it was probably much better to use them first and preemptively than to sit back and take a first hit—made them especially destabilizing.

Despite the deep animosity and mistrust between the United States and the Soviet Union, efforts were made to constrain both vertical— the superpower competition in strategic arms—and horizontal (proliferation) nuclear arms races. Some of these efforts were most likely driven by propaganda goals, whereas others were more serious. On the instructions of President Harry S. Truman, American policy-makers Dean Acheson and David Lilienthal cowrote a 1946 report proposing ideas for the international control of nuclear materials. Though the proposal was never acted on, it was followed up by other efforts—some more serious than others—including the creation of the International Atomic Energy Agency in 1957, the signing of a Partial Test Ban Treaty in 1963, a Nuclear Nonproliferation Treaty limiting the spread of nuclear weapons, and 1972 treaties limiting both strategic nuclear weapons (SALT I and SALT II) and weapons to defend against nuclear attack (ABM treaty). Furthermore, global grassroots movements advocated for reigning in the bomb. In general, much of the world, and especially the superpowers, recognized that after the Cuban missile crisis of 1962, in particular, efforts to avoid the use of nuclear weapons had to be a global priority.

While these efforts had some success, in fact the first decades after World War II witnessed intense nuclear arms races on various fronts. The number of states that acquired nuclear weapons rose from one—the United States—to nine. The Soviet Union acquired the bomb in 1949, Great Britain in 1952, France in 1960, and the People's Republic of China in 1964. Israel was suspected of developing an atomic weapon sometime in the 1960s (though it has never formally acknowledged the act), India detonated what they called a "peaceful" nuclear blast in 1974, Pakistan reciprocated in 1998, and North Korea tested in 2006. Today, dozens of other states possess civilian nuclear technology that would allow them, if they so chose, to develop nuclear weapons in relatively short order. Tools from coercion to persuasion were used to keep a wide range of states, from American allies such as West Germany and South Korea, to adversaries such as Iran, non-nuclear. Like all tools and leverage, they might, with a crisis or a change of thinking, prove inadequate.

The fierce strategic arms competition between the Cold War rivals, the Soviet Union and the United States, witnessed massive quantitative buildups, which saw each side possessing as many as tens of thousands of weapons. Finally, there was a less obvious but arguably more destabilizing competition in the types of nuclear delivery systems and the strategies under which they were deployed. At times, each side strove for weapons with greater destructive power, while at others the superpowers sought weapons of greater stealth, speed, and accuracy. Both the Soviet Union and the United States embraced strategies that called for massive and early, even pre-emptive, use of weapons. The SALT and ABM treaties of the 1970s were meant to tame this competition and generate the conditions for peace. For a brief time, with détente, they succeeded. The SALT and ABM treaties had unintended, negative effects, however:

> An unimpeachable belief in the strategy and arms-control community is that SALT I and SALT II were unalloyed goods, the cornerstone of strategic stability. An alternative view holds that negative reactions within the United States poisoned foreign policy debates and gave rise to neoconservatism. The Soviet military was furious as well, which may have led to the deployment of SS-20 missiles. The SALT agreements inspired great mistrust and dissatisfaction among many of America's European allies, and the deployment of the SS-20s generated a crisis in NATO. These efforts to establish strategic stability, it could be argued, perversely helped undermine détente by the late 1970s.[14]

For many others, however, the nuclear arms race was a recipe for disaster, and no effort should be spared to rid the world of these monstrous weapons. Early skeptics of arms control and disarmament simply believed that achieving meaningful and verifiable limits was not feasible. Over time, however, another view emerged: The possible use of nuclear weapons was horrific and catastrophic. Those very characteristics, however, may have given states pause, made them more cautious, made war unlikely. In other words, nuclear weapons may have deterred conflict from taking place and thereby served an important purpose in stabilizing international politics and promoting world peace.

During the thirty-one years that preceded the U.S. atomic bombing of Japan, the nations of the world fought two global wars, which in actuality were many murderous conflicts in almost every region of the globe. These wars had also fostered violent revolution, depression, famine and epidemics, and genocide. The horrific bloodlust killed many tens of millions of people, and many tens of millions more were maimed, dislocated, or disenfranchised. Empires collapsed, new states emerged, and political instability was the rule rather than the exception. Many of the issues that had driven these conflicts—expansionist ideologies, the industrialization of war, great-power competition, imperialism and colonial struggle, the race for resources—had been exacerbated, not resolved, by war. In 1945 most people expected a third world war to follow the second and first, only more murderous and terrifying. With the recent past as their guide, many expected the worst.

World War III, however, never came. In fact, the kind of great-power land wars that had devastated Europe and Asia for a century more or less disappeared. There was conflict, to be sure—smaller proxy wars, civil wars, insurgencies and counterinsurgencies, and dangerous crises. But nothing like what had marked the previous three decades. What explained what John Lewis Gaddis came to call "the Long Peace"?[15]

A variety of explanations were offered, from the increasing power of norms abhorring war to the shifting demographic and economic patterns. Expanding and intensifying globalization deepened economic and political links between states that, to many, made war unthinkable. Many analysts, however, said that the massive decrease in the number, length, and ferocity of great-power wars was derived from the power of nuclear deterrence. Nuclear deterrence was paradoxical—these weapons were so devastating and so hard to defend against that there was almost no political objective worth the risk of a retaliatory nuclear strike on your territory. As Gaddis points out in his famous article written as the Cold War was winding down,

It is worth recalling that World War I grew out of the unsuccessful management of a situation neither created nor desired by any of the major actors in the international system. There were simply no mechanisms to put a lid on escalation: to force each nation to balance the short-term temptation to exploit opportunities against the long-term danger that things might get out of hand. The nuclear deterrent provides that mechanism today. . . . The development of nuclear weapons has had, on balance, a stabilizing effect on the postwar international system.[16]

Furthermore, nuclear weapons had little offensive purpose—unlike tanks or armies that would seize land, nuclear blasts would render whatever territory was conquered unusable, undesirable, and, for sure, uninhabitable. You could not use nuclear weapons to invade a country and take its land, but you could use them to deter an invader from trying. As President Dwight D. Eisenhower stated, "The only thing worse than losing a global war was winning one."[17] In short, by making great-power war in the nuclear age an unthinkable absurdity, nuclear weapons may have actually saved tens of millions of lives. To misuse the famous quote from the cultural historian Paul Fussell, many thought, "Thank God for the atom bomb."[18]

There were many contested debates over how deterrence worked, what actions or policies could or could not be deterred, and what types and how many weapons were needed to achieve the ideal stability. Some worried that nuclear weapons in certain low numbers and in vulnerable positions were actually destabilizing, by inviting attack. Others pointed out that possession of too great a number was either destabilizing or useless. Might a nuclear war begin by accident? Questions arose about whether certain types of leaders or regimes would understand or follow (or exploit) the logic of deterrence. But a view did take hold that some number of nuclear weapons was, from the perspective of global stability, far better than no nuclear weapons.

For those who still embraced the logic of disarmament baked into the idea of international institutions and collective security, the deterrent arguments were wrongheaded and dangerous. There were other reasons for the absence of great-power war, they reasoned, and even if deterrence had worked to this point, it only had to fail once for the consequences to be catastrophic. Ward Wilson claims that an "examination of the record of nuclear deterrence shows doubtful successes and proven failures" that "undermine the apparent certainty and success that often seem to surround nuclear deterrence."[19] He argues that the deterrent advocates' argument about the Long Peace cannot be proved and is likely wrong.

> But we don't accept proof by absence in any circumstance where there is real risk. We wouldn't fly an airline that claimed to have invented a device that prevented metal fatigue, proved it by equipping 100 planes with the devices for one year without a single crash, and then suddenly ceased all metal-fatigue inspections and repairs, and decided instead to rely solely on these new devices.[20]

What were the odds that a world system whose stability was based on the threat of using nuclear weapons could last forever without those weapons being used? Over time, the risks of miscalculation and accidents could outweigh the benefits of deterrence. To many, the logic of disarmament remained powerful.

These arguments resumed with a renewed focus when the Cold War ended and the Soviet Union collapsed. Nuclear disarmament may not have been a plausible policy option for American leaders as long as their geopolitical and ideological rival was challenging the United States. But the post–Cold War period, like the end of all periods of war or conflict, offered an opportunity to remake the international order. Perhaps Wilson's vision of a world shaped by international institutions, law, democracy, and collective security could take place. Even among those with more realist views, the United States' overwhelming advantage in conventional and economic power offered an opportunity to reconsider the nuclear deterrent order. In 2007 the so-called four horsemen—former secretary of defense William Perry, former secretary of state Henry Kissinger, former senator Sam Nunn, and former secretary of state George Schultz—shocked the world by embracing the goal of a world free of nuclear weapons:

> Reassertion of the vision of a world free of nuclear weapons and practical measures toward achieving that goal would be, and would

be perceived as, a bold initiative consistent with America's moral heritage. The effort could have a profoundly positive impact on the security of future generations. Without the bold vision, the actions will not be perceived as fair or urgent. Without the actions, the vision will not be perceived as realistic or possible.[21]

As the post–Cold War order unfolded, however, the United States and the other nuclear powers resisted giving up what they saw as the benefits of nuclear deterrence. Both Russia and the United States, it is true, massively decreased their nuclear stockpiles. They also moved to secure loose nuclear materials and make nuclear accidents less likely. But new players entered the arena: India and Pakistan, bitter rivals since their founding, tested nuclear devices in 1998. North Korea abandoned the so-called Agreed Framework to build nuclear weapons. Other states with less-than-ideal international and domestic political records—Libya, Iran, and Syria—had nuclear weapons programs. The United States launched a war against Saddam Hussein's Iraq, based in large part on inaccurate suspicions that the regime was developing nuclear weapons. In the aftermath of the 9/11 attacks on the United States, the world was seen by some as too dangerous, too risky, to allow pursuit of nuclear disarmament.

In the past decade, the distance between those who see nuclear disarmament as the best policy for global peace and stability and those who see nuclear deterrence as the cornerstone of the world order has increased. The division is often stark and binary, with little middle ground, save for the world's greatest nuclear power, the United States, who confusingly appears to pursue both, mutually exclusive policies simultaneously.

A World without Nuclear Weapons?

Would the world be better off without nuclear weapons, or are they the best guarantee against the return of the horrors of great-power world war that terrorized the globe in the first half of the twentieth century? Who is right—Noam Chomsky, who said, "It's a near miracle that nuclear war has so far been avoided," or Margaret Thatcher, who noted during a speech in March 1987 at a banquet in the Soviet Union, "A world without nuclear weapons would be less stable and more dangerous for all of us"? The answers to these crucial questions can never be known for sure, and we can only hope they never will be. We cannot really know why a thermonuclear war has not happened, though we have strong suspicions. More to the point, how should one think about the various trade-offs, and in particular, the risks of nuclear use versus the benefits that nuclear deterrence may bring? Is there some way to capture the benefits of nuclear deterrence while avoiding the dangers of nuclear use?

While the goal is laudable, it is not entirely clear how to might be achieved. It is hard to deny that eight decades of the nuclear age have been far less bloody and are getting less bloody all the time. Though it is impossible to prove why a World War III has not happened, the intuition that nuclear deterrence played an important if not deciding role is powerful and convincing. While we have forgotten what that prenuclear world was like, the basic anarchy of world politics, competing ideologies, and rivalries among states could, in a world without deterrence, see the return of great-power war. It would be unwise to simply ignore the advantages nuclear deterrence has brought and discount the dangers that might return in its absence.

There is also the issue of the connection between our current nuclear order and the future of nuclear proliferation. The United States provides a security guarantee, or nuclear umbrella, to many states. It promises to use its own nuclear weapons, and expose itself to risk of nuclear retaliation, for the purpose of defending its allies. To make this threat credible, the United States not only needs nuclear weapons; it also needs weapons in large enough numbers and deployed in a strategy that credibly convinces its allies and adversaries alike that it would use these weapons. If the United States deemphasized nuclear weapons in its own strategy or eliminated them all together, states that are protected by the United States might face strong temptations to acquire or develop their own arsenals. The nuclearization of several of these non-nuclear states—Germany, Japan, and South Korea, for example—would be deeply upsetting to their neighbors and potentially destabilizing to world politics. Some believe this could unleash rapid proliferation—so-called nuclear dominoes or tipping points. It is hard to see how the United States could seek nuclear disarmament while maintaining its alliance commitments and suppressing the spread of nuclear weapons around the world.

The nuclear age was and remains terrifying. We now know that the danger of nuclear use, both advertent and inadvertent, has been present throughout. The purposeful use of nuclear weapons loomed in crises in Korea, Berlin, Cuba, and South Asia and at the Chinese-Russian border. Recent histories have highlighted the real dangers of accidental detonations of nuclear devices that were narrowly averted.[22] Was the world simply lucky, and would it be wise simply to hope for such good fortune to continue? Even if nuclear deterrence did play a role in stabilizing world politics in the early decades after World War II, one might argue that in more recent years other factors—norms, globalization and the spread of democracy, changes in conventional weaponry, the collapse of many aggressive ideologies and regimes—can secure some of the benefits of deterrence at a lower price.

Furthermore, it is increasingly incredible that any responsible state would use nuclear weapons except under the most extreme and dire circumstances, and perhaps not even then. This doubt existed even when the Cold War confrontation was at its sharpest. Henry Kissinger shocked his European audiences in 1979 when he laid out the truth about nuclear weapons:

> I have sat around the NATO Council table in Brussels and elsewhere and have uttered the magic words which had a profoundly reassuring effect. . . . My successors have uttered the same reassurances, and yet if my analysis is correct these words cannot be true, and . . . we must face the fact it is absurd to base the strategy of the West on the credibility of mutual suicide.[23]

This attitude is, if anything, even more strongly held today and might hold even in the absence of mutual suicide. Can a threat so obviously incredible maintain its power to deter and preserve the peace?

Can deterrence be maintained without nuclear weapons? Even in the absence of disarmament, the credibility of nuclear deterrence may fray.

What are some possible ways to accomplish this? A variety of thoughtful suggestions have been made. One idea is to revisit elements of the early Acheson-Lilienthal-type plans, whereby nuclear materials are banked in a global institution, though the challenges to this idea are many. In the mid-1980s, several analysts suggested what they called "virtual deterrents," whereby nuclear weapons were disassembled so they could not be used immediately but could be reconstructed in a crisis. This idea had a brief life and then disappeared, only to reappear over the past few years. Might this hold the possibility of reducing the dangers associated with nuclear use while retaining the benefits of deterrence?

Another possibility lies in what has been called a revolution in conventional and nonkinetic military capabilities. The United States has developed weapons whose accuracy, speed, and stealth may allow them to fulfill many of the missions that nuclear weapons were once called on to carry out. Combined with missile defense and extraordinary space and cyber capabilities, including the coordinated and integrated acquisition, processing, and provision of timely and accurate intelligence through land, sea, air, and space platforms, the United States possesses command of the commons in such a way that might allow it to prevent a nuclear attack before it occurs. Should the United States fully develop this capacity and maintain an edge over rivals with nuclear weapons, it may become more comfortable with deemphasizing nuclear weapons in its own strategy.

In short, a combination of shifting norms, empowered international institutions, the resolution of underlying geopolitical conflicts, and new technologies, along with the growing reawakening of awareness of the dangers of nuclear weapons, may create the circumstances to move toward some of the goals of disarmament without undermining the benefits of deterrence. In the future, one might imagine the United States strengthening an existing liberal international institution, such as the International Atomic Energy Agency—or creating a new one—to generate the trust, transparency, and technical capabilities necessary to achieve this goal.

Regardless of the specifics of the plans that are pursued, the essential goal must be to move the debate away from the unresolvable binary positions of deterrence and disarmament. Only by attempting to capture the best of both positions, while recognizing the challenges in both, can we make progress in reducing the dangers of nuclear use while once and for all relegating total, great-power wars of conquest to the ashbin of history.

Conclusion

On August 6, 1945, Tsutomu Yamaguchi was in Hiroshima on a business trip for his employer, Mitsubishi Heavy Industries, when the atomic bomb detonated. Miraculously, he survived his injuries and returned to his home in Nagasaki, only to survive a second atomic bombing three days later. Few possess his credibility on speaking of the horrors of nuclear war, nor his insight into a solution. "The only people who should be allowed to govern countries with nuclear weapons are mothers, those who are still breastfeeding their babies."[24]

Nuclear weapons are horrific, and their intentional use is, fortunately, largely unthinkable. Their existence, however, may have left us in a better world, one in which, ironically, we may be able to move away from continued dependence on them for our security. Despite widespread examples of political and cultural discontent, both in the United States and around the globe, the world is an undeniably healthier, wealthier, less violent place than it was in the past. Great-power war has decreased, homicide rates have collapsed, major diseases have been eliminated, international law and institutions have blossomed, and, though not a linear process, more people have left poverty and live in regimes that, if not fully liberal democracies, are more tolerant and open than ever before.[25] This is not to say there has not been and will not be backsliding, that hypernationalism or great-power war cannot return, or that terrifying new threats, from pandemics to a climate catastrophe, will not emerge. That being said, it is remarkable how the world has changed along the lines Wilson hoped for and recommended in his original Fourteen Points. What a century ago would have seemed foolish idealism is now largely a reality.

This may be the best argument for pursuing the benefits of deterrence and disarmament, regardless of sharply divided viewpoints or how difficult it appears to us now. Wilson was not exactly clear on how to fashion a world where great-power war and want diminished dramatically; nor can we be precisely sure how we will achieve this new aim. At the very least, it will require American leadership, sacrifice, and an innovative recommitment to American ideals of promoting a vibrant, transparent, and secure liberal world order. As President Obama made clear in his 2009 Prague speech, the path to a world without nuclear weapons will be a long one. This does not mean, however, that we should not pursue this ambitious goal as soon and as vigorously as possible. As President John F. Kennedy said in his own call to "bring the absolute power to destroy other nations under the absolute control of all nations," let us begin.[26]

NINE

Rethinking Nuclear Weapons and American Grand Strategy

Nuclear weapons and the role they play in American grand strategy are an issue of fundamental importance. Any use of these fearsome tools of destruction, whether intentionally or by mistake, would be catastrophic. Nuclear weapons also buttress much of American grand strategy, explicitly and more often implicitly, to a far greater extent than is acknowledged. The mere existence of these weapons shapes strategy, statecraft, and the international system in profound, powerful, and often puzzling ways.

Despite the obvious importance of the bomb, its role is largely taken for granted by the American public, even among foreign policy experts. The purpose of nuclear weapons in American grand strategy draws little focused attention and few probing questions. There are discussions about aspects of U.S. nuclear policy: debates over whether the U.S. nuclear deterrent should be modernized, what the consequences would be if a particular arms-control agreement were signed or abandoned, or worries about the possible nuclearization of a rogue state. These discussions, however, are episodic. They tend to fade quickly from headlines, and only rarely do they bring to the surface underlying assumptions about the role of nuclear weapons in U.S. grand strategy.

Academic discussion of the bomb has its own challenges. Within the most influential school of thought in security studies, nuclear weapons' effect on foreign policy and international relations is largely understood as a settled question. This is not to suggest that there is consensus among academics: more so than many fields of inquiry, nuclear studies is plagued by intellectual stove-piping, methodological disputes, and disciplinary divides. Within these academic worlds, moreover, much of the debate over nuclear issues focuses on peripheral questions and is often divorced from the realities of policymaking. Most telling, discussions of nuclear weapons are rarely connected to larger questions surrounding American politics, policy, and purpose in the world. Most of these disputes center on competing versions of the past. And the academic discipline of history—the field that could arbitrate these disagreements—marginalizes the study of nuclear weapons and rarely contributes to these debates.

This chapter seeks to disturb this complacency about the role of nuclear weapons in U.S. grand strategy to explore important questions: What is the rationale for these weapons? And how do they advance America's interests in the world? In seeking to better understand the purpose and consequences of nuclear weapons in American grand strategy, it is helpful to interrogate widely held assumptions and beliefs, with a goal of updating the intellectual architecture undergirding analysis of the role of the bomb.

Unfortunately, much of the conventional wisdom surrounding these issues is incomplete, lacks falsifiability, and, at times, is simply wrong. This is not the result of a lack of effort or intellect in the academy. To be clear, the body of scholarly work on nuclear weapons is enormous and impressive. Rather, the nature of nuclear weapons and the unusual and unexpected role of the bomb in American grand strategy have often been perplexing, hard to measure and assess, and even contradictory. This has led to confusion and unproductive, sometimes sharp, disagreements among scholars of nuclear weapons and international relations. Decisionmakers often share this confusion. There are five key arguments and insights to help gain better clarity on the question of nuclear weapons and American grand strategy.

First, the leading theoretical approach to nuclear politics, known as the nuclear revolution school, has failed to predict and explain critical aspects of U.S. nuclear policies, including nuclear strategy and nonproliferation. The most important insight from this approach is correct: few if any political objectives are worth the extraordinary costs of a thermonuclear war. The theory, however, does not offer much insight into almost eight decades of U.S. "exceptional" behavior with the bomb—or policies at odds with the predictions of the nuclear revolution framework.

Second, our understanding of the history of U.S. nuclear weapons policies, and the bomb's role in American grand strategy, is often incomplete, misleading, and even wrong. Much of this stems from a shameful lack of attention to the subject by academic historians, leaving largely unchallenged a decades-old, stylized narrative crafted by participants and scholars of security and strategic studies who lack access to key archival sources. America's nuclear past is more complex than the conventional wisdom allows. There are at least four complementary and competing strands of U.S. nuclear history— intellectual, rhetorical, operational, and presidential—that should be recognized and reconciled. Furthermore, U.S. nuclear history should be understood as distinct from, if inextricably interwoven with, other powerful streams of world history since 1945, including the Cold War, decolonization, and globalization.

Third, the inadequacies of theory and history in explaining the policies of the United States are not surprising, since the nature of nuclear statecraft presents severe methodological and rhetorical challenges to getting the "right" answer. Furthermore, nuclear weapons raise profound moral considerations, making it difficult to distinguish between scholarly arguments and advocacy. These challenges demand intellectual humility and are ignored at great peril.

Fourth, emerging challenges—technological, geopolitical, and normative—will make questions of nuclear weapons and American grand strategy both more difficult and more consequential in the years and decades to come. Some of these forces make the use of nuclear weapons increasingly unthinkable, while others appear to make use of the bomb more likely, both with consequences for American grand strategy. The tensions and contradictions in U.S. policy—between nuclear activism and nuclear abstinence—will make an already difficult situation increasingly unsustainable in the future.

Fifth, America's often puzzling nuclear policies are best understood through a grand strategic lens. What does such a framework reveal about the United States? While such policies have often appeared uncertain, ambiguous, and inconsistent, when assessed over time it is clear that the United States has persistently used nuclear weapons to achieve one overriding grand strategic goal: to resist the elements of the nuclear revolution that limit America's freedom of action in the world and expose it to vulnerability. This was true during the Cold War and after the Cold War ended, and it remains true to this day. Washington has sought to eliminate its vulnerability and promote freedom of action through policies and behaviors that often appear to be in tension or even contradictory. Academics have often missed this important point, which is often intuitively understood by American policymakers.

How did the United States pursue this grand strategic goal? At times, the U.S. government has pursued nuclear activism by treating nuclear weapons as the most important element of its grand strategy. It did this, for example, by prizing nuclear superiority and by adopting strategies to use these weapons early and first in a crisis. At other times, Washington has pursued policies of nuclear abstinence, highlighting how unusable and even repugnant nuclear weapons are and encouraging other states to eschew their benefits. Many times, American grand strategy has been to pursue both, seemingly incompatible, positions. This split was driven less by strategic ambiguity than real uncertainty about the best path forward and a desire to fully cover its bet. When it comes to activism or abstinence, the United States, like a switch-hitter in baseball choosing between batting left or right, chooses the option with the greatest odds of achieving its grand strategic goals.

The Wrong Revolution?

How should nuclear weapons affect U.S. strategy and statecraft? What does the leading theory—the nuclear revolution school—say about how American grand strategy should be influenced by the bomb?

Under the nuclear revolution framework, assessing the purpose and consequences of the bomb through a grand strategic lens can make for an awkward fit. After all, grand strategy is about making choices, determining what means and instruments, including war, states and their leaders select to achieve desired ends in geopolitical competition in international relations. It reflects "a purposeful and coherent set of ideas about what a nation seeks to accomplish in the world, and how it should go about doing so."[1] Grand strategies vary enormously over time, location, individuals, and regimes. The United States has pursued a variety of grand strategies since its founding, and debate is fierce over what grand strategy it should pursue today and what means it should employ.

The nuclear revolution school argues that the bomb severely constrains and limits—and at times eliminates—the grand strategic choices that were available to states and statesmen in the past. Robert Jervis, the leading thinker in the nuclear revolution school, has argued that "force and the threat of it cannot support foreign policy in the same way that it did in the past."[2] The historian Lawrence Freedman agrees, suggesting that nuclear strategy "is a contradiction in terms."[3]

What is the nuclear revolution framework, and what predictions and explanations does it offer? While scholars differ on some aspects,* Stephen Walt has nicely defined its broad outlines: "As refined by scholars like [Bernard] Brodie, Thomas Schelling, Glenn Snyder, Robert Jervis, Kenneth Waltz, and Stephen Van Evera, nuclear weapons are said to provide states with the ability to protect their sovereignty and independence not via direct defense but rather through *deterrence*." Walt continues that, "according to the "logic of the 'nuclear revolution,' therefore, states with second-strike capabilities were secure against attack and didn't need to worry very much about their sovereignty or independence." The nuclear revolution "means that 'nuclear superiority' was a meaningless concept. . . . A handful of survivable weapons makes it very unlikely that another state will attack you directly or try to invade and take over your country."[4]

According to Jervis, nuclear weapons "can kill but not influence."[5] Nuclear weapons even "eliminate the security dilemma," the phenomena that many scholars believe drove international conflict for centuries, making cooperation among states more likely.[6] Nor can they be used for much else besides deterrence. As Todd Sechser and Matthew Fuhrmann argue in a recent study, "For all the money spent on atomic bombs, they have bought precious little coercive leverage for states."[7]

The nuclear revolution should have had important consequences for proliferation dynamics, nonproliferation policies, and alliances. Joshua Rovner explains that according to the nuclear revolution view, "if nuclear weapons were great for deterrence but lousy for

---

*While there are a range of perspectives within the nuclear revolution framework, most derive and share the assumptions of defensive realism, which may be the predominant theoretical approach to international relations within the field of American political science. For an interesting take on efforts by different realist camps to understand the effects of nuclear weapons on world politics, see Zanvyl Krieger and Ariel Ilan Roth, "Nuclear Weapons in Neo-Realist Theory," *International Studies Review* 9, no. 3 (2007), 369–84.

battle, then Washington should have been sanguine as new countries went nuclear. It might even have been optimistic, since proliferation would, under this theory, lead countries to become cautious."[8] Even if the United States wanted to stem the spread of nuclear weapons, however, the effort would be futile. According to Kenneth Waltz, "If countries feel insecure and believe that nuclear weapons would make them more secure, America's policy of opposing the spread of nuclear weapons will not prevail."[9] Waltz, the most influential international relations theorist of modern times and one of the more extreme advocates of the nuclear revolution framework, went further still, arguing that nuclear weapons "make alliances obsolete."[10] The mere presence of the bomb would override the grand strategic choices made by a particular state or leader. "Nuclear weapons can carry out their deterrent task no matter what other countries do."[11]

The key insight of this framework is that the bomb is a defensive weapon of such powerful force that it transforms strategy and statecraft, constraining the grand strategic options available to states and leaders before the nuclear age, regardless of a state's history, geography, culture, or regime type. According to Waltz, "American estimates of what is required for deterrence were absurdly high." In other words, "not much is required to deter."[12]

Summing up the conventional wisdom among scholars in this tradition, Charles Glaser and Chaim Kauffman argue that the nuclear revolution reveals that "this technology so heavily favors defense that when all the major powers have nuclear weapons *variation in other factors* becomes relatively unimportant."[13] According to Stephen Van Evera, "The nuclear revolution gave defenders a large military advantage," so large that conquest "became virtually impossible."[14] John Mearsheimer similarly concludes that "there is no question . . . the presence of nuclear weapons makes states more cautious about using military force of any kind against each other."[15]

How well did the theory of the nuclear revolution do in predicting American nuclear weapons policy and explaining the role of the bomb in U.S. grand strategy? The framework's key point—that nuclear weapons made total, thermonuclear war a horrifying absurdity to be avoided at all costs—is, of course, a profound insight. As the historian John Lewis Gaddis argued during the Cold War, "It seems inescapable that what has really made a difference in inducing this unaccustomed caution has been the workings of the nuclear deterrent."[16]

Yet the implications of this incontrovertible truth for American grand strategy are both contested and uncertain. Did the United States accept mutual vulnerability with nuclear-armed adversaries, as the theory would have predicted? Was the bomb understood only as a defensive weapon to defend American sovereignty and territorial integrity? Were American leaders nonplussed as other states expressed interest in the bomb, and, even if concerned, did they recognize and accept that there was little they could do to stop proliferation? Did alliances become less important, and was the United States less likely to use force of any kind? Perhaps most critical, did the United States behave like any other state in the system, bowing before the constraints the nuclear revolution imposed on its strategy and statecraft?

Taken to its logical end, this school of thought suggests that many states should seek nuclear weapons and that the United States should or could do little to stop other states from pursuing and attaining their own bomb. When building arsenals, the ease of securing a second-strike capability meant that seeking quantitative or qualitative advantages beyond a certain point would be a foolish goal for a state: At best it would be wastefully expensive; at worst, destabilizing and dangerous. According to the theory, strategic stability, both in dyadic competitions and on a broader, horizontal scale, should emerge naturally from the nuclear revolution.[17] Nor should the particular circumstance, history, leadership or regime type, or interests of the nuclearizing state affect the powerful, systemwide effects of these weapons.

Or so went the story largely crafted by American academics specializing in security and strategic studies.[18] As Rovner has noted,

> If the nuclear revolution affected grand strategy, the United States should have settled for a small arsenal for the sole purpose of deter-

rence. It would never have sought to integrate nuclear and conventional forces, because nuclear weapons were fundamentally different in that they could never be used. U.S. leaders should have recognized that defenses against nuclear attack were futile, and avoided pouring time and money into such efforts. And they should have managed the process of proliferation so that states, great and regional powers alike, enjoyed the security benefit of a reliable second-strike capability. None of these things happened.[19]

Why not?

Exceptional, but Not for the Reasons Many Think

The nuclear revolution framework provides a powerful lens to understand two of the most important aspects of world politics since 1945: the disappearance of great-power war and the nonuse of nuclear weapons against adversaries after the United States dropped atomic bombs on Hiroshima and Nagasaki, Japan, in August 1945. It is less helpful in explaining other aspects of U.S. grand strategy in the nuclear age. The United States' behavior and policies diverged from expectations of the nuclear revolution school in at least three ways.

The first involves American leaders' interest in making nuclear weapons such a core element in U.S. grand strategy. According to the nuclear revolution school, the most powerful role of nuclear weapons is as invasion insurance, to prevent the conquest of sovereign territory. Whatever the fears raised by the Japanese attack on Pearl Harbor, the United States has faced almost no threat of conquest since the Civil War ended in 1865. A United States without nuclear weapons—in 2019 or in 1955 or 1975 or any other year—faced almost zero threat of conquest. Rarely has a state had less need for the bomb to guarantee its immediate territorial integrity, sovereignty, and security.*

---

* Protecting the territorial sovereignty of the homeland is obviously not the only U.S. national interest. The United States fought two world wars, in large part to prevent any state from consolidating Europe and using it as a base to threaten the Americas. The United States has been obsessed with expelling great-power influences from its hemisphere and guaranteeing that conflict takes place far

Yet no state has invested greater resources in developing and deploying nuclear weapons, nor has any other state relied more heavily on nuclear weapons to implement its grand strategy. The United States has spent astronomical sums on nuclear weapons since 1940, dwarfing the expenditures of other rivals.[20] Between 1940 and 1996, the United States spent $5.5 trillion on nuclear weapons. It plans to spend an additional $1.2 trillion over the next thirty years.[21]

This is not to suggest that it is surprising the United States pursued and developed the bomb, or even that it pursued a survivable nuclear capability. What is surprising, however, is the central and expensive role that nuclear weapons have played in American grand strategy. Advocates of strategic stability and the nuclear revolution framework, to say nothing of the historians of American grand strategy before 1950, would probably struggle to explain the United States' experiments with nuclear sharing with its allies, its willingness to use nuclear weapons first in a conflict, and predelegating authority to launch the bomb to military commanders in the field.[22]

Second, extraordinary new scholarship is making it increasingly clear that the United States never permanently abandoned its efforts to achieve nuclear superiority.[23] For a decade and a half after the United States lost its nuclear monopoly, it strove diligently to build far more deliverable nuclear weapons than any other country.[24] It is true that the United States began to accept quantitative equality with its primary adversary, the Soviet Union, by the late 1960s and 1970s. Two points are in order. First, the United States accepted parity only reluctantly. As James Cameron astutely observes, "Nixon hated MAD, believed its logic was defeatist and naïve, yet he signed agreements that enshrined it at the heart of the United States' relations with the Soviet Union."[25] Mired in a disastrous war in Southeast

---

away from its homeland. Historically, however, that is a rare luxury for a great power—even Britain and Japan, as well as the continental great powers, have had to worry far more about invasion of the homeland. And the United States developed nuclear weapons during World War II because of fears that Nazi Germany was developing the bomb.

Asia and facing both economic and domestic political constraints on military spending, the United States pulled in its horns. Second, while American policymakers accepted quantitative parity, they still sought qualitative primacy over U.S. adversaries.

How did the United States seek this superiority? Concurrent to American policymakers negotiating and accepting the SALT I and II and ABM treaties, the U.S. government undertook a massive, extraordinary effort to develop and deploy more sophisticated nuclear weapons and systems to support them. This allowed the United States to exploit its natural advantages over the Soviet Union. As John Mauer has argued, "American leaders raced the Soviets in military technologies where the United States was perceived to enjoy significant advantages, while simultaneously entangling the Soviet Union in an arms control regime that would limit areas of Soviet strength. By combining arms racing and arms control, the United States pursued a holistic offset strategy.[26] As the historians Niccolo Petrelli and Giordana Pulcini reveal, between 1969 and 1976 the Nixon and Ford administrations "actively sought to transcend nuclear parity."[27]

In the years after quantitative parity was accepted, the United States developed and deployed a number of technologically sophisticated and expensive capabilities, including the Pershing II, MX, Trident D-5, as well as cruise missiles. It also invested enormous resources into missile defense; antisubmarine warfare (that is, targeting and eluding Soviet nuclear submarines); and command, control, communications, and intelligence capabilities.[28] As Austin Long and Brendan Green demonstrate in their pathbreaking work, the United States "invested massive resources into intelligence capabilities for a first strike, including successful innovation in tracking submarines and mobile missiles."[29] These expenditures were oriented toward systems whose characteristics and capabilities, such as speed, stealth, intelligence, and accuracy, were best suited to a nuclear posture that focused on counterforce, damage limitation, and even preemptive uses. In other words, the nuclear forces built in the decades after the SALT and ABM treaties made little sense if the United States had fully embraced the consequences of mutual vulnerability spelled out by the nuclear revolution school. This is certainly how the Soviet Union perceived these efforts. Because of the "development of American counterforce capabilities," Soviet leaders "were uncertain they could indefinitely maintain a secure second strike in spite of their strenuous efforts."[30]

This interest in maintaining superior nuclear capabilities continued after the Cold War ended.[31] As a 2003 RAND report observed,

> The force is larger than it needs to be if deterrence by threat of nuclear retaliation is the sole objective of U.S. nuclear strategy. Even a mildly expanded target base that included selected targets in emerging nuclear powers as well as chemical and biological weapons facilities in a larger set of countries would not necessarily require the sort of force that the United States plans to maintain. What the planned force appears best suited to provide beyond the needs of traditional deterrence is a *preemptive counterforce capability against Russia and China*. Otherwise, the numbers and the operating procedures simply do not add up.[32]

It has been argued that bureaucratic and organizational politics were the primary drivers of these expensive, risky, and politically polarizing nuclear postures.[33] Organizational and bureaucratic factors no doubt played some role, but the fact that the search for qualitative superiority has spanned decades, encompassing multiple administrations and great shifts in global politics, undermines such interpretations. As Green and Long argue, "In sum, it was international politics, not domestic politics, which killed hopes for nuclear stability."[34]

Why did the United States seek nuclear primacy? The United States asked more of its nuclear weapons in its grand strategy than any other nuclear state.* Most states seek nuclear weapons to protect

---

*This is not to say there is not variation in the nuclear strategies, as Vipin Narang lays out brilliantly in his book about regional nuclear strategies. In addition to assured-retaliation postures, regional nuclear powers can choose catalytic or asymmetric escalation postures, both of which imply first use. See Vipin Narang, *Nuclear Strategy in the Modern Era: Regional Powers and International Conflict* (Princeton University Press, 2014).

themselves from invasion and conquest. This is a scenario the United States has not had to worry about, and even if it did, such protection would not require the massive, sophisticated nuclear forces and related systems the U.S. government built. Instead, the United States employed its nuclear forces to achieve far more ambitious, historically unprecedented goals. From the early 1950s onward, the United States pursued an audacious strategy of relying on its massive nuclear capabilities to both protect far-flung allies from nuclear attack or conventional invasion while also inhibiting the nuclear desires of those same allies. As Green and Long demonstrate, "Successive administrations discovered that the threat of retaliation and the existential risk of nuclear escalation posed by stability doctrines were not a sufficient military solution for their perceived geopolitical challenges."[35]

There has long been a tension between the goal of strategic stability and extending deterrence to America's allies. As analysts from RAND pointed out in 1989, there was a clash between the "objectives of enhancing first-strike stability, on the one hand, and extending deterrence and limiting damage, on the other," such that the more robust the Soviets believed stability was "the less they might hesitate to precipitate a deep crisis by engaging in serious aggression."[36] As Earl Ravenal explained in 1982, extending deterrence demanded expensive and potentially destabilizing counterforce capabilities, employed in first-strike strategies. "Such a damage-limiting attack, to have its intended effect, must be preemptive."[37] Permanently extending deterrence while inhibiting proliferation have been cornerstones of American grand strategy for so long it is easy to forget how historically unusual, difficult, and demanding this ambition is.

There was, of course, great tension between the goal of a preemptive strategy and strategic stability. Ravenal makes clear that counterforce strategies were not about mutual vulnerability:

Counterforce and first nuclear strike are mutually dependent. A first strike implies counterforce targeting, since the only initial attack that makes sense is a damage-limiting strike, the destruction of as much of the enemy's nuclear force as possible. And counterforce targeting,

202

in return, implies a first strike, a preemptive attack, because a second strike against the enemy's missiles is useless to the extent that one's missiles would hit empty holes.

As an assistant to Defense Secretary Robert McNamara told a reporter in the mid-1960s, "There could be no such thing as primary retaliation against military targets after an enemy attack. If you're going to shoot at missiles, you're talking about first strike."[38]

To be clear, this is not to argue that American leaders seriously contemplated a first strike or even made full-out efforts to acquire meaningful first-strike forces.[39] While American presidents refused to accept qualitative parity with the Soviet Union and pursued expensive and arguably dangerous counterforce options, they also shied away from seeking a full-scale, first-strike capability. One of the great unanswered questions of the nuclear age involves what U.S. leaders thought they were getting with this qualified superiority.* Strategies of inhibition required strategic forces that went far beyond mutual vulnerability, but such postures might dangerously undermine strategic stability.[40] One promising explanation is Glenn Kent and David Thaler's idea of "optimum instability"—developing enough counterforce to make the other side think you might go first in a crisis but without making your adversary think you are eager to do so. "Indeed, one might argue that an optimal amount of first-strike instability is possible: that is, enough to deter the Soviets from generating a major crisis (say, by invading Western Europe), but not enough to allow a major crisis to spiral out of control."[41]

This aggressive posture was pursued, in large measure, to inhibit

---

* Logically, it would seem debatable that possessing increased potential for damage limitation well short of perfect first-strike capabilities would increase U.S. willingness to risk nuclear war to protect allies and enhance extended deterrence and even coercive leverage. Yet the historical record demonstrates that American leaders were willing to pay quite a bit—financially, politically, and in terms of risk—to acquire these capabilities and, perhaps more important, that the Soviet Union and U.S. allies took these efforts seriously.

the development of independent nuclear weapons programs among ostensible allies. The United States went to great lengths to prevent what might otherwise have been a natural development in world politics: the emergence of independent, capable states with their own nuclear weapons. Nuclear weapons would, after all, effectively guarantee their possessors against invasion and conquest for the first time—ever. Rare was the state in history that turned away from an effective military technology or turned over its security to another state. Washington, however, aggressively pursued a wide range of policies to achieve inhibition, including threats of force or abandonment, forward deployed forces, enacting sanctions, selling arms, and encouraging treaties and norms.[42] To achieve its goals of inhibition, the United States often cooperated with its most bitter ideological and geopolitical adversary, the Soviet Union, at the expense of U.S. partners and allies.[43]

It is easy to lose sight of how strange, even radical, these grand strategic choices were when they were developed in the 1950s and the extent to which they remain so today. There is little in the nuclear revolution theory that can explain the cost, number, and technological sophistication of America's nuclear weapons systems nor the aggressive postures in which they were employed. Imagine explaining in the early twentieth century that the United States was going to risk a global war that would kill tens of millions of people to defend a conventionally indefensible portion of a city—West Berlin—100 miles within enemy territory that had no geostrategic value whatsoever. Imagine that everyone would think this was normal (and call it "extended deterrence"). Imagine the weapons and military strategy necessary to convince an adversary that was far closer, that had superior conventional arms, and that, arguably, had more at stake that this was a credible commitment. Try to imagine a parallel in world history for this situation before 1950.

Then think about how the strategists who constructed these theories did so based largely on their view of how this story unfolded between 1958 and 1963. The United States, which had little need for nuclear weapons to prevent an invasion or nuclear attack upon its homeland, built, at great expense, the largest and most sophisticated nuclear forces in the world and placed them within forward-leading and often preemptive strategies, backed by military technologies that potentially undermined strategic stability. American leaders worked feverishly, often with adversaries, to prevent the rise of independent nuclear weapons states—ally, enemy, or neutral—and this remains a cornerstone of U.S. grand strategy. These strategies were exceptional.

In one sense, however, nuclear weapons did revolutionize American grand strategy. Before 1949, the United States had no permanent peacetime alliances. America demobilized during peacetime, and it typically pursued slow strategies of attrition when conflict did arise. Congress was widely perceived as the more powerful foreign policy actor during peacetime, while military leaders were afforded little leeway. All of that changed dramatically after the early 1950s, across administrations and shifts in the structure of the international system.[44] The United States developed strategies that would escalate quickly—even preemptively—with nuclear weapons, and it concentrated enormous power to initiate war into the hands of the American presidency, all on behalf of defending a sprawling set of countries around the world. Simply put: There was a (thermo) nuclear revolution that shaped American grand strategy—but it was a much different revolution from what the conventional wisdom puts forward.

Limitations of Nuclear Histories

What is the history of U.S. nuclear weapons and their role in American grand strategy? Careful assessment of what is known—and whether these accounts accurately capture the past—is critical. Most theories and policy analysis are based on assumptions and beliefs about what happened in the past. Unfortunately, less is known about U.S. nuclear history and its role in American grand strategy than is presumed, and what many people do know is often overly simplistic, misleading, or otherwise problematic.

Why is this the case? The major works that cover the history of U.S. nuclear weapons policy were, for the most part, written some time ago—before many primary documents were released. These works were often penned not by historians but by policy participants, scholars of strategic and security studies, or analysts outside of the academy. Many of these works are excellent first cuts at history.[45] Most, however, are older, do not engage recent archival finds, and often accept the logic of the nuclear revolution school to explain U.S. policy.

What of the discipline of academic history? To be sure, impressive international research has been conducted into various elements of global nuclear history, especially the issues surrounding various state decisions about whether to build a bomb.[46] There are also excellent monographs exploring particular aspects of U.S. nuclear history.[47] Writ large, however, treatment of American nuclear weapons history has been episodic rather than systematic. This is part of a larger, and unfortunate, decades-old trend within history departments. As Hal Brands has argued, "The historical profession in the United States has simply deprioritized the study of statecraft and international relations, at least as those subjects were conventionally understood."[48] This is especially true in nuclear history, where there is almost no participation by scholarly historians on these contested issues. The academic discipline of history "has largely abandoned studying important issues such as international security and nuclear weapons and is in the midst of a four-decade, slow-motion act of collective suicide. There simply is not, nor will there be anytime soon, a critical mass of diplomatic and military historians available to research these important questions or make use of these amazing materials."[49]

Even when scholarly historians do focus on issues of foreign policy or international relations, nuclear questions often get short shrift. Large, synthetic accounts of the Cold War either accept the nuclear revolution framework or do not break new ground on nuclear issues.[50] Arguably far more is known about the development of U.S. human rights policies, for example, or the role of race and gender in American foreign policy, than about how U.S. decisionmakers have discussed and debated the purpose and consequences of the bomb in its relations with the rest of the world. Given the extraordinary importance and potential consequences of American nuclear weapons policies and the massive increases in primary documents available to researchers, the failure of the American historical profession to support and undertake this work is shameful.

Challenges of Writing Nuclear History

What would a comprehensive history of U.S. nuclear weapons policy and its role in grand strategy look like? To be fair, undertaking historical work on nuclear issues is particularly difficult. There are the methodological challenges that are laid out in the next section: assessing historical evidence and making causal claims is difficult when the issues at stake—deterrence, assurance, credibility, and resolve— are unobservable. Speeches and written evidence are often hard to interpret. Top-secret deliberations often reveal American presidents taking contradictory approaches or blowing off steam. U.S. officials' public pronouncements are frequently intended to convey signals to various audiences and may not represent operational policy. Furthermore, the decisions behind nuclear policies and strategies are some of the government's most carefully guarded activities, and access to top-secret documents is heavily restricted. While the situation has improved considerably in recent years, archival materials on nuclear policy are notoriously difficult to declassify, and even when they are released, they are often heavily redacted. With important pieces of evidence unavailable, constructing an all-inclusive, seamless narrative remains enormously challenging.

A larger question looms: What does it mean to talk about nuclear history? The history of nuclear weapons was once told as the history of the Cold War (and the converse is also true). It is now understood that they were not the same. Sometimes nuclear history and Cold War history overlapped, while at other times they moved on independent paths, so much so that it is often hard to determine whether nuclear weapons prevented the bipolar competition from breaking out into war or dangerously exacerbated underlying tensions. A history that conflates Cold War and nuclear dynamics could not, for example, fully explain why the United States cooperated with the Soviet Union to deny their respective allies nuclear weapons.[51] Alliances once ascribed solely to Cold War dynamics, in Europe, the Middle East, and Asia, have not only persisted since that struggle ended but have broadened and deepened in ways that show that nuclear considerations (among other non-Cold War factors) were always at their root. It is essential to disentangle the interconnected but distinct histories of the nuclear age and the geopolitical and ideological rivalry between the superpowers.[52]

The Cold War was not, however, the only powerful historical force interacting with, shaping, and being shaped by nuclear history. Decolonization, whose deep roots in imperialism and resistance date back centuries, had an enormous influence—in many cases, more than the Cold War—on shaping nuclear decisionmaking in Great Britain, France, Israel, South Africa, India, and Pakistan, as well as other states that decided not to acquire the bomb. Other factors, such as regional dynamics and the effects of globalization, influenced American grand strategy and approach to nuclear weapons. Disentangling competing global histories since the end of World War II is a difficult but necessary task when trying to understand how nuclear weapons influence international relations.

There is also the question of periodization and chronology. Is the nuclear age one continuous stream, beginning in August 1945—if not earlier—and continuing to the present? Or are there sharp breaks dictated by key technological advances such as the development of thermonuclear weapons or intercontinental ballistic missiles? Important political events had profound consequences for nuclear history: the emergence of Soviet nuclear parity and the negotiation of major arms-control treaties, the end of the Cold War, and the collapse of the Soviet Union. Is there such a thing as a second nuclear age, and, if so, how is it different from the first? Defining nuclear history and its scope is difficult, and calculating how American grand strategy incorporates and reacts to these shifts even more so.

Competing Histories

The most important historical challenge is reconciling contending and often contradictory narratives that chronicle the past. This is especially true when trying to understand the American experience with the bomb. There are at least four competing histories of how nuclear weapons influenced U.S. grand strategy and vice versa: intellectual, rhetorical, operational, and presidential. Assessing which of these strands is most important, and how they interact with one another, is challenging.

The first strand is the intellectual history of the United States. For many within the security studies community, the most familiar strand is what might be called the "Wizards of Armageddon" story. In this tale, smart strategists, typically civilians from universities and think tanks such as the RAND Corporation, wrestled with and explained to the wider world the new realities created by nuclear weapons. In the process, great thinkers such as Bernard Brodie, Thomas Schelling, and Albert Wohlstetter made sense of "the unthinkable," created modern deterrence theory, transformed U.S. policy and grand strategy, and probably prevented World War III. This history is both familiar and comforting—to the extent that nuclear history can be comforting—because it explains the rise of the field of security studies and provides the intellectual architecture for the ideas behind nuclear peace. Because a key part of the stylized telling is how the wizards transformed American policy (and saved the world!), it also suggests that scholarly ideas matter to policymakers. As Marc Trachtenberg points out, however, analysis by the civilian nuclear strategists often suffered from being both "apolitical in substance" and "ahistorical in method."[53] Bruce Kuklick is even more harsh: The strategists "professed deep understanding" but actually "groped in the dark," and their ideas "had little causal impact."[54] The problem is that, as history, the story of the "Wizards of Armageddon" is, at best, overstated and misleading; at worst, it bears little relation to what actually happened.[55]

The second history is rhetorical. Through speeches and published documents, the United States government has used public declarations to indicate its views on nuclear weapons. Prominent examples include the Eisenhower administration's Secretary of State John Foster Dulles's "massive retaliation" speech given at the Council on Foreign Relations in 1954, Defense Secretary Robert McNamara's University of Michigan commencement address in 1962 laying out the flexible-response doctrine and his 1967 doctrine on missile defense, Nixon administration Defense Secretary James Schlesinger's announcement of a new doctrine in January 1974, and the discussion surrounding President Jimmy Carter's Presidential Directive 59.[56] Understandably, these public declarations are analyzed to better understand the role of nuclear weapons in American grand strategy. Interpreting policy rhetoric is always challenging, however, especially when nuclear strategy is involved. These speeches and documents were often vehicles to send signals to a variety of audiences—domestic, allied, and adversarial—that involved assurance, reassurance, inhibition, and deterrence missions.[57] Cameron notes that American policymakers frequently played a "double game," struggling to "balance the demands of presenting a front of strategic coherence" when, behind the scenes, things were far more complicated and uncertain.[58] Many public missions and messages of nuclear strategy were at cross purposes. For example, "the rhetoric of flexible response . . . was convenient to top U.S. policymakers for reasons that had little to do with enhancing deterrence or winning a nuclear war."[59] Moreover, nuclear rhetoric is often imprecise, unrealistic, and easily drained of meaning.

The third strand is the operational history of the United States and nuclear weapons. The United States devoted enormous resources to develop certain kinds of nuclear weapons systems, deployed in surprising ways and places, as part of often-extraordinary strategies. It is critical to understand what weapons were developed and why, where and how they were deployed and targeted, and in what strategies. This history is closely guarded, but these operational decisions appear to have been driven by a complex brew of technological factors, alliance relations, and geopolitical competition as well as bureaucratic and organization interests and domestic political considerations. The intellectual history, as told by the "Wizards of

Armageddon," and the rhetorical history laid out by political leaders often bears little resemblance to the acquisition, deployment, and use plans developed as core parts of U.S. grand strategy. As the historian David Alan Rosenberg argues, "Nuclear strategy does not, in reality, consist of concepts or even policy statements. It consists of concrete decisions regarding war plans, budgets, forces, and deployments."[60]

The fourth strand of history is both the most important and the most obscure: presidential history. The structure, laws, and customs of war-making in the United States combined with the unique characteristics of nuclear weapons provides the president extraordinary power and singular responsibilities over nuclear weapons.[61] What a president thought about nuclear weapons—whether and under what circumstances he might threaten or even use nuclear weapons—is of fundamental importance. How can scholars get at these beliefs and how they informed decisions?[62] How did such beliefs change over time—both across and within administrations? How did thinking about nuclear use, or avoiding nuclear use, shape particular decisions about larger issues surrounding U.S. foreign policy and grand strategy? Even when the question of using nuclear weapons was not explicit, it no doubt cast a shadow over multiple policies. Understanding and reconstructing this past is extraordinarily difficult.[63] What is one to make, for example, of Nixon's loose rhetoric about nuclear use in private, when his actions and policies often revealed quite careful and responsible considerations? Or Dean Acheson's advice to President John F. Kennedy that he never reveal whether he would use nuclear weapons? As former secretary of defense Robert McNamara told Rosenberg, "Nuclear strategy . . . is determined by the President's views and intentions, not by policy or planning documents, or even force structures. The President alone determines how nuclear war will be fought, by virtue of his position in a highly centralized command and control structure."[64]

Reconstructing America's nuclear past and explaining how it both shaped and was shaped by U.S. grand strategy is a daunting task. It demands integrating all four strands of this history, while deconflicting contradictory elements and assessing what forces and factors are most important. It also requires figuring out how nuclear history interacts with, and is distinct from, other powerful historical forces as varied as regional rivalries, decolonization, and the Cold War. This task is made all the more difficult by the challenges laid out in the next section: Ultimately, the past scholars and analysts are exploring is a history that cannot be observed, analyzed, or measured—the history of thermonuclear war.

Language of Nuclear History

It should not be surprising that neither international relations theory nor history has satisfactorily explained the role of nuclear weapons in American grand strategy. Two reasons for this are baked into the nature of the nuclear enterprise.

First, nuclear weapons present profound and often unsettling moral challenges that can make discussing their role in grand strategy difficult and divisive. It can also cause scholarship to bleed into advocacy. Second, there are profound methodological challenges in trying to understand the role of nuclear weapons. When scholars analyze the role of nuclear weapons in American grand strategy, we are most interested in phenomena that have not occurred, such as thermonuclear war, and policy outcomes that are difficult to observe and measure—such as deterrence, assurance, and resolve—or even to prove operative.

These challenges pull in different directions. Analysts understandably hold strong views about nuclear weapons, which drives them to speak with authority and passion about the role and purpose of the bomb in American grand strategy. Yet many of these deep-seated beliefs are difficult, even impossible, to prove with history or with theory. A debate that should be marked by humility and respect is often polarizing and unproductive.

Talking about the Unthinkable

The moral problem surrounding nuclear weapons is basic and unsettling. How should one speak about and analyze something that is unthinkable—detonating nuclear weapons against another nation? Use of these weapons would be catastrophic. It would reflect a historic failure of policy and, in many cases, would amount to mass murder. Yet the threat to use these weapons in a variety of scenarios—including many that do not involve an attack on the United States or an adversary's use of nuclear weapons—has been the backbone of American grand strategy for decades. The language used to discuss these dilemmas rarely captures the magnitude of nuclear decision-making, and both academic and policy discourse often drift into a world of insider jargon and toothless acronyms that mask the extraordinary potential consequences of this debate. More than thirty years ago, Carol Cohn highlighted "the elaborate use of abstraction and euphemism, of words so bland that they never forced the speaker or enabled the listener to touch the realities of nuclear holocaust that lay behind the words."[65] As Michael Quinlan wisely recommends, "Thinking about nuclear weapons must be constantly on the alert—the more so in the absence of historical experience to anchor and calibrate discussion—to probe behind words and customary expressions so as to recall the underlying realities."[66]

The colorless language used to describe elements of this strategy and the underlying threat of nuclear confrontation that undergirds it—deterrence, credibility, signaling, escalation—is often eerily disconnected from the realities behind the words. Nina Tannenwald observes a "disconnect between how ordinary people" thought about nuclear weapons and how academic deterrence theory discussed these issues. "These game theoretic analyses, I found, had little to say about issues of revulsion and morality."[67] Reid Pauly has termed this "rhetorical evaporation," whereby the words policymakers and scholars use to describe U.S. nuclear policies are drained of meaning.[68] This rhetorical evaporation goes to the heart of a grand strategic problem the United States has faced since the start of the thermonuclear age: The most important goal of American nuclear weapons policy is to guarantee that they are never used. This policy tautology was bound, over time, to undermine the threat needed to project deterrence and arguably has driven the United States to greater and more strenuous actions to demonstrate the credibility of an action no one really believes it would take.

The lack of clarity about language and meaning surrounding the purposes of nuclear weapons has consequences for policy. An October 2016 report by the Center for Strategic and International Studies connected poor morale and dysfunction among American officials responsible for nuclear weapons to the difficulties of clearly communicating what role the bomb served in American grand strategy. Looking over years of nuclear policies, the report pointed out that "a coherent narrative about the fundamental role of U.S. nuclear weapons has not been sufficiently stated and promulgated" to those in the military responsible for nuclear weapons. The report criticized how U.S. nuclear weapons policy "is described in highly sophisticated strategic logic that is not very accessible to the general public or the junior nuclear personnel." It is filled with "concepts and jargon that are not routinely defined and explained" and focuses on "what nuclear weapons will not do," supplemented by "descriptions of decline, reduction, and diminishment."[69] The inability to connect these fearsome weapons to explicit U.S. interests in a convincing manner arguably plays into a culture burdened by accidents and scandal.[70]

The lack of clear language to describe a willingness to do the unthinkable, in order to avoid the unthinkable, is only one challenge. It would be impossible to wrestle with these issues without engaging deep moral considerations, a stance that presents difficulties for a purely "social scientific" approach. The lines between analysis and advocacy are often easily—if understandably—blurred. Robert Jervis admirably has acknowledged that mutual second-strike capabilities may not "have been as secure as I and most others believed" in the 1980s. In May 2018, he explained, "Although I stand behind the arguments I made in *The Illogic of American Nuclear Strategy* and *The Meaning of the Nuclear Revolution*, and believe that they represent a significant scholarly contribution, they were also interventions in a fierce political debate. . . . I was trying to persuade as well as analyze."[71]

This moral and rhetorical challenge is especially pointed for the

United States. One can imagine, for example, a state's using nuclear weapons as a last resort to repel a more powerful enemy that seeks to conquer its territory. The United States, however, fields nuclear weapons to achieve a variety of goals that fall well below the level of existential, including extending deterrence over allies while inhibiting their nuclear ambitions and seeking coercive advantages during crises with adversaries. These goals require more nuclear weapons in far more aggressive strategies than simply deterring invasion or nuclear attack on the American homeland. Relying on such profoundly powerful instruments to achieve less-than-existential goals inevitably generates credibility issues. How believable are American nuclear policies? The United States has worked hard to ameliorate these credibility concerns over the years using a variety of tactics, including diplomacy and consultation with allies, nuclear sharing, developing and deploying counterforce delivery capabilities, and a willingness to use nuclear weapons first, in addition to foreign policy and military commitments that would, in a non-nuclear world, be puzzling at best.*

Given the fundamental role of nuclear weapons in American grand strategy, will these words, commitments, weapons, and strategies remain convincing and credible in years to come? Within decades after the close of World War II—a war of savage conquest and genocide—analysts began to doubt that the United States would use nuclear weapons against a bitter ideological and geopolitical rival committed to its downfall. In today's far different world, marked by relative peace, stability, and the apparent disappearance of war between the great powers, does anyone—ally or foe—know the cir-

---

* Of course, the United States has also tried to demonstrate credibility by fighting wars that otherwise make little geostrategic sense from a narrow, traditional, non-nuclear "self-interest" perspective, such as in Korea in the early 1950s and in Southeast Asia in the 1960s and 1970s. One might ask how U.S. decisionmaking toward limited wars would have proceeded in a world without nuclear weapons, where the demands of credibility would have been, presumably, smaller.

cumstances that would prompt the United States to use nuclear weapons? Does Russia or China believe that the United States would use nuclear weapons in response to an attack on Estonia or Taiwan, for example? How and in what ways will that matter for the future of American grand strategy?

Measuring the Unobservable, Observing the Immeasurable

The second, and bigger, challenge to understanding nuclear weapons and U.S. grand strategy is the methodological conundrum. The most important question surrounding nuclear weapons involves a nonevent: the nonoccurrence of a thermonuclear war. As John Lewis Gaddis pointed out while the Cold War was still ongoing, "Anyone attempting to understand why there has been no third world war confronts a problem not unlike that of Sherlock Holmes and the dog that did not bark in the night: how does one account for something that did not happen?"[72]

The factors that start or prevent thermonuclear war are arguable since such a war has never taken place. Nuclear deterrence and assurance, in all their forms, are ultimately connected to estimates about the causes and likelihood of thermonuclear war that are difficult, if not impossible, to calculate.

Social science relies on observations and measurements to identify patterns and causal paths to generate theories that drive predictions and inform policies. History requires accumulating, sorting, and making sense of evidence about things that happen in the world. How does one generate reliable theories, histories, and policy recommendations about phenomena for which there are few or no observations or measurements? Analysts have used a variety of plausible proxies, such as how nuclear weapons affect state behavior, both in normal circumstances and crises, but the insights of such approaches have limits. It is hard enough for scholars to find consensus on things that actually happened, such as the origins of World War I.[73] Developing a consensus about a nonevent one cannot observe, measure, or assess is obviously harder.

This challenge plagues any assessment of the U.S. nuclear posture and its role in grand strategy. Desired outcomes such as deterrence, extended deterrence, assurance, reassurance, and credibility are elusive and can be proved only ex post, if at all. As Quinlan notes, "We have no further empirical data about how events may run if nuclear weapons are used, or if nuclear powers come seriously to blows with one another without such use."[74] Even if deterrence and credibility could, somehow, be observed and measured, they are characteristics and phenomena driven by intangible qualities such as fear, uncertainty, and resolve. These psychological factors depend far more on context and circumstance than the material factors that make up much of international politics. Furthermore, these are human characteristics, and it is unclear how to aggregate such feelings from the level of individuals to the policies and behaviors of institutions and states. These challenges affect understanding of other important nuclear behavior, such as why states that our theories would have expected to develop nuclear weapons—a wide-ranging group that might include Australia, Brazil, Egypt, Indonesia, Japan, Sweden, Switzerland, and Yugoslavia—never developed the bomb. Decisions against doing things—not to detonate a nuclear device during a war, not to acquire nuclear weapons—are difficult to fully assess.[75]

Even though many of these phenomena are elusive, analysts intuit that nuclear weapons cast a powerful shadow over foreign policy and grand strategy. Nuclear weapons obviously matter enormously, even if precisely how cannot always be demonstrated. Consider the heated controversy over whether and how nuclear superiority—if it could be properly measured—is important to outcomes in the world. Perhaps the best that can be done is to acknowledge, as Philip Zelikow writes, that "U.S. nuclear superiority mattered. And, at some level, it also didn't. At times both of these propositions were, at one and the same time, true."[76]

These challenges—linguistic, moral, and methodological—should not prevent the development of rigorous theories and histories of nuclear weapons and American grand strategy. If anything, they invite working harder to surface underlying assumptions and rigorous examination of both the deductive and inductive foundations of these arguments. What is most important here is to better recognize the challenges and barriers to certainty and proceed with humility in the face of daunting questions that have profound policy consequences. As Quinlan notes, the "limitation in our knowledge ought to instill in all who make predictive statements about these issues a degree of humility not always evident."[77] American grand strategy with nuclear weapons is based on a variety of deeply held assumptions that have rarely been tested and are difficult to prove.

Our Uncertain Nuclear Future

The incomplete understanding of nuclear history and dynamics has consequences for present and future American grand strategy. If these theories and histories are problematic or questionable, it may affect how nuclear policies and grand strategies that are chosen in the future are evaluated. Even if little changed in the contemporary nuclear landscape, it is critical to have a far better, more comprehensive understanding of the past. The circumstances and environment in which nuclear decisions are made will change enormously in the years to come. Four trends stand to be especially consequential.

The Return of Geopolitics

The first trend is geopolitical. World politics is changing in at least three ways that might influence how nuclear weapons and U.S. grand strategy interact.

First, the structure of world politics has shifted from bipolarity during the Cold War to unipolarity in the years since the demise of the Soviet Union to the possible emergence of multipolarity or even, as Richard Haass has dubbed it, nonpolarity.[78] Contemporary analysts and decisionmakers have no experience with nuclear dynamics in such a transformed international system. Will states increase their desire for and efforts to acquire the bomb? Would states be more willing to threaten and even use nuclear weapons in a postbipolar and postunipolar world?

This relates to the second change: the increased geopolitical assertiveness of America's primary nuclear-armed competitors, China and Russia.[79] Both countries are modernizing their nuclear forces (albeit at different paces and in different ways), and both have made efforts to reexamine their nuclear doctrines. There are dangerous scenarios—such as a crisis over Taiwan, a clash over disputed territories in the South China Sea, or an attack on a NATO member in the Baltics—in which nuclear weapons might plausibly be engaged, either on purpose or inadvertently.

Third, U.S. allies and adversaries, as well as neutral countries, will continue to make their own choices about nuclear capabilities based in part on their beliefs about the role of nuclear weapons in American grand strategy. This can take many forms. Changes in the international environment or American grand strategy, perceptions of declining U.S. credibility or power, intensifying regional rivalries, or technological developments might contribute to shifts in the global nuclear landscape. The use of nuclear weapons by regional adversaries—India and Pakistan, for example—might entangle the United States and its nuclear forces in unforeseen and unwelcome ways. Smaller, arguably less responsible countries such as North Korea or Iran could expand their nuclear programs. Geopolitical shifts are taking place today under a U.S. administration whose policies on nuclear weapons and grand strategies can most generously be described as erratic; meanwhile, America's role in the world, regardless of who is in the White House, is uncertain.

Brave New World

The second trend affecting nuclear weapons and American grand strategy is technological. As Keir Lieber and Daryl Press argue, "Changes in technology . . . are eroding the foundations of nuclear deterrence."[80] Three forces in particular are expected to have important consequences for nuclear weapons' role in American grand strategy: changes in nuclear technology and the systems that support nuclear weapons; emerging technologies such as cyber and artificial intelligence; and the blurring of the once-stark line between nuclear and non-nuclear capabilities.

Changes in nuclear technology will continue to have profound consequences for American grand strategy. The nuclear revolution school often portrays the bomb in a binary fashion: as a technology that, once achieved, needs little change or improvement. In this thinking, what matters is whether or not one possesses a bomb, not what kind one has, where it is held, or how it is delivered or supported. Analysts often forget, however, three crucial characteristics about nuclear weapons. One, as Michael Horowitz has written, "Nuclear weapons and missiles are relatively old technologies," within the reach of many if not most modern states.[81] Two, nuclear weapons are not a static technology but one that has changed and will continue to shift over time. Finally, nuclear bombs are only one aspect of the technology that affects American grand strategy. Enormous changes to intelligence, surveillance, and reconnaissance; command, control, and communications; and the capabilities to deliver nuclear bombs have had and will continue to have profound consequences for nuclear strategy and statecraft. As Lieber and Press point out, synergistic revolutions in computing power and remote sensing make nuclear forces "far more vulnerable than before."[82]

These changes will intensify in the decades to come. The United States has committed to spending more than $1 trillion on modernizing its capabilities over the next thirty years—a remarkable commitment in a time of competing demands. Much of this modernization, moreover, focuses on advancing characteristics—accuracy, speed, stealth, and miniaturization—that could make nuclear weapons appear more usable in a crisis. This massive, multidecade investment began during the previous U.S. administration, despite being seemingly at odds with President Barack Obama's 2009 pledge "to seek the peace and security of a world without nuclear weapons."[83]

In addition, technologies are emerging that may influence and potentially shape the future nuclear environment. Cyber and artificial intelligence, robotics, unmanned aerial vehicles, hypersonic and directed energy, nanotechnology, and as-yet-undeveloped technologies will have unknown effects. A recent RAND study, for example, warned that "artificial intelligence (AI) might portend new capabilities that could spur arms races or increase the likelihood of states escalating to nuclear use—either intentionally or accidentally—during a crisis."[84] Cyber capabilities present similar challenges. As a recent Chatham House report explained, "During peacetime, offensive cyber activities would create a dilemma for a state as it may not know whether its systems have been the subject of a cyberattack. This unknown could have implications for military decisionmaking, particularly for decisions affecting nuclear weapons deterrence policies. At times of heightened tension, cyberattacks on nuclear weapons systems could cause an escalation, which results in their use."[85] These capabilities would have direct bearing on the role and use of nuclear weapons in American grand strategy.

Meanwhile, the United States has already developed impressive non-nuclear and nonkinetic weapons capable of carrying out missions that were once the sole provenance of the bomb, including holding an adversary's nuclear capabilities at risk. This shift has the potential to blur the line between conventional and nuclear war. As Rovner points out, there is an increasing worry that "inadvertent escalation may occur when conventional attacks put the adversary's nuclear force at risk."[86] Caitlin Talmadge argues that American military action could easily be misunderstood by China as a direct threat to its retaliatory capabilities, and so "Chinese nuclear escalation in the event of a conventional war with the United States is a significant risk."[87] New technologies, combined with how the United States has prosecuted its recent wars, may leave a nuclear adversary uncertain as to whether its nuclear forces are being targeted for elimination, possibly inciting "use it or lose it" pressures. Michael Kofman controversially suggests that "the Pentagon remains wholly committed to the fantasy of having conventional wars with nuclear states, where they will let us win, accepting defeat without a nuclear exchange."[88]

How should one think about conventional capabilities, or nonkinetic tools, that potentially blunt or eliminate a country's ability to use its nuclear weapons? How to define and respond to a cyberattack that undermines a country's secure deterrent yet did not kill or injure a single person? Much existing analysis of the role of nuclear weapons assumes a stark divide between nuclear and non-nuclear conflict, a distinction that may become dangerously cloudy over time. According to Andrew Krepinevich, "The firebreak between conventional and nuclear war is slowly disappearing."[89] As a recent study explains,

> The future of nuclear deterrence is complicated further by the proliferation of conventional military technologies that may undermine traditional modes of escalation management, and as a consequence, nuclear stability. Much attention has already been given to the possible effects of several such technologies, to include stealthy unattended ground sensors, uninhabited aerial vehicles, micro-satellites, and ballistic missile defenses. Comparatively little attention, however, has been given to the possible implications of autonomous systems and artificial intelligence for nuclear stability.[90]

James Acton perceptively notes that the "emerging interactions between nuclear and nonnuclear weapons . . . may prove to be a defining risk of the current nuclear age."[91]

Changing Global Norms

The third trend is global public opinion. While the major nuclear powers are modernizing their forces, much of the rest of the world has been clamoring for a reduction—indeed elimination—of nuclear weapons. As Nina Tannenwald explains in her magisterial study, *The Nuclear Taboo*, outside of the nuclear powers, "Nuclear deterrence has not been viewed as a legitimate practice for most of the other states of the world."[92]

This is not new. Since the start of the nuclear age, many non-state actors and governments have lobbied fiercely for nuclear reductions and disarmament. Nearly three decades after the Cold War ended, however, much of the non-nuclear world questions why more progress has not been made toward ridding the world of the bomb. As Heather Williams and Patricia Lewis make clear, "Civil society groups and the majority of states have not yet given up on nuclear disarmament."[93] Pope Francis has declared that "nuclear deterrence and the threat of mutually assured destruction cannot be the basis for an ethics of fraternity and peaceful coexistence among peoples and states."[94] In 2017 the U.N. General Assembly passed a treaty prohibiting nuclear weapons. This emerged in large part from the popular global campaign to highlight the humanitarian impact of nuclear weapons. Conversations about nuclear weapons take a much different form in Sydney, Rio de Janeiro, Cape Town, Vienna, and Washington, DC.

It is hard to assess how and to what extent emerging global norms will shape U.S. policies in the years to come. Tannenwald has identified the power of the nuclear taboo on state behavior, and John Mueller has highlighted the rise of powerful norms on issues such as slavery and dueling that could eventually affect not simply nuclear use but also nuclear possession. Norms and public opinion may not be determinative, but they also cannot be ignored. Tannenwald's work suggests that even in states with nuclear weapons, "national leaders do take the notion of world opinion seriously."[95] There may come a time when the majority of the world sees mere possession of nuclear weapons, let alone use of them, as wrongheaded and immoral.

Credibility of Nuclear Threats

A fourth trend involves the consequences for American grand strategy of the decreasing credibility of threats of nuclear use that undergird nuclear deterrence. Short of a bolt-from-the-blue nuclear attack by an adversary—and possibly even then—how does one evaluate and assess the credibility of U.S. threats to use nuclear weapons? The probability of an invasion of the United States has not increased. The credibility issues surrounding U.S. nuclear guarantees to allies—a deep challenge even during the Cold War—may increase over time. Tannenwald captures this dynamic well:

> Even though US leaders came to believe that nuclear weapons should not really be used, they were not willing to give up nuclear *deterrence*. But they were caught in the paradox recognized early on by nuclear strategists: making deterrence credible (especially in the face of the threat of mutual assured destruction) required convincing the

adversary that the United States would actually use such weapons. As such threats became less credible over time for both deterrence and normative reasons, more numerous and more elaborate strategies were sought in an effort to bolster credibility.[96]

There is conflicting evidence about Americans' willingness to support the use of nuclear weapons. A report chaired by the former commander of America's strategic nuclear forces posited that "there is no conceivable situation in the contemporary world" where it would be in either Russia's or the United States' "national security interest to initiate a nuclear attack against the other side."[97] Important studies suggest that Americans would support nuclear use under certain circumstances,[98] while other evidence suggests that in simulated crises it has always been difficult to get approval to use nuclear weapons.[99] If elite war games designed and played by Thomas Schelling, Henry Kissinger, and others in the 1960s found it extremely difficult to get players to initiate a nuclear war, even when the games were rigged to make nuclear use easier, how likely are scholars today to get anyone to think about using nuclear weapons? That nuclear use is becoming increasingly unthinkable is obviously a good thing. If the bomb is unusable, however, an American grand strategy that relies heavily on nuclear weapons to achieve many of its key missions may be increasingly untenable.

Collectively, these trends should make understanding the role of nuclear weapons in U.S. grand strategy even more difficult in the years to come—and more critical.

Resisting the Revolution, or Revolution à la Carte

Why is a grand strategic lens the best way to understand nuclear weapons and their consequences, especially in the case of the United States? And how best to understand the role and purpose of nuclear weapons in American grand strategy?

There are two criticisms of using a grand strategic approach to America's nuclear weapons policies. First, some are skeptical of the concept of grand strategy, arguing that it falsely conveys a picture of policy coherence.[100] The lack of coherence marks U.S. policy in particular.[101] Second, many believe the transformative power of nuclear weapons reduces and even eliminates the choices that leaders and states can make. The power of nuclear deterrence and the reality of mutual vulnerability remove many of the grand strategic options and maneuvers available to states in nuclear competition, tying the hands of leaders.

While there is some merit to these critiques, they are not ultimately convincing. Although it is unable to overcome all of the methodological, linguistic, and normative challenges surrounding nuclear behavior, grand strategy does recognize an obvious but often overlooked point: that nuclear weapons are, first and foremost, tools for states to accomplish their goals in the world. These goals, and the capabilities to achieve them, vary significantly across time, countries, leaders, and circumstance. A grand strategic frame best captures such variance, as well as the radical uncertainty, risk profiles, trade-offs, moral challenges, and unintended consequences that policymakers face when deciding about an unknowable future.[102] Grand strategy recognizes the "crucible of uncertainty and risk" where decisions are made.[103]

What insights might a grand strategic lens provide about the role of nuclear weapons in U.S. policies? Considered broadly, the most important observation is that the United States never fully accepted the consequences of the nuclear revolution. In fact, the United States has, from the start of the nuclear age, worked eagerly to resist and overcome many of the revolutionary consequences of the bomb. It has done so with one overriding goal: to escape vulnerability, to the extent possible, and to obtain and maintain the greatest freedom of action it could to pursue its grand strategic interests in the world.[104]

This should not surprise anyone. Since 1945, the United States has been the leading power in the international system, at times possessing conventional military, economic, and cultural-ideological capabilities far in excess of any other state. Creating strategic stability, maintaining the international status quo, and avoiding war were not the only goals of American grand strategy since 1945, nor were they always the most important objectives. Many times, the United States wanted to avoid being deterred and constrained by the bomb.[105]

Nuclear deterrence looks one way to a status quo, medium-size state that lacks global ambitions and whose primary concern is to avoid being invaded, conquered, or intimidated. It looks quite different to the most powerful state in the system, one facing no risk of invasion or conquest and whose conventional military and economic strength, absent nuclear deterrence, would allow it great freedom of action (and far less vulnerability) in the world. It is natural that the United States would seek to resist deterrence and get around the constrictions the bomb effectively places on its freedom of action.

It was not always obvious, however, how this extremely ambitious goal could be achieved. American policymakers faced fateful choices, and few actions were preordained. In the years after World War II, for example, American leaders could have invested their enormous political capital in pursuing nuclear disarmament or international control of the bomb.[106] At the other extreme, the United States might have launched preventive attacks against the Soviet Union and its nascent nuclear capabilities, while threatening to do the same to any other country that attempted to develop nuclear weapons.[107]

Both options were at least discussed and ultimately dismissed. In later years, American leaders could have developed policies that relied less on extended nuclear deterrence by building up conventional forces that matched those of the Soviet Union in Central Europe. Or U.S. policymakers might have encouraged Western European and Asian allies to acquire and develop their own nuclear capabilities, which would have guaranteed their security without an expensive American military commitment that exposed the United States to attack. During the 1970s and 1980s, the United States could have abandoned arms-control efforts and engaged in a quantitative arms race with the Soviet Union; or American presidents might have avoided massive investments in qualitative improvements in nuclear capabilities and simply embraced parity and mutual vulnerability. These were plausible options available to U.S. presidents for how nuclear weapons would be incorporated into grand strategy. How were these choices made, and how should the alternatives be evaluated? This question should be the focus of renewed research by historians and international relations scholars attempting to understand and evaluate America's choices with the bomb.

While one purpose of America's grand strategy is to overcome the constraints of nuclear deterrence, this goal was pursued in ways that often appear to be in tension, even contradiction, with each other. At times, U.S. leaders pursued what might be labeled "nuclear activism"—the idea that nuclear weapons are crucial instruments of statecraft and that advantages in capabilities versus adversaries were both achievable and would translate into important policy outcomes in the world. This can be seen in America's persistent and expensive efforts over the past eight decades to develop and deploy sophisticated nuclear systems in forward-leaning strategies on behalf of expansive grand missions such as extended deterrence. It can also be seen in the extraordinary U.S. efforts to prevent other states from acquiring nuclear weapons.

At other times, the U.S. government advocated forms of what could be called "nuclear abstinence." Strategic stability, mutual vulnerability, and both vertical and horizontal arms control were actively encouraged. The United States went further at points, denigrating the political utility of nuclear weapons and suggesting that the burdens, costs, and dangers of the bomb were not worth its benefits and that the world might be better off free of all nuclear weapons. For much of its nuclear history, however, the United States has put forward both nuclear activism and abstinence, as it does when it seeks strategic nuclear advantages to limit the spread of nuclear weapons to its friends and allies. What explains this apparent contradiction?

Perhaps the best way to understand these tensions and contradictions—seeking both nuclear primacy and nonproliferation, embracing the first use of nuclear weapons while advocating a world free of them—is to imagine American policymaking as akin to the choice of a switch-hitter in baseball, deciding whether to bat right-handed or left-handed. In the end, it simply chooses the side that offers the best chance for success, defined as reducing U.S. vulnerability and increasing its freedom of action in the world.

Sometimes, the choice of whether to bat left or right is obvious; but it has not always been clear which side—nuclear activism or abstinence—would provide the best outcomes for the United States. On the one hand, nuclear weapons provided American leaders with certain advantages. The United States developed nuclear weapons first, and for most of the nuclear age it has possessed superiority, often enormous superiority, in qualitative capabilities—if not always quantity—over any of its competitors, an advantage that is likely to persist. Nuclear weapons have, arguably, allowed the United States to pursue strategies that may have otherwise been too difficult or expensive, such as the defense of Western Europe against the Soviet Union's large and close armies after World War II. On the other hand, the risks of a nuclearized environment are terrifying. In an international system based on deterrence, the bomb could be used by others to constrain the United States and dilute the effect of other forms of American power. As Jervis points out, "One could argue that it is only nuclear weapons that stand between the US and world domination, at least as far as the use and threat of force are concerned."[108]

The United States, obviously, does not reject every aspect of the nuclear revolution. After almost fifty years of murderous conflict and world war during the first half of the twentieth century, the stabilizing and peace-inducing qualities of nuclear deterrence were no doubt welcome, by American leaders and others. Rather, American policymakers often reject and try to overcome those aspects of nuclear weapons power that they do not like while maintaining those that advance their interests. Through nuclear activism and abstinence and everything in between, the United States takes an à la carte view of the nuclear revolution.

Did these choices make for wise grand strategy? It is difficult to identify and assess the causal effects of nuclear weapons on important outcomes in American foreign policy and world politics. Answering these and similar questions requires engaging counterfactual reasoning and at the same time making assumptions about the purpose and effects of nuclear weapons.[109] These conjectures are almost impossible to test and verify. Perhaps great-power war would have decreased, if not disappeared, in a non-nuclear world, driven out by the increased lethality of war, demographics and interdependence, or shifting norms.[110] Maybe in a non-nuclear world, Berlin's political status would have been easily resolved or would have been the cause of a third world war.[111] Perhaps it was the expense of the arms race that accelerated Soviet decline, or perhaps the communist state would have collapsed from its internal rot regardless of what nuclear weapons system or strategies the United States did or did not deploy. In a postwar world with a less engaged, more restrained United States, more independent nuclear-weapons states may have emerged, with uncertain consequences.

The nuclear revolution, and America's responses to it, also may have transformed other elements of U.S. grand strategy in ways that are underappreciated. The power of nuclear deterrence and the dangers of escalation in the nuclear age may have shifted by who, how, and for how long the United States has been prepared to fight with conventional weapons. American leaders have been obsessed with demonstrating resolve and credibility since 1945, including pursuing military action in areas of the world where it was difficult to identify vital U.S. interests. Would the United States invest blood and treasure in Southeast Asia, for example, in a world without nuclear weapons? Would it still have fought two costly wars in Iraq? Even where nuclear weapons are not explicitly engaged, they cast a long shadow over grand strategic decisions.

Even with all these caveats, and recognizing numerous self-inflicted wounds and disastrous military interventions, one can imagine grand strategic choices surrounding nuclear weapons with far worse outcomes. After all, the United States prevailed in its Cold War struggle against the Soviet Union without a nuclear exchange or great-power war. It maintains extraordinary power and influence in a world where the streak of nuclear nonuse has continued and where, despite dire predictions to the contrary, the number of nuclear-weapons states remains in the single digits. It is not hard to construct plausible alternative histories with far graver outcomes. That said, it is right to ask whether the United States' heavy reliance on the bomb in its grand strategy has outlived its utility.

Conclusion

The cover of a recent *Foreign Affairs* asks, "Do nuclear weapons matter?" As the introduction to the issue explained, nuclear weapons "are purchased, deployed, and discussed on separate tracks from the rest of the foreign policy agenda, and they are largely ignored, with little apparent consequence."[112] This chapter makes clear that this lack of scrutiny courts trouble. There is much we do not know about the purpose and effects of America's nuclear posture, and much of what we think we know deserves rigorous interrogation. Without a doubt, many other pressing and significant issues confront American policymakers, world leaders, and scholars. Nevertheless, no discussion or debate about United States grand strategy—to say nothing of the future prospects for and the shape of world order—can proceed without coming to terms with the nuclear question. As Beatrice Fihn has pointed out, "If there's nuclear war, there's no other agenda to talk about."[113]

What is the future role of nuclear weapons in American grand strategy? Significant changes in technology, geopolitics, and global public opinion present American decisionmakers with crucial questions. Should the United States continue to rely heavily on nuclear weapons to underwrite grand strategic missions beyond defending the homeland? Will the United States be forced to overcome its credibility gap by continuing to massively invest in capabilities and postures, nuclear and non-nuclear, that decrease American vulnerability to nuclear attack while increasing U.S. abilities to preempt threats? Or should the United States encourage nuclear abstinence in an effort to remove the constraining effects on its own freedom of action while inhibiting new, independent nuclear programs? Will other capabilities—conventional, space, or cyber—augment or replace the role of nuclear weapons? In all likelihood, the answer will continue to be "all of the above," as American grand strategy retains its confusing, frustrating balance between relying heavily on nuclear deterrence and trying mightily to overcome its constraints.

In shaking our complacency about American grand strategy and the bomb, we need a vigorous debate and discussion that interrogates many of our deeply held assumptions and convictions. For example, perhaps it is worth considering whether a grand strategy that seeks a world with fewer nuclear weapons, or even none at all, might advance U.S. interests the most. Can the United States find a way to retain the advantages that nuclear weapons have provided in the past, while limiting and even eliminating the challenges of a grand strategy centered on the bomb in the future? As far-fetched as that may seem, the United States has long reveled in opposing constraints imposed from the outside while pushing its own revolutionary ideas on the world. Few could have predicted that the United States would have resisted the nuclear revolution as successfully as it has. Might a far-sighted United States grand strategy accomplish what is often seen as both impossible and irresponsible: eliminating the role of nuclear weapons in international relations while advancing American interests in the world?

NOTES

CHAPTER ONE

1. As discussed in chapter 7, this volume.

2. Scott D. Sagan, "Two Renaissances in Nuclear Security Studies," paper prepared for H-Diplo/ISSF Forum, "What We Talk about When We Talk about Nuclear Weapons," Stanford University, June 15, 2014. The entire forum is available at http://issforum.org/ISSF/PDF/ISSF-Forum-2.pdf.

3. For a summary of the work in political science, albeit reflecting the author's preferences, see Jacques E. C. Hymans, "No Cause for Panic: Key Lessons from the Political Science Literature on Nuclear Proliferation," *International Journal* 69, no. 1 (2014), 85–93.

4. What follows is a small sample of the new research on national nuclear programs, much of it supported by the pathbreaking Nuclear Proliferation International History Project (NPIHP) at the Woodrow Wilson International Center for Scholars (www.wilsoncenter.org/program/nuclear-proliferation-international-history-project). On Australia, see Christine M. Leah, *Australia and the Bomb* (New York: Palgrave Macmillan, 2014); on Brazil, see Carlo Patti, "Origins and Evolution of the Brazilian Nuclear Program (1947–2011)," NPIHP, November 15, 2012; on Israel, see Avner Cohen, *The Worst-Kept Secret: Israel's Bargain with the Bomb* (Columbia University Press, 2013); on Italy, see Leopoldo Nuti, "Italy's Nuclear Choices," *UNISCI Discussion Papers*, no. 25 (2011), 167–81; on Japan, see Fintan Hoey Sato, *America and*

the Cold War: U.S.-Japanese Relations, 1964–1972 (New York: Palgrave Macmillan, 2015); on Pakistan, see Feroz Khan, *Eating Grass: The Making of the Pakistani Bomb* (Stanford University Press, 2012); on Romania, see Eliza Gheorghe, "Atomic Maverick: Romania's Negotiations for Nuclear Technology, 1964–1970," *Cold War History* 13, no. 2 (2013), 373–92; on South Korea, see Se Young Jang, "Dealing with Allies' Nuclear Ambitions: U.S. Nuclear Non-Proliferation Policy towards South Korea and Taiwan, 1969–1981," Ph.D. dissertation, Graduate Institute of International and Development Studies, 2015; on Sweden, see Thomas Jonter, "The Swedish Plans to Acquire Nuclear Weapons, 1945–1968: An Analysis of the Technical Preparations," *Science and Global Security* 18, no. 2 (2010), 61–86; on West Germany, see Andreas Lutsch, "The Persistent Legacy: Germany's Place in the Nuclear Order," Working Paper 5, NPIHP, May 2015.

5. On hedging and nuclear reversal, see Ariel E. Levite, "Never Say Never Again: Nuclear Reversal Revisited," *International Security* 27, no. 3 (2002), 59–88; for recessed deterrence, see Ashley Tellis, *India's Emerging Nuclear Posture between Recessed Deterrent and Ready Arsenal* (Santa Monica, CA: RAND, 2001); on nuclear threshold states, see Maria Rost Rublee, "The Nuclear Threshold States: Challenges and Opportunities Posed by Brazil and Japan," *Nonproliferation Review* 17, no. 1 (2010); on opacity, see Avner Cohen and Marvin Miller, "Bringing Israel's Bomb Out of the Basement," *Foreign Affairs* 89, no. 5 (2010), 31; on latency, see Scott Sagan, "Nuclear Latency and Nuclear Proliferation," in *Forecasting Nuclear Proliferation in the 21st Century,* edited by William C. Potter and Gaukhar Mukhatzhanova (Stanford University Press, 2010).

6. Francis J. Gavin, "Strategies of Inhibition: U.S. Grand Strategy, the Nuclear Revolution, and Nonproliferation," *International Security* 40, no. 1 (2015), 9–46.

7. Elisabeth Roehrlich, "The Cold War, the Developing World, and the Creation of the International Atomic Energy Agency (IAEA), 1953–1957," *Cold War History* 16, no. 2 (2016), 195–212.

8. As Steve Walt notes, one reason is that there has not been much new to say about the subject; "the essential features of deterrence theory are well established by now, and the infeasibility of any sort of nuclear war seems to be pretty well understood (at least let's hope so)." Stephen M. Walt, "A Renaissance in Nuclear Security Studies?," *Foreign Policy,* January 21, 2010 (http://foreignpolicy.com/2010/01/21/a-renaissance-in-nuclear-security-studies/). This belief in the infeasibility of nuclear war has come into doubt in recent years, in part because of statements and policies of the Donald Trump administration. For a fascinating look into the questions surrounding an order to use nuclear

weapons by an American president, see Alex Wellerstein and Avner Cohen, "If a President Wants to Use Nuclear Weapons, Whether It's 'Legal' Won't Matter," *Washington Post*, November 22, 2017.

9. For my take on the failings of the most widely read and influential work on nuclear proliferation and nonproliferation, the debate between Scott Sagan and Kenneth Waltz, see Francis J. Gavin, "Politics, History, and the Ivory Tower–Policy Gap in the Nuclear Proliferation Debate," *Journal of Strategic Studies* 35, no. 4 (2012), 573–600. For my critique of quantitative work on nuclear studies, see Francis J. Gavin, "What We Talk about When We Talk about Nuclear Weapons: A Review Essay H-Diplo/ISSF Forum, June 15, 2014 (http://issforum.org/ISSF/PDF/ISSF-Forum-2.pdf); and Francis J. Gavin, "What We Do, and Why It Matters: A Response to FKS," Response to Forum, no. 2 (2014) (http://issforum.org/ISSF/PDF/ISSF-Forum-2-Response.pdf).

10. For an effort to overcome these challenges and apply historical work to aid policymakers, especially on nuclear issues, see Francis J. Gavin and James B. Steinberg, "Mind the Gap: Why Policymakers and Scholars Ignore Each Other, and What Can Be Done about It?," *Carnegie Reporter* 6, no. 4 (2012) (http://teaching-national-security-law.insct.org/wp-content/uploads/2012/07/Carnegie-Corporation-of-New-York%C2%A0Mind-the-Gap.pdf).

11. William H. McNeill, *The Pursuit of Power: Technology, Armed Force, and Society since A.D. 1000* (University of Chicago Press, 1982). See also Charles Tilly, *Coercion, Capital, and European States: AD 990–1992* (Cambridge: Wiley-Blackwell, 1992).

12. Paul Fussell, *Thank God for the Atom Bomb and Other Essays* (New York: Summit, 1990).

13. Russell F. Weigley, *The American Way of War: A History of United States Military Strategy and Policy* (Indiana University Press, 1960).

14. Gavin, "Strategies of Inhibition"; see also Marc Trachtenberg, "The Nuclearization of NATO and U.S.–West European Relations," in *History and Strategy*, edited by Marc Trachtenberg (Princeton University Press, 1991), 153–68.

15. John Lewis Gaddis, "The Long Peace: Elements of Stability in the Postwar International System," *International Security* 10, no. 4 (1986), 99–142.

16. For a good overview of some of this work, see Erik Gatzke and Matthew Kroenig, "Nukes with Numbers: Empirical Research on the Consequences of Nuclear Weapons for International Conflict," *Annual Review of Political Science* 19 (2016): 397–412.

17. Steven E. Miller and Scott D. Sagan, "Nuclear Power without Nuclear Proliferation?," *Daedalus* 138, no. 4 (2009), 7–18.

18. John Lewis Gaddis, "The Long Peace: Elements of Stability in the Postwar International System," *International Security*, 1986, 10, no. 4, 99–142.

19. Eric Schlosser, *Command and Control: Nuclear Weapons, the Damascus Accident, and the Illusion of Safety* (New York: Penguin Press, 2013).

20. On the taboo, see the pathbreaking work of Nina Tannenwald, *The Nuclear Taboo: The United States and the Non-Use of Nuclear Weapons since 1945* (Cambridge University Press, 2007). For a push back against the power of this norm, see Scott D. Sagan and Benjamin A. Valentino, "Revisiting Hiroshima in Iran: What Americans Really Think about Using Nuclear Weapons and Killing Noncombatants," *International Security* 42, no. 1 (2017), 41–79. For an overview of the declaratory policies of different nuclear weapons states, see Ankit Panda, " 'No First Use' and Nuclear Weapons," *Backgrounder,* Council on Foreign Relations, July 17, 2018.

21. For overviews of the academic literature on nuclear proliferation, see Alexandre Debs and Nuno P. Monteiro, "Conflict and Cooperation on Nuclear Nonproliferation," *Annual Review of Political Science* 20, no. 1 (2017), 331–49; Erik Gartzke and Matthew Kroenig, "Nukes with Numbers: Empirical Research on the Consequences of Nuclear Weapons for International Conflict," *Annual Review of Political Science* 19, no. 1 (2016), 397–412; Jacques E. C. Hymans, "Theories of Nuclear Proliferation: The State of the Field," *Nonproliferation Review* 13, no. 1 (2006), 455–65; Alexander Montgomery, and Scott Sagan, "The Perils of Predicting Proliferation," *Journal of Conflict Resolution* 53, no. 2 (2009), 302–28.

22. Francis J. Gavin, *Nuclear Statecraft: History and Strategy in America's Atomic Age* (Cornell University Press, 2012).

23. William Burr, "A Scheme of 'Control': The United States and the Origins of the Nuclear Suppliers' Group, 1974–1976," *International History Review* 36, no. 2 (2014), 252–76.

24. See the articles in "The Origins of the Nuclear Nonproliferation Regime," edited by Roland Popp and Andreas Wenger, special issue, *The International History Review* 36, no. 2 (2014), 195–323; also the articles in "Extended Deterrence in Europe and East Asia during the Cold War: A Reappraisal," edited by Leopoldo Nuti and Christian Ostermann, special issue, *Journal of Strategic Studies* 39, no. 4 (2016).

25. There were differences among them, however, in how many forces had to survive to maintain a credible deterrent and how easy or difficult it was to achieve that goal.

26. A. W. Marshall, *Long-Term Competition with the Soviets: A Framework for Strategic Analysis,* report prepared for the U.S. Air Force Project Rand, R-862-PR, April 1972.

27. Thomas C. Schelling, *Arms and Influence* (Yale University Press, 1966).

28. See, for example, Alex Wellerstein's excellent analysis in his paper, "The

Kyoto Misperception: What Truman Knew, and Didn't Know, about Hiroshima," in *The Age of Hiroshima,* edited by Michael D. Gordin and G. John Ikenberry (Princeton University Press, forthcoming).

29. Daniel J. Sargent, *A Superpower Transformed: The Remaking of American Foreign Relations in the 1970s* (Oxford University Press, 2014).

30. Robert Jervis, *System Effects: Complexity in Political and Social Life* (Princeton University Press, 1997).

31. Bruce Kuklick, *Blind Oracles: Intellectuals and War from Kennan to Kissinger* (Princeton University Press, 2006).

32. David Alan Rosenberg, "The Origins of Overkill: Nuclear Weapons and American Strategy, 1945–1960," *International Security* 7, no. 4 (1983), 3–71.

33. Francis J. Gavin, "NATO's Radical Response to the Nuclear Revolution," in *NATO: Past, Present, and Future*, edited by Ian Shapiro and Adam Tooze (Yale University Press, forthcoming).

34. See especially Justin Vaisse, *Neoconservatism: The Biography of a Movement* (Cambridge: Harvard University Press, 2010).

35. Odd Arne Westad, "The Fall of Détente and the Turning Tides of History," in *The Fall of Détente: Soviet-American Relations during the Carter Years,* edited by Odd Arne Westad (Oslo: Scandinavian University Press, 1997), 15. For further details of the Soviet reaction and the theory that Brezhnev may have allowed the SS-20 deployment to placate a Soviet military angry over SALT I and SALT II negotiations, see David Holloway, "The Dynamics of the Euromissile Crisis, 1977–1983," in *The Euro Missile Crisis and the End of the Cold War*, edited by Leopoldo Nuti, Frédéric Bozo, Marie-Pierre Rey, and Bernd Rother (Washington, DC: Woodrow Wilson Center Press, 2015).

36. See especially *The Crisis of Détente in Europe: From Helsinki to Gorbachev, 1975–1985,* edited by Leopoldo Nuti (New York: Routledge, 2009). On documents relating to the Euromissile crisis, see *The Euromissiles Crisis and the End of the Cold War: 1977–1987,* edited by Timothy McDowell (Washington, DC: Woodrow Wilson International Center for Scholars, 2009).

37. For the idea that obscure debates over nuclear strategies and deployments masked deeper differences in geopolitical outlooks, particularly in the United States, see Francis J. Gavin, "Wrestling with Parity: The Nuclear Revolution Revisited," in *The Shock of the Global: The 1970s in Perspective*, edited by Niall Ferguson and others (Harvard University Press, 2010), 189–204.

38. One example was the Obama administration's effort to apply the principles of distinction and proportionality to nuclear targeting. See the thoughtful essay by Jeffrey G. Lewis and Scott D. Sagan, "The Nuclear Necessity Principle: Making U.S. Targeting Policy Conform with Ethics and the Laws of War," *Daedalus* 145, no. 4 (2016), 62–74.

CHAPTER TWO

1. Scott D. Sagan and Kenneth N. Waltz, *The Spread of Nuclear Weapons: A Debate* (New York: W. W. Norton, 1995).

2. Scott D. Sagan and Kenneth N. Waltz, *The Spread of Nuclear Weapons: A Debate Renewed* (New York: W. W. Norton, 2002).

3. Scott D. Sagan and Kenneth N. Waltz, *The Spread of Nuclear Weapons: An Enduring Debate* (New York: W. W. Norton, 2012).

4. Ibid., 42.

5. Ibid., 43.

6. Scott D. Sagan, "More Will Be Worse," in Scott D. Sagan and Kenneth N. Waltz, *The Spread of Nuclear Weapons: A Debate* (New York: W.W. Norton & Company, 1995), 75.

7. One organization that is doing extraordinary work to identify, declassify, and make accessible declassified documents on nuclear statecraft from around the world is the Nuclear Proliferation International History Project, an effort led by Christian Ostermann and Leopoldo Nuti (www.wilsoncenter.org/program/ npihp). This project is part of the Woodrow Wilson's Cold War International History Project, which has produced countless documents, briefs, and reports on nuclear issues over the past twenty years. Two other notable organizations declassifying and publishing important documents on nuclear statecraft include the Parallel History Project (www.php.isn.ethz.ch/collections/index.cfm) and the National Security Archive (http://www.gwu.edu/~nsarchiv/index.html). Two recent international conferences give just a small sample of the work being done—one hosted by the Nobel Institute in Oscarsborg, Norway, in June 2009 and another hosted by Center for Security Studies in Zurich in June 2010 (www.css.ethz.ch/events/archive/academic_research/Uncovering_Sources_ EN). Each conference brought together more than a dozen scholars using new archival materials to analyze the origins, developments, and consequences of nuclear programs around the world, including those in Pakistan, India, Brazil, Argentina, South Africa, Yugoslavia, and Italy. The papers from the Zurich conference have not yet been published, but some of the papers from the Nobel Conference can be found in *Nuclear Proliferation and International Order: Challenges to the Non-Proliferation Treaty,* edited by Olav Njølstad (New York: Routledge, 2011).

8. Ibid., xi.

9. Marc Trachtenberg, "Review: Waltzing to Armageddon?," *National Interest*, no. 69 (fall 2002), 144–52.

10. Thomas C. Schelling, *Arms and Influence* (Harvard University Press, 1966), 176.

11. Kenneth N. Waltz, *Theory of International Politics* (New York: McGraw-Hill, 1979), 180.

12. Trachtenberg, "Waltzing to Armageddon," 149.

13. Telegram from the Embassy in the Soviet Union to the Department of State, May 24, 1961, *Foreign Relations of the United States [FRUS],* 1961–1963, vol. 14, *The Berlin Crisis, 1961–1962,* edited by Charles S. Sampson and Glenn W. LaFantasie (Washington, DC: U.S. GPO, 1993), Document 24, 67.

14. Sagan and Waltz, *Enduring Debate,* 6.

15. Memorandum of Conversation on Meeting between President Kennedy and Chairman Khrushchev in Vienna, June 4, 1961, *FRUS, 1961–1963,* vol. 5, Soviet Union, edited by Charles S. Sampson, John Michael Joyce, and David S. Patterson (Washington, DC: GPO, 1998), Document 87, 218.

16. Kennedy clearly appreciated the high stakes for the Soviet leader. "Khrushchev is losing East Germany. He cannot let that happen. If East Germany goes, so will Poland and all of Eastern Europe." Frederick Kempe, *Berlin 1961* (New York: Putnam, 2011), 293.

17. Memorandum of Conversation with President Eisenhower and Secretary of State Dulles, November 30, 1958, *FRUS, 1958–1960,* vol. 8, Berlin Crisis, 1958–1960, eds. Charles S. Sampson and Glenn W. LaFantasie (Washington, DC: GPO, 1993), Document 80, 143. At another point, President Eisenhower suggested in a conversation with John Foster Dulles, "We should not have committed ourselves as deeply as we had to Berlin" and that "the situation was basically untenable, as in the case of Quemoy and Matsu." Memorandum of Conversation between President Eisenhower and Secretary of State Dulles, November 18, 1958, *FRUS, 1958–1960,* vol. 8, Berlin Crisis, 1958–1959, Document 47, 85.

18. Kempe, *Berlin 1961,* 220. "God knows I am not an isolationist, but it seems particularly stupid to risk killing a million Americans over an argument about access rights on an Autobahn in the Soviet zone of Germany, or because the Germans want Germany reunified." W. R. Smyser, *Kennedy and the Berlin Wall* (New York: Rowman & Littlefield Publishers, 2009), 75.

19. Quoted in Alexsandr Fursenko and Timothy Naftali, *Khrushchev's Cold War: The Inside Story of an American Adversary* (New York: W. W. Norton, 2007), 243–44.

20. Frederick Taylor, *The Berlin Wall: A World Divided, 1961–1989* (New York: Harper, 2007), 116.

21. Ibid.

22. Ibid., 105.

23. Telegram from the Embassy in the Soviet Union to the Department of State, May 27, 1961, *FRUS, 1961–1963,* vol. 14, Document 28, 77.

24. Position Paper Prepared in the Department of State, "Berlin and Germany," May 25, 1961, *FRUS, 1961–1963*, vol. 14, Document 26, 74.

25. Memorandum from the President's Assistant for National Security Affairs (Kissinger) to President Nixon, January 24, 1969, *FRUS: 1969–1976*, vol. 40, Germany and Berlin, 1969–1972, eds. David C. Geyer and Edward C. Keefer (Washington, DC: GPO, 2008), Document 4, 9.

26. Draft Memorandum of Conversation, Bonn, February 26, 1969, *FRUS, 1969–1976*, vol. 40, Document 16, 44.

27. Telegram from the Mission in Berlin to the Department of State, January 8, 1969, *FRUS, 1969–1976*, vol. 40, Document 2, 5.

28. Editorial Note, March 3, 1969, *FRUS, 1969–1976*, vol. 40, Document 17, 49.

29. Editorial Note, October 22, 1970, *FRUS, 1969–1976*, vol. 40, Documber 129, 377.

30. Memorandum from the President's Assistant for National Security Affairs (Kissinger) to President Nixon, January 25, 1971, *FRUS, 1969–1976*, vol. 40, Document 166, 495.

31. Ibid.

32. Conversation among President Nixon, German Chancellor Brandt, the President's Assistant for National Security Affairs (Kissinger), and the German State Secretary for Foreign, Defense, and German Policy (Bahr), June 15, 1971, *FRUS, 1969–1976*, vol. 40, Document 254, 741–48.

33. M. Taylor Fravel and Evan S. Medeiros, "China's Search for Assured Retaliation: The Evolution of Chinese Nuclear Strategy and Force Structure," *International Security* 35, no. 2 (2010), 48–87.

34. Kier Lieber and Daryl Press, "The End of MAD? The Nuclear Dimension of U.S. Primacy," *International Security* 30, no. 4 (2006), 7–44.

35. See especially Justin Vaïsse, *Neoconservatism: The Biography of a Movement* (Harvard University Press, 2010).

36. Odd Arne Westad, "The Fall of Détente and the Turning Tides of History," in *The Fall of Détente: Soviet-American Relations during the Carter Years*, edited by Odd Arne Westad (Scandinavian University Press, 1997), 15. For further details of the Soviet reaction, and the theory that Brezhnev may have allowed the SS-20 deployment to placate a Soviet military angry over SALT I and SALT II negotiations, see David Holloway, "The Dynamics of the Euromissile Crisis, 1977–1983," in *The Euro Missile Crisis and the End of the Cold War*, edited by Leopoldo Nuti, Frédéric Bozo, Marie-Pierre Rey, and Bernd Rother (Washington, DC: Woodrow Wilson Center Press, 2015).

37. See especially *The Crisis of Détente in Europe: From Helsinki to Gorbachev, 1975–1985,* edited by Leopoldo Nuti (New York: Routledge,

2009). On documents relating to the Euromissile crisis, see "The Euromissiles Crisis and the End of the Cold War: 1977–1987," by Timothy McDowell, the Wilson Center (www.wilsoncenter.org/publication/the-euromissiles-crisis-and-the-end-the-cold-war-1977-1987).

38. For the idea that obscure debates over nuclear strategies and deployments masked deeper differences in geopolitical outlooks, particularly in the United States, see Francis J. Gavin, "Wrestling with Parity: The Nuclear Revolution Revisited," in *The Shock of the Global: The 1970s in Perspective*, edited by Niall Ferguson and others (Harvard University Press, 2010), 189–204.

39. Kenneth N. Waltz, "The Spread of Nuclear Weapons: More May Be Better," *Adelphi Papers*, no. 171 (London: International Institute for Strategic Studies, 1981).

40. Shane Maddock also identifies the persistent U.S. goal of atomic supremacy but ascribes this policy to ideological rather than power-political motives. See Shane J. Maddock, *Nuclear Apartheid: The Quest for Atomic Supremacy from World War II to the Present* (University of North Carolina Press, 2010).

41. Rusk to State Department, August 7, 1963, National Security File, box 187, John F. Kennedy Presidential Library, Boston, MA.

42. See Francis J. Gavin and Mira Rapp-Hooper, "The Copenhagen Temptation: Rethinking Prevention and Proliferation in the Age of Deterrence Dominance," working paper, prepared for Tobin Project conference, "Power through Its Prudent Use," 2010.

43. On West Germany, see Thomas Alan Schwartz, *Lyndon Johnson and Europe: In the Shadow of Vietnam* (Harvard University Press, 2003), and Marc Trachtenberg, *A Constructed Peace: The Making of the European Settlement, 1946–1963* (Princeton University Press, 1999); on Israel, see Avner Cohen, *Israel and the Bomb* (Columbia University Press, 1998); on the desire of many top U.S. policymakers to get the British out of the nuclear business, see Richard Neustadt, *Report to JFK: The Skybolt Crisis in Perspective* (Cornell University Press, 1999).

44. Francis J. Gavin, "Blasts from the Past: Nuclear Proliferation and Rogue States before the Bush Doctrine," *International Security* 29, no. 3 (2004/2005), 110.

45. On Pakistan, see "Congressional Consultation on Pakistan," State Department Cable 235372 to US Embassy, Vienna, 15 September 1978, 3–4, National Security Archive, Pakistan Nuclear Development Collection. On South Korea and Taiwan, see Lewis A. Dunn, "Half Past India's Bang," *Foreign Policy*, no. 36 (Autumn 1979), and Rebecca K. C. Hersmann and Robert Peters, "Nuclear U-Turns: Learning from South Korean and Taiwanese Rollback," *Nonproliferation Review* 13, no. 3 (2006), 547–48.

46. "Arizona Senator's Support Sought for New START Pact," April 20, 2010, Global Security Newswire (www.nti.org/gsn/article/arizona-senators-support-sought-for-new-start-pact/).

47. For three excellent unpublished papers that look at this issue, see Matthew Fuhrmann and Todd S. Sechser, "Signaling Alliance Commitments: Hand-Tying and Sunk Costs in Extended Nuclear Deterrence," paper prepared for the Texas Triangle Security Conference, Austin, Texas, February 2012; Alexander Lanoszka, "Protection States Trust? Superpower Patronage, Nuclear Behavior, and Alliance Dynamics," Princeton University, January 23, 2012; Dan Reiter, "Security Commitments and Nuclear Proliferation," *Foreign Policy Analysis* 10, no. 1 (2014), 61–80. For a terrific article that uses new archival sources to show the link between U.S. extended deterrence and Australia's decision to stay non-nuclear, highlighting the crucial differences between nuclear umbrellas in Asia and Europe, see Christine M. Leah, "U.S. Extended Nuclear Deterrence and Nuclear Order: An Australian Perspective," *Asian Security* 8, no. 2 (2012), 93–114.

48. Gavin, "Blasts from the Past," 115–22.

49. Matthew Kroenig, *Exporting the Bomb: Technology Transfer and the Spread of Nuclear Weapons* (Cornell University Press, 2010) 3.

50. Michael C. Horowitz, *The Diffusion of Military Power: Causes and Consequences for International Politics* (Princeton University Press, 2010), 106.

51. Stanley Kurtz, "Why We Must Invade Iraq," *National Review Online*, September 16, 2002 (www.freerepublic.com/focus/f-news/751583/posts).

52. Richard K. Betts, "Universal Deterrence or Conceptual Collapse? Liberal Pessimism and Utopian Realism," in *The Coming Crisis: Nuclear Proliferation, U.S. Interests, and World Order,* edited by Victor A. Utgoff (MIT Press, 2000), 65. In other words, the international system may prefer Waltz, but the United States—and any system-leading power—will prefer Sagan, albeit for reasons other than those he lays out.

53. Sagan and Waltz, *Enduring Debate*, 100.

54. Ibid., 103.

55. Ibid., 106.

56. Ibid., 224.

57. Ibid., 221.

58. "Les Aspin, when he was chairman of the house [*sic*] Armed Services Committee, put this thought in the following words: 'A world without nuclear weapons would not be disadvantageous to the United States. In fact, a world without nuclear weapons would actually be better. Nuclear weapons are still the big equalizer, but now the United States is not the equalizer but the equilizee.'" Sagan and Waltz, *Enduring Debate*, 107.

59. "In the twenty years dating from 1983, we invaded six of them, beginning and ending with Iraq. Yet since the end of World War II, states with nuclear weapons have never fought one another." Ibid., 220.

60. Francis J. Gavin, "Same As It Ever Was: Nuclear Alarmism, Proliferation, and the Cold War," *International Security* 34, no. 3 (2009/2010), 7–37.

61. Waltz, *Theory of International Politics*, 109.

62. Kenneth N. Waltz, *Man, the State, and War: A Theoretical Analysis* (Columbia University Press, 1959), 238. In this classic work, Waltz identified three frames or "images" through which international politics can be understood: the first individuals, the second the state, and the third the international system. For Waltz, the third image, or the structure of the international system, was the most important variable by which to explain questions of war and peace.

63. Campbell Craig, *Total War in the Realism of Niebuhr, Morgenthau, and Waltz* (Columbia University Press, 2003), 118.

64. Waltz, *Theory of International Politics*, 180.

65. Ibid., 181.

66. Ibid., 182.

67. Craig, *Total War*, 161.

68. I am grateful to Mariana Carpes for this insight, which is the focus of her very promising research project, "Bringing the Region In: A Neoclassical Realist Approach for the Study of Rising Powers Nuclear Strategies."

69. The best study of these questions, which combines policy insight and academic rigor, is Colin H. Kahl, Melissa G. Dalton, and Mathew Irvine, *Risk and Rivalry: Iran, Israel, and the Bomb* (Washington, DC: Center for a New American Security, 2012).

70. For a discussion of the challenges decisionmakers confront weighing risks in the face of radical uncertainty and lamenting how rarely academics capture these factors, see Francis J. Gavin and James B. Steinberg, "Mind the Gap: Why Policymakers and Scholars Ignore Each Other, and What Should De Done about It," *Carnegie Reporter* 6, no. 4 (2012) (http://carnegie.org/publications/carnegie-reporter/single/view/article/item/308/).

71. Kenneth Waltz, "Why Iran Should Get the Bomb," *Foreign Affairs* 91, no. 4 (2012), 2–5.

72. I am grateful to Leopoldo Nuti for explaining this fascinating story to me.

CHAPTER THREE

1. Josh Freedman, "It's Not You, It's Quantitative Cost-Benefit Analysis," *McSweeney's*, February 5, 2013 (www.mcsweeneys.net/articles/its-not-you-its-quantitative-cost-benefit-analysis). See also Jory John, "Nate Silver Offers Up a

Statistical Analysis of Your Failing Relationship," *McSweeney's,* September 26, 2013 (https://www.mcsweeneys.net/articles/nate-silver-offers-up-a-statistical-analysis-of-your-failing-relationship).

2. "When an incorrect statement appears in presidential memoirs, writers go on repeating it year after year and all the political scientists and historians in the country are unable to prevent its continued currency." See George V. Allen to Alexander George, June 4, 1969, Papers of George V. Allen, Correspondence File, 1945–1969, box 1, Harry S. Truman Presidential Library. I am grateful to Brian Muzas for this reference, which comes from his doctoral dissertation, "Sign of Contradiction? Religious Cultural Heritage and the Nuclear Paradox of Truman, Eisenhower, and Reagan," University of Texas at Austin, 2013.

3. For a nice summary of the competing arguments, see Kenneth M. Pollack, *The Persian Puzzle: The Conflict between Iran and America* (New York: Random House, 2004), 44–48, and 440n35. Iran ultimately reneged on its agreement with the Soviet Union.

4. Bernard Brodie, ed., *The Absolute Weapon* (New York: Harcourt, Brace, 1946), 76.

5. Todd S. Sechser and Matthew Fuhrmann, "Crisis Bargaining and Nuclear Blackmail," *International Organizations* 67, no. 1 (2013), 173–95; Matthew Kroenig, "Nuclear Superiority and the Balance of Resolve: Explaining Nuclear Crisis Outcomes," *International Organizations* 67, no. 1 (2013), 141–71.

6. Kroenig, "Nuclear Superiority and the Balance of Resolve," 142.

7. Fuhrmann has written an important book that shows how countries receiving civilian nuclear assistance are more likely to develop a weapons program: see Matthew Fuhrmann, *Atomic Assistance: How "Atoms for Peace" Programs Cause Nuclear Insecurity* (Cornell University Press, 2012). Kroenig's monograph smartly recognizes (in a way most defensive realists do not) that superpowers do not like proliferation because it deters them themselves. See Matthew Kroenig, *Exporting the Bomb: Technology Transfer and the Spread of Nuclear Weapons* (Cornell University Press, 2010).

8. While many qualitative books and articles deal with these issues, the most important and impressive work in this tradition on these questions remains Richard K. Betts, *Nuclear Blackmail and Nuclear Balance* (Washington, DC: Brookings Institution Press, 1987). In addition, see an excellent study based on deep archival work and rigorous theory that focuses on the 1958–1962 period: Daryl G. Press, *Calculating Credibility: How Leaders Assess Military Threats* (Cornell University Press, 2006), 80–141.

9. Sechser and Fuhrmann, "Crisis Bargaining and Nuclear Blackmail," 192; Kroenig, "Nuclear Superiority and the Balance of Resolve," 143.

10. See, for example, the online debate between Kroenig, Sechser, and Fuhrmann beginning with "Debating the Benefits of Nuclear Superiority for Crisis Bargaining, Part I," Duck of Minerva, March 3, 2013 (https://duckofmin erva.com/2013/03/debating-the-benefits-nuclear-superiority-for-crisis-bargain ing-part-i.html).

11. Sechser and Fuhrmann, "Crisis Bargaining and Nuclear Blackmail," 192.

12. Kroenig, "Nuclear Superiority and the Balance of Resolve," 143. Although as Dan Nexon points out, one could argue that Kroenig's scholarship and policy recommendations are in tension; Iran's acquiring a small nuclear force that would be vastly inferior to that of the United States would support a relatively passive policy response, that is, such inferior forces would be useful for deterrence only. See Dan Nexon, "Scholarship and Advocacy: Bomb Iran Edition (Updated)," December 22, 2011 (https://duckofminerva.com/2011/12/scholarship-and-advocacy-bomb-iran.html). Kroenig's policy recommendations on Iran have generated strong critiques. For the original policy piece, see Matthew Kroenig, "Time to Attack Iran: Why a Strike Is the Least Bad Option," *Foreign Affairs* 91, no. 1 (2012), 76–80; 82–86. For the critiques, see, for example, Colin H. Kahl, "Not Time to Attack Iran: Why War Should Be a Last Resort," *Foreign Affairs* 91, no. 2 (2012), 166–73; Paul R. Pillar, "Worst-Casing and Best-Casing Iran," *National Interest*, December 22, 2011 (http://nationalinterest.org/blog/paul -pillar/worst-casing-best-casing-iran-6307); Stephen M. Walt, "The Worst Case for War with Iran," *Foreign Policy*, December 21, 2011 (https://foreign policy.com/2011/12/21/the-worst-case-for-war-with-iran/). Basing his recommendation on the article reviewed here, Kroenig recently criticized President Obama's proposal to further reduce Russian and American strategic nuclear weapons. See "The Case for Overkill—Obama's Wrong: America Does Need Thousands of Nukes," *Foreign Policy*, June 18, 2013 (www.foreignpolicy.com/ articles/2013/06/19/the_case_for_overkill).

13. For a thoughtful critique of the notion of a "hard" or "critical" test, see James Fearon and David Laitin, "Integrating Qualitative and Quantitative Research Methods," in *The Oxford Handbook of Political Methodology*, edited by Janet M. Box-Steffensmeier, Henry E. Brady, and David Collier. (Oxford University Press, 2008).

14. Speech by Soviet Premier Nikita S. Khrushchev at a Soviet-Polish Meeting in Moscow, November 10, 1958, German History in Documents and Images (http://ghdi.ghi-dc.org/sub_document.cfm?document_id=3089).

15. While there are some disagreements over the causes and course of the standoff, most historians see the 1958–1962 period as a singular crisis. "The Cuban Missile Crisis was the climax of the great Berlin crisis of 1958–1962."

Marc Trachtenberg, "The Structure of Great Power Politics, 1963–1975," in *The Cambridge History of the Cold War,* vol. 2, *Crises and Détente,* edited by Melvyn Leffler and Odd Arne Westad (Cambridge University Press, 2010), 483.

16. Marc Trachtenberg, *A Constructed Peace: The Making of the European Settlement, 1945–1963* (Princeton University Press, 1999), 247.

17. McGeorge Bundy, *Danger and Survival: Choices about the Bomb in the First Fifty Years* (New York: Random House, 1988), 358–59.

18. I deal with these puzzles, dilemmas, and contradictions at greater length in "Nuclear Weapons, Statecraft, and the Berlin Crisis, 1958–1962," in Francis J. Gavin, *Nuclear Statecraft: History and Strategy in America's Atomic Age* (Cornell University Press, 2012), 57–74.

19. Telegram from the Embassy in the Soviet Union to the Department of State, May 24, 1961, *Foreign Relations of the United States [FRUS], 1961–1963,* vol. 14, Berlin Crisis, 1961–1962, edited by Charles S. Sampson (Washington, DC: GPO, 1993), Document 24, 67.

20. Frederick Kempe, *Berlin 1961* (New York: Putnam, 2011), 201. It is important to note that similar conversations occurred secretly among officials in both governments as they tried to assess the strategic importance of Berlin to both sides. See Gavin, *Nuclear Statecraft,* 57–59; 62–71.

21. President's Report of His Private Session with Khrushchev, September 27, 1959, *FRUS, 1958–1960,* vol. 9, Berlin Crisis, 1959–1960, Germany, Austria, edited by David M. Baehler and Charles S. Sampson (Washington, DC: GPO, 1993), Document 15, 46.

22. By far the best analysis of the role of nuclear weapons during this period, including the argument that Soviet actions were motivated by fears of a nuclearized Bundeswehr, can be found in Trachtenberg, *A Constructed Peace,* especially 251–351.

23. Alexandr Fursenko and Timothy Naftali, *Khrushchev's Cold War: The Inside Story of an American Adversary* (New York: W. W. Norton, 2006), 220.

24. The fact that not only in public but also in private, each side thought its stakes were higher than those of the other reveals that the public statements were not simply made for bargaining purposes.

25. Fursenko and Naftali, *Khrushchev's Cold War,* 243–44.

26. McGeorge Bundy, cited in Campbell Craig, *Destroying the Village: Eisenhower and Thermonuclear War* (Columbia University Press, 1998), 132.

27. It is not only quantitative models that have difficulty recognizing these subtleties. For a recent formal model that fails to recognize the Kennedy administration was worried that conventional mobilization might signal a weakening of its resolve to use nuclear weapons during a crisis, see Scott Wolford, "Show Restraint, Signaling Resolve: Coalitions, Cooperation, and Crisis Bargaining,"

American Journal of Political Science 58, no. 1 (2014), 144–56, especially 149.

28. For a discussion, based on primary documents and interviews, of the first-strike plan and the ensuing debate, see Fred Kaplan, "JFK's First Strike Plan," *Atlantic Monthly* October 2001, 81–86. Look also at the documents at "First Strike Options and the Berlin Crisis, September 1961," National Security Archive, September 21, 2001 (https://nsarchive2.gwu.edu/NSAEBB/NSAEBB56/).

29. Although Robert Jervis makes the fascinating point that the United States' willingness to protect an exposed Western Europe may have created mutual vulnerability far earlier than expected.

> The problem of extended deterrence has another aspect that is little remarked upon. The basic logic is that the American threat was credible to the extent that the Soviets believed that the U.S. would believe that an attack on Europe was a prelude to an attack on it or that the Americans saw the Europeans as so much like themselves that they would respond to an attack on the former as though it were directed against the U.S. homeland. The latter argument was the one that was repeated most often—and the repetition was partly intended to make it a self-fulfilling prophesy. But neither observers nor policy-makers paid much attention to the opposite side of this coin. If the Americans really valued the Europeans to this extent, then the Soviets' ability to destroy West Europe gave them great leverage over the U.S., and they gained the equivalent of a second-strike capability long before they could retaliate against the American homeland. It is perhaps not surprising that those in office did not want to dwell on this implication of their policy because it is not an entirely comfortable one, but the silence of scholars is more puzzling.

Robert Jervis, "Response," *H-Diplo Roundtable Review* 15, no. 1 (2013), 34.

30. Summary Record of the 517th Meeting of the National Security Council, Washington, September 12, 1963, 11 a.m., *FRUS, 1961–1963*, vol. 8, *National Security Policy*, edited by David W. Mabon (Washington, DC: GPO, 1996). A taped recording of the meeting is available at the John F. Kennedy Archives (www.jfklibrary.org/Asset-Viewer/Archives/JFKPOF-MTG-110-004.aspx).

31. Kroenig, "Nuclear Superiority and the Balance of Resolve," 149.

32. For a good summary of this situation, see Austin Long, review of *Nuclear Statecraft: History and Strategy in America's Atomic Age*, by Francis J. Gavin, *H-Diplo Roundtable* 15, no. 1 (2013). As a high-level Soviet military official said, the U.S. superiority in qualitative factors such as command, control, communications, and intelligence meant that "Soviet superiority in the number of launchers

did not give them any real advantage. The numerical superiority reflected a mechanistic, wasteful approach to force building." Interview with A. S. Kalashnikov, April 1993, in *Soviet Intentions 1965–1985,* edited by John Hines and others, vol. 2, *Soviet Post–Cold War Testimonial Evidence* (McLean, VA: BDM Federal, 1995), 90. As another high-level Russian defense planner pointed out, "Several factors, especially accuracy, for example, increased the power of the U.S. arsenal by a factor of three." Interview with Vitalii Leonidovich Kataev, June 23, 1993, ibid., 100. Kroenig does have a variable for second-strike forces, but it seems clear that these forces (and any damage limitation capability) make sense only if used first, a fact the Soviets fully understood. "We assumed that the U.S. would launch first and, given your focus on accuracy and relatively smaller yields per warhead, that you intended to strike our weapons and control systems in an attempt to disarm us." Interview with Kataev, 100. According to Kalashnikov, the Soviet Union's Achilles' heel was its inability to "create a sophisticated, survivable, integrated command, control and communication system" on par with the United States, which meant that after an "all-out nuclear strike" the Soviets would be able to launch only 2 percent of their missiles. Interview with Kalashnikov, 90.

33. "Power-projecting states, states with the ability to project conventional military power over a particular target, have a lot to lose when that target state acquires nuclear weapons. . . . Once that state acquires nuclear weapons, however, this strategic advantage is certainly placed at risk and may be fully lost. For these reasons, power-projecting states fear nuclear proliferation to both allied and enemy states." Matthew Kroenig, *Exporting the Bomb: Technology Transfer and the Spread of Nuclear Weapons* (Cornell University Press, 2010), 3.

34. See chapter 2, this volume.

35. Fursenko and Naftali, *Khrushchev's Cold War,* 384.

36. Trachtenberg, *A Constructed Peace,* 379–80.

37. Fursenko and Naftali, *Khrushchev's Cold War,* 5.

38. Kroenig implies that changing the coding on any one case will not challenge the robustness of his findings. I leave it to others to decide whether my analysis of how these models explain the 1958–1962 period affects their confidence in his overall findings, theories, and policy recommendations. See Kroenig, "Nuclear Superiority and the Balance of Resolve," 154–55n69.

39. There is no consensus on how threatening the 1983 crisis actually was. For an argument that the crisis was quite dangerous, see Dmitry Dima Adamsky, "The 1983 Nuclear Crisis: Lessons for Deterrence Theory and Practice," *Journal of Strategic Studies* 36, no. 1 (2013), 4–41. For a convincing argument, based on Soviet documents, that the fears of a nuclear war in 1983 have been overblown, see Mark Kramer, "The Able Archer 83 Non-Crisis: Did Soviet

Leaders Really Fear an Imminent Nuclear Attack in 1983?," paper presented at the Conference on Challenges, Concepts, and Ideas During the Cold War of the 1970s and 1980s, Collaborative Research Center, University of Tübingen, Tübingen, Germany, September 2013.

40. In addition to the 1958–1962 period, the winter of 1950–1951, after the People's Republic of China intervened in the Korean War and nearly threw the Americans off the peninsula, was extraordinarily dangerous. The United States had lost the atomic monopoly and had not yet implemented the defense buildup called for in NSC-68, and Western Europe and Japan were still economically feeble, militarily impotent, and largely unprotected. American policymakers not only worried about a war but also felt that if one came they might lose it. These two superpower standoffs strike one as being in categories of their own, significantly more dangerous than any other listed in either data set.

41. Thomas C. Schelling, *Arms and Influence* (Yale University Press, 1966), 69–91.

42. One of the only efforts to test the difference can be found in Walter J. Petersen, "Deterrence and Compellence: A Critical Assessment of Conventional Wisdom," *International Studies Quarterly* 30, no. 3 (1986), 269–94. Petersen's study suggests that compellence is not harder than immediate deterrence.

43. James D. Fearon, "Domestic Political Audiences and the Escalation of International Disputes," *American Political Science Review* 88, no. 3 (1994), 577–92.

44. Fearson notes,

Surprisingly, in the model, neither the balance of forces nor the balance of interests has any direct effect on the probability that one side rather than the other will back down once both sides have escalated. The reason is that in choosing initially whether to threaten or to resist a threat, rational leaders will take into account observable indices of relative power and interest in a way that tends to neutralize their impact if a crisis ensues. For example, a militarily weak state will choose to resist the demands of a stronger one only if it happens to be quite resolved on the issues in dispute and so is relatively willing to escalate despite its military inferiority. The argument implies that observable aspects of capabilities and interests should strongly influence *who gets what in international politics but that their impact should be seen more in uncontested positions and faits accomplis than in crises.* Which side backs down in a crisis should be determined by relative audience costs and by unobservable, privately known elements of states' capabilities and resolve. Ibid., 578, italics added.

See also ibid., 586:

Two of the most common informal claims about state behavior in international crises are that (1) the militarily weaker state is more likely to back down and (2) the side with fewer "intrinsic interests" at stake is more likely to back down. These arguments are problematic. If relative capabilities or interests can be assessed by leaders prior to a crisis and if they also determine the outcome, then we should not observe crises between rational opponents: if rational, the weaker or observably less interested state should simply concede the issues without offering public, costly resistance. . . .

A second striking result from the equilibrium analysis is that observable measures of the balance of capabilities and balance of interests should be unrelated to the relative likelihood that one state or the other backs down in crises where both sides choose to escalate.

Less formally, the result suggests that rational states will "select themselves" into crises on the basis of observable measures of relative capabilities and interests and will do so in a way that neutralizes any subsequent impact of these measures. Possessing military strength or a manifestly strong foreign policy interest does deter challenges, in the model. But if a challenge occurs nonetheless, the challenger has signaled that it is more strongly resolved than initially expected and so is no more or less likely to back down for the fact that it is militarily weaker or was initially thought less interested.

I am grateful to Marc Trachtenberg for identifying and explaining the meaning and importance of Fearon's arguments to understanding these issues.

45. Eugene Gholz and Daryl Press make this recommendation to deal with selection effects in their paper, "Untangling Selection Effects in Studies of Coercion," unpublished working paper, University of Texas at Austin and University of Pennsylvania, 2006 (http://utip.lbj.utexas.edu/colloquium/Gholz.pdf).

46. Marc Trachtenberg, *History and Policy* (Princeton University Press, 1991), 231.

47. This is the core theme of Trachtenberg's *A Constructed Peace*.

48. Gavin, *Nuclear Statecraft*, 72–73. Also see *FRUS, 1969–1976,* vol. 40, *Germany and Berlin, 1969–1972,* edited by David C. Geyer (Washington, DC: GPO, 2008).

49. Conversation among President Nixon, German Chancellor Brandt, the President's Assistant for National Security Affairs (Kissinger), and the German State Secretary for Foreign, Defense, and German Policy (Bahr), June 15, 1971,

FRUS, 1969–1976, vol. 40, Germany and Berlin, edited by David C. Geyer (Washington, DC: GPO, 2008), Document 254, 742.

50. Ibid., 744.

51. Ibid., 743.

52. Paul Huth and Bruce Russett, "What Makes Deterrence Work? Cases from 1900 to 1980," *World Politics* 36, no. 4 (1984), 29–45.

53. Paul Huth and Bruce Russett, "Deterrence Failure and Crisis Escalation," *International Studies Quarterly* 32, no. 1 (1988).

54. Richard Ned Lebow and Janice Gross Stein, "Deterrence: The Elusive Dependent Variable," *World Politics* 42, no. 3 (1990); Paul Huth and Bruce Russett, "Testing Deterrence Theory: Rigor Makes a Difference," *World Politics* 42, no. 4 (1990).

55. James D. Fearon, "Selection Effects and Deterrence," *International Interaction* 28, no. 1 (2002), 5–29. See also Frank Harvey, "Rational Deterrence Theory Revisited: A Progress Report," *Canadian Journal of Political Science* 28, no. 2 (1995), and James D. Fearon, "Signaling versus the Balance of Power and Interests: An Empirical Test of a Crisis Bargaining Model," *Journal of Conflict Resolution* 38, no. 2 (1994).

56. The best source for U.S. nuclear decisionmaking during the 1958–1962 period is the U.S. Department of State's *Foreign Relations of the United States* series, many (including all cited here) of which are available online (http:// history.state.gov/historicaldocuments). See, among other volumes, *FRUS, 1958–1960*, vol. 3, *National Security Policy; Arms Control and Disarmament*, edited by Edward C. Keefer and David W. Mabon (Washington, DC: GPO, 1996); *FRUS, 1958–1960*, vol. 3, *National Security Policy; Arms Control and Disarmament, Microfiche Supplement; FRUS, 1958–1960*, vol. 8, *Berlin Crisis, 1958–1959*, edited by Charles S. Sampson (Washington, DC: GPO, 1993); *FRUS, 1958–1960*, vol. 9; *FRUS, 1961–1963*, vol. 5, *Soviet Union*, edited by Charles S. Sampson and John Michael Joyce (Washington, DC: GPO, 1998); *FRUS, 1961–1963*, vol. 6, *Kennedy-Khrushchev Exchanges*, edited by Charles S. Sampson (Washington, DC: GPO, 1996); *FRUS, 1961–1963*, vol. 7, *Arms Control and Disarmament*, edited by David W. Mabon and David S. Patterson (Washington, DC: GPO, 1995); *FRUS, 1961–1963*, vol. 11, *Cuban Missile Crisis and Aftermath*, edited by Edward C. Keefer, Charles S. Sampson, and Louis J. Smith (Washington, DC: GPO, 1996); *FRUS, 1961–1963*, vol. 14; Charles S. Sampson, ed., *FRUS, 1961–1963*, vol. 15, *Berlin Crisis, 1962–1963* (Washington, DC: GPO, 1994).

57. The National Security Archive has a microfiche collection devoted to this very subject: *The Berlin Crisis, 1958–1962*, available online (www.gwu.

edu/~nsarchiv/nsa/publications/berlin_crisis/berlin.html) and at most research libraries. It also has a searchable digital archive and a long list of online briefing books, including almost seventy related to nuclear history (www.gwu. edu/~nsarchiv/NSAEBB/index.html).

58. U.S. Declassified Documents Online, Gale, a Cengage Company, 2019.

59. "Macmillan Cabinet Papers, 1957–1963: Sources from the National Archives, UK," Adam Matthew, a SAGE Publishing Company, 2018.

60. Aleksandr Fursenko, ed., *Prezidium TsK KPSS, 1954–1964: Chernovye protokol'nye zapisi zasedanii stenogrammy* [The Presidium of the Central Committee of the Communist Party of the Soviet Union, 1954–1964: Rough stenographic meeting minutes] (Moscow: Rosspen, 2003). Some of those transcripts pertaining to the Cuban missile crisis can be found in "The Global Cuban Missile Crisis at 50," *Bulletin*, no. 17/18, Cold War International History Project, Wilson Center, especially 303–15. My sincere thanks to Simon Miles for identifying these and other important Russian source materials.

61. To give three important examples, two of which have been translated to English: Anatoly Dobrynin, *In Confidence: Moscow's Ambassador to America's Six Cold War Presidents* (New York: Times Books, 1995); Nikita Khrushchev, *Memoirs of Nikita Khrushchev*, vol. 3, *Statesman*, edited by Sergei Khrushchev (Pennsylvania State University Press, 2007); and Georgii Kornienko, *Kholodnaia voina: Svidetel'stvo ee uchastnika* [The Cold War: Testimony of a participant] (Moscow: Olma, 2001).

62. There are quite a few, but one can get very far with the following three excellent books: Fursenko and Naftali, *Khrushchev's Cold War*; Hope Harrison, *Driving the Soviets Up the Wall: Soviet-East German Relations, 1953–1961* (Princeton University Press, 2003); William Taubman, *Khrushchev: The Man, His Era* (New York: Free Press, 2005).

63. Marc Trachtenberg, *The Craft of International History: A Guide to Method* (Princeton University Press, 2006), xiii–xix.

64. Hal Brands and Francis J. Gavin, "The Historical Profession Is Committing Slow-Motion Suicide," *War on the Rocks*, December 10, 2018 (https://warontherocks.com/2018/12/the-historical-profession-is-committing-slow-motion-suicide/).

65. For an excellent "inside baseball" review of many of the problems that plague quantitative work in political science, see Christopher H. Achen, "Toward a New Political Methodology: Microfoundations and ART," *Annual Review of Political Science 5* (2002), 423–50. "Even at the most quantitative end of the profession, much contemporary empirical work has little long-term scientific value. . . . The present state of the field is troubling. For all our hard work, we have yet to give most of our new statistical procedures legitimate

theoretical micro-foundations, and we have had difficulty with the real task of quantitative work—the discovery of reliable empirical generalizations." Ibid., 424. Like my critique of the articles reviewed here, Achen fears many statistical models do not think hard enough about what is being compared in the analysis or correctly identifying the universe of like events, and he worries that the absence of any logical theory of how the variables interact prevents the correct econometric tools from being chosen, as opposed to canned models with lots of commonly used control variables.

66. For an excellent guide to when it is appropriate to use qualitative or quantitative methods in international relations research, see Stephen Van Evera, "Director's Statement: Trends in Political Science and the Future of Security Studies," MIT Security Studies Program, Annual Report 2009–10, MIT (http://web.mit.edu/ssp/publications/annual/ssp_annual_report2010.pdf), 6–9.

67. Furthermore, if I am right about the state of the field of history (and I truly hope I am not), it is hard to see how political scientists can accurately code these events if there is not a good historical literature to rely on.

68. For an excellent caution on the accuracy of participant memoirs, see Robert Jervis, review of Melvyn Leffler, "The Foreign Policies of the George W. Bush Administration: Memoirs, History, and Legacy," *Diplomatic History* 37, no. 2. For a classic example of this, see Fred I. Greenstein and Richard H. Immerman, "What Did Eisenhower Tell Kennedy about Indochina? The Politics of Misperception," *Journal of American History* 79, no. 2 (1992), 568–87.

69. Gavin, *Nuclear Statecraft*, chap. 5.

70. Meeting between President Nixon and Committee on Arms Control and Disarmament, March 21, 1972, Editorial Note, *FRUS, 1969–1976*, vol. 14, Soviet Union, October 1971–May 1972, edited by David C Geyer, Nina D. Howland, and Kent Sieg (Washington, DC: GPO, 2006), Document 66, 218.

71. Conversation between President Nixon and his Assistant for National Security (Kissinger), April 4, 1972, *FRUS, 1969–1976*, vol. 14, Soviet Union, October 1971–May 1972, edited by David C. Geyer, Nina D. Howland, and Kent Sieg (Washington, DC: GPO, 2006), Document 82, 258.

72. For my critique of this view, and the whole way the nuclear proliferation question has been handled in much of the strategy literature, see Francis J. Gavin, "Politics, History, and the Ivory Tower–Policy Gap in the Nuclear Proliferation Debate," *Journal of Strategic Studies* 35, no. 4 (2012), 573–600. For Sagan and Waltz's response, see Scott D. Sagan and Kenneth N. Waltz, "Political Scientists and Historians in Search of the Bomb," *Journal of Strategic Studies* 6, no. 1 (2013), 143–51.

73. Summary Record of the 517th Meeting of the National Security Council.

74. Philip Zelikow, review of *Nuclear Statecraft: History and Strategy in*

America's Atomic Age, by Francis J. Gavin, *H-Diplo Roundtable* 15, no. 1 (2013), 27–29.

75. As Jacques Hymans notes, statistical efforts by Dong-Joon Jo and Erik Gartze to understand nuclear proliferation dynamics produced different answers from those of the quantitative model of Sonali Singh and Christopher Way. While Hymans suggests both quantitative efforts are "sophisticated," the "differences in their results may reflect a more basic problem for quantitative attacks on this question: the lack of a reliable data set on which to base worldwide statistical tests. . . . In light of this confusion about the basic historical facts, it may be premature to attempt large-N analyses of the proliferation phenomenon." Jacques E. C. Hymans, "The Study of Nuclear Proliferation and Nonproliferation: Toward a New Consensus?," in *Forecasting Nuclear Proliferation in the 21st Century: The Role of Theory,* edited by William C. Potter with Gaukhar Mukhatzhanova, vol. 1 (Stanford University Press, 2010), 21–22. For an excellent critique of what has been called the second wave of quantitative studies on nuclear proliferation, see Alex H. Montgomery and Scott Sagan, "The Perils of Predicting Proliferation," *Journal of Conflict Resolution* 53, no. 2 (2009), 302–28. "First, nuclear programs' initiation and completion dates are ambiguous and difficult to code, but findings are rarely subjected to sufficient robustness tests using alternative codings. Second, independent variables overlook important factors such as prestige and bureaucratic power and often use poor proxies for concepts such as the nonproliferation regime. Third, methodologies and data sets should be tightly coupled to empirical questions but are instead often chosen for convenience. Fourth, some findings provide insights already known or believed to be true. Fifth, findings can ignore or gloss over data crucial for policy making and wider debates" (302).

76. For the first time he laid out this argument, see Kenneth Waltz, "The Spread of Nuclear Weapons: More May Be Better," *Adelphi Papers,* no. 171 (London: International Institute for Strategic Studies, 1981). For the last time, see Kenneth Waltz, "Why Iran Should Get the Bomb: Nuclear Balancing Would Mean Stability," *Foreign Affairs* 91, no. 4 (2012), 2–5.

77. For a good exploration of this issue, see Philip Zelikow, "The Nature of History's Lessons," paper prepared for History and Policy conference, Duke University, May 16, 2013; for the challenges facing decisionmakers confronting radical uncertainty, with a particular focus on Iran's nuclear ambitions, see Francis J. Gavin and James B. Steinberg, "The Unknown Unknowns," *Foreign Policy,* February 14, 2012 (https://foreignpolicy.com/2012/02/14/the-unknown-unknowns/); Francis J. Gavin and James B. Steinberg, "Mind the Gap: Why Policymakers and Scholars Ignore Each Other, and What Can Be Done about It?" *Carnegie Reporter,* Spring 2012 (http://carnegie.org/publica

tions/carnegie-reporter/single/view/article/item/308/). For an important effort to improve expert judgment to make better policy predictions, see Michael C. Horowitz and Philip E. Tetlock, "Trending Upwards: How the Intelligence Community Can Better See into the Future," *Foreign Policy*, September 6, 2012 (www.foreignpolicy.com/articles/2012/09/06/trending_upward). For an excellent example of research that exploits international relations theory and history to provide policymakers with real-world policy guidance on nuclear questions, see Colin H. Kahl, Melissa Dalton, and Matthew Irvine, "Risk and Rivalry: Iran, Israel, and the Bomb," Report, Center for a New American Security, June 2012; and Colin H. Kahl, Melissa Dalton, and Matthew Irvine, "Atomic Kingdom: If Iran Builds the Bomb, Will Saudi Arabia Be Next?," Report, Center for a New American Security, February 2013.

CHAPTER FOUR

1. Inhibition includes both nonproliferation and counterproliferation policies.

2. For the history of and logic behind the United States' strategies of containment during the Cold War, see John Lewis Gaddis, *Strategies of Containment: A Critical Appraisal of American National Security Policy during the Cold War* (Oxford University Press, 2005). The openness mission is also often referred to as liberal internationalism. For the best summary of its origins and motivations, see G. John Ikenberry, *The Liberal Leviathan: The Origins, Crisis, and Transformation of American World Order* (Princeton University Press, 2011).

3. For a sense of these debates, see *America's Strategic Choices*, edited by Michael E. Brown and others, rev. ed. (MIT Press, 2000); and Elbridge Colby, "Grand Strategy: Contending Contemporary Analyst Views and Implications for the U.S. Navy" (Arlington, VA: Center for Naval Analyses, November, 2011); Michèle Flournoy and Shawn Brimley, eds., *Finding Our Way: Debating American Grand Strategy* (Washington, DC: Center for a New American Security, 2008). The best version of the restraint case can be found in Barry R. Posen, *Restraint: A New Foundation for U.S. Grand Strategy* (Cornell University Press, 2014); the best critique can be found in Ikenberry, *Liberal Leviathan,* and Stephen G. Brooks, G. John Ikenberry, and William C. Wohlforth, "Don't Come Home, America: The Case against Retrenchment," *International Security* 37, no. 3 (2012–2013), 7–51.

4. Nuclear nonproliferation is not discussed at all in Gaddis's *Strategies of Containment* and only in passing in Ikenberry's *Liberal Leviathan*. U.S nonproliferation policy is overlooked in the most recent works on American grand strategy, including Hal Brands, *What Good Is Grand Strategy? Power and Pur-*

pose in American Statecraft from Harry S. Truman to George W. Bush (Cornell University Press, 2015); Colin Dueck, *Reluctant Crusaders: Power, Culture, and Change in American Grand Strategy* (Princeton University Press, 2008); and William C. Martel, *Grand Strategy in Theory and Practice: The Need for an Effective American Foreign Policy* (Cambridge University Press, 2015). Robert Art identifies preventing the spread of nuclear, biological, and chemical weapons to rogue states and terrorists as a post–September 11, 2001, priority but does not believe the United States should be overly concerned by what he calls "normal states" with nuclear weapons. See Robert J. Art, *A Grand Strategy for America* (New York: Century Foundation, 2003). Barry Posen also sees nuclear nonproliferation as a post–Cold War priority, arguing that U.S. "grand strategy today is fixated on preventing nuclear proliferation." Posen thinks this unwise: the U.S. nonproliferation effort, which "assumes the risks and responsibilities of defending other capable states around the world, and fights and threatens preventive wars to deny potential adversaries nuclear capabilities, is costly and risky, and ultimately futile." Posen, *Restraint*, 72–73. Stephen M. Walt recognizes that the United States pursued nuclear nonproliferation for strategic reasons that preceded the end of the Cold War, but he also believes that, for purposes other than preventing nuclear terrorism, recent U.S. nuclear nonproliferation policies are costly and ineffective: "Earlier efforts to halt the spread of nuclear weapons were only partly successful, and they required the United States to offer considerable inducements to would-be proliferators (including security guarantees, access to nuclear technology, and a U.S. pledge . . . eventually to reduce its own nuclear arsenal)." Stephen M. Walt, *The Taming of American Power: The Global Response to U.S. Primacy* (New York: W. W. Norton, 2005), 139–40.

5. Scott D. Sagan, "Two Renaissances in Nuclear Security Studies," paper prepared for H-Diplo/ISSF Forum, "What We Talk about When We Talk about Nuclear Weapons," Stanford University, June 15, 2014. For the increased availability of previously classified documents on nuclear dynamics from capitals around the world, see Francis J. Gavin, "What We Talk about When We Talk about Nuclear Weapons: A Review Essay," in the same roundtable. The entire forum is available at http://issforum.org/ISSF/PDF/ISSF-Forum-2.pdf.

6. This effort began against Germany even before the United States had used atomic bombs against Japan. As the war in Europe ended, the

U.S. and U.K. forces moved aggressively to prevent the proliferation of this nucleus of nuclear capability. They promptly seized the scientists and materials in their own zones of occupation and snatched some from the agreed zones of France and the USSR ahead of their advancing armies. They even destroyed by air attack the Auer Company plant, in the prospective Soviet zone, that had produced the uranium metal for the German program. They interned near London the ten ranking scientists . . . and only after Hiroshima did they release them under such conditions that they would not want to go to the USSR.

7. Brands, *What Good Is Grand Strategy?*, vii.

8. Posen, *Restraint*, 1.

9. See Brands, *What Good Is Grand Strategy?*, 3.

10. George F. Kennan laid out his view in "The Sources of Soviet Conduct," *Foreign Affairs* 25, no. 4 (1947), 566–82. Kennan ultimately distanced himself from how U.S. policymakers came to understand and implement containment. See John Lewis Gaddis, *George F. Kennan: An American Life* (New York: Penguin, 2011).

11. For a sample of discussions over the pros and cons of attempting to contain Iran, see Kenneth M. Pollack, "Containing Iran," in *The Iran Primer: Power, Politics, and U.S. Policy,* edited by Robin Wright (Washington, DC: U.S. Institute of Peace Press, 2010), 209–11. For a discussion of containment in the context of Iraq, see Eric K. Graben, "Policy Brief: The Case for Containing Iraq," *Middle East Quarterly* 1, no. 2 (June 1994); for the debate over containing China, see David Shambaugh, "Containment or Engagement of China? Calculating Beijing's Responses," *International Security* 21, no. 2 (1996), 180–209.

12. U.S. support for European integration was driven by both the openness and containment missions. On the security considerations behind U.S. support, see Sebastian Rosato, *Europe United: Power Politics and the Making of the European Community* (Cornell University Press, 2011).

13. The best source is Tony Smith, *America's Mission: The United States and the Worldwide Struggle for Democracy in the 20th Century* (Princeton University Press, 1994). See also Frank Ninkovich, *The Wilsonian Century: U.S. Foreign Policy since 1900* (University of Chicago Press, 1999).

14. Marc Trachtenberg, "Preventive War and U.S. Foreign Policy," *Security Studies* 16, no. 1 (2007), 1–31; and Francis J. Gavin and Mira Rapp-Hooper, "The Copenhagen Temptation: Rethinking Prevention and Proliferation in the Age of Deterrence Dominance," unpublished paper (www.tobinproject.org/sites/tobinproject.org/files/assets/Gavin%26Rapp-Hooper_US_Preventive_War_Thinking.pdf).

15. Such attacks might generate economic instability and uncertainty, which would not be good for the goals of the openness mission.

16. Nicholas L. Miller, "The Secret Success of Nonproliferation Sanctions," *International Organization* 68, no. 4 (2014), 913–44.

17. Gene Gerzhoy, "Coercive Nonproliferation: Security, Leverage, and

Nuclear Reversals," Ph.D. dissertation, University of Chicago, 2014; Gene Gerzhoy, "Alliance Coercion and Nuclear Restraint: How the United States Thwarted West Germany's Nuclear Ambitions," *International Security* 39, no. 4 (2015), 91–129; Alexander Lanoszka, "Protection States Trust: Major Power Patronage, Nuclear Behavior, and Alliance Dynamics," Ph.D. dissertation, Princeton University, 2014.

18. For example, the United States made economic concessions to West Germany while privileging inhibition over containment and openness because of "the explosive set of issues surrounding the German and nuclear question." See Francis J. Gavin, *Gold, Dollars, and Power: The Politics of International Monetary Relations, 1958–1971* (University of North Carolina Press, 2004), 12; see also 89–116, 135–64. Similar logic also infused American calculations on trade and international monetary relations with Japan.

19. Jeffrey W. Knopf, ed., *Security Assurances and Nuclear Nonproliferation* (Stanford University Press, 2012); and Makreeta Lahti, "Security Cooperation as a Way to Stop the Spread of Nuclear Weapons? Nuclear Nonproliferation Policies of the United States towards the Federal Republic of Germany and Israel, 1945–1968," Ph.D. dissertation, University of Potsdam, 2008.

20. One might argue that these are not, in fact, alliances. Historically, alliances have been temporary, threat specific, and additive. These relationships appear to be permanent, persist regardless of threat, and are suppressive.

21. Kenneth N. Waltz, "Nuclear Myths and Political Realities," *American Political Science Review* 84, no. 5 (1990), 738.

22. Austin Long and Brendan Rittenhouse Green, "Stalking the Secure Second Strike: Intelligence, Counterforce, and Nuclear Strategy," *Journal of Strategic Studies* 38, no. 1/2 (2015), 38–73; Keir A. Lieber and Daryl Press, "The End of MAD? The Nuclear Dimension of U.S. Primacy, " *International Security* 30, no. 4 (2006), 7–44.

23. The U.S. government will spend $160 billion on strategic nuclear delivery systems and weapons and $52 billion on nuclear-related command, control, communications, and early warning systems. Congressional Budget Office, "Projected Costs of U.S. Nuclear Forces, 2015 to 2024," January 2015.

24. Hal Brands, "Non-Proliferation and the Dynamics of the Middle Cold War: The Superpowers, the MLF, and the NPT," *Cold War History* 7, no. 3 (2007), 389–423; Andrew J. Coe and Jane Vaynman, "Collusion and the Nuclear Nonproliferation Regime," *Journal of Politics* 77, no. 4 (2015), 983–97; Vladimir Orlov, Roland Timerbaev, and Anton Khlopkov, *Nuclear Nonproliferation in U.S.-Russian Relations: Challenges and Opportunities Report*, Center for Policy Studies in Russia (Moscow: Raduga, 2002); William C. Potter, "The Soviet Union and Nuclear Proliferation," *Slavic Review* 44, no.

3 (1985), 468–88; Dane Swango, "The Nuclear Nonproliferation Treaty: Constrainer, Screener, or Enabler?," University of California, Los Angeles, 2009; Joseph S. Nye Jr., "U.S.-Soviet Cooperation in a Nonproliferation Regime," in *U.S.-Soviet Security Cooperation: Achievements, Failures, Lessons,* edited by Alexander L. George, Philip J. Farley, and Alexander Dallin (Oxford University Press, 1988), 336–52; Peter R. Lavoy, "Learning and the Evolution of Cooperation in U.S. and Soviet Nuclear Nonproliferation Activities," in *Learning in U.S. and Soviet Foreign Policy,* edited by George W. Breslauer and Philip E. Tetlock (Boulder, CO: Westview Press, 1991), 735–83. Elisabeth Roehrlich demonstrates that the two superpowers acknowledged a shared interest in nuclear nonproliferation during the negotiations to create the International Atomic Energy Agency during the Eisenhower administration. See Elisabeth Roehrlich, "Cold War Dynamics and North-South Divisions in the Creation of the IAEA, 1953–1957," paper prepared for the Nuclear Studies Research Initiative, Austin, Texas, October 2013.

25. No scholar has identified nuclear nonproliferation as an independent driver of U.S. grand strategy with its own strategic logic.

26. For a sample of writings on grand strategy that share one or more of these assumptions, see Robert J. Art, "Defensible Defense: America's Grand Strategy after the Cold War," *International Security* 15, no. 4 (1991), 5–53; Shawn Brimley, "Finding Our Way," in *Finding Our Way,* edited by Flournoy and Brimley, 9–22; Ashton B. Carter, William J. Perry, and John D. Steinbruner, *A New Concept of Cooperative Security* (Washington, DC: Brookings Institution, 1992): G. John Ikenberry, "An Agenda for Liberal International Renewal," in *Finding Our Way,* edited by Flournoy and Brimley, 43–60; G. John Ikenberry and Anne-Marie Slaughter, "Final Paper of the Princeton Project on National Security" (Princeton, NJ: Princeton Project on National Security, 2006); Charles Krauthammer, "The Unipolar Moment," *Foreign Affairs* 70, no. 1 (1991), 23–33; Sarah Sewall, "A Strategy of Conservation: American Power in the International System," in *Finding Our Way,* edited by Flournoy and Brimley, 103–22.

27. "The end of the Cold War offered an opportunity to reduce the incentives for acquiring nuclear weapons. Instead, a new class of weak and insecure states that are either seeking or expanding their nascent nuclear capability has emerged. . . . These states' internal weakness, however, poses a new problem because of the uncertainties associated with the state implosion of a nuclear power." Sewall, "A Strategy of Conservation," 109.

28. "Proliferation of destructive technology casts a shadow over future U.S. security in a way that cannot be directly addressed through superior force readiness. . . . And even when U.S. interests are not directly at risk, the United States bears an unavoidable responsibility for the world order." See Carter, Perry, and

Steinbruner, *A New Concept of Cooperative Security*, 4. See also Walter Russell Mead's interesting argument that "Jeffersonian logic on disarmament was widely accepted; every president from Kennedy through Reagan engaged in serious efforts to limit the development and spread of nuclear weapons." See Walter Russell Mead, *Special Providence: American Foreign Policy and How It Changed the World* (New York: Routledge, 2002), 212.

29. "What is most striking [in the post–Cold War era] is not the preeminence of one threat but the scope and variety of threats. Global warming, health pandemics, nuclear proliferation, jihadist terrorism, energy scarcity. . . . The point is that none of these threats is, in itself, so singularly preeminent that it deserves to be the centerpiece of American grand strategy in the way that anti-fascism and anti-communism did in an earlier era." Ikenberry, "An Agenda for Liberal International Renewal," 49.

30. One of the reasons the United States viewed collective nuclear sharing arrangements such as the Multilateral Force as nonproliferation tools was that these agreements were far preferable to independent nuclear programs.

31. Kenneth N. Waltz, "The Spread of Nuclear Weapons: More May Be Better," *Adelphi Papers*, no. 171 (London: International Institute for Strategic Studies, 1981).

32. Robert Jervis, *The Illogic of American Nuclear Strategy* (Cornell University Press, 1984).

33. Rusk to State Department, August 7, 1963, National Security files, box 187, folder "USSR—Gromyko Talks—Rusk," John F. Kennedy Presidential Library, Boston.

34. Memorandum of Conversation, Secretary Dulles and Foreign Minister Gromyko, October 5, 1957, document 225897-i1-6, reproduced in *Declassifed Documents Reference System* (Farmington Hills, MI: Gale, 2014).

35. For an excellent treatment of catalytic strategies, see Vipin Narang, *Nuclear Strategy in the Modern Era: Regional Powers and International Conflict* (Princeton University Press, 2014).

36. On Israel, Pakistan, and South Africa, see ibid. On France, see Trachtenberg, *A Constructed Peace*, 338n192: "One measure of how bad relations had become is that Rusk at one point even threatened the French with an American nuclear attack if they dared to act independently in a crisis."

37. "Report on Strategic Developments over the Next Decade for the Interagency Panel," October 12, 1962, National Security files, box 376, John F. Kennedy Presidential Library, Boston, 52.

38. For a compelling argument that the United States was very worried about nuclear tipping points, see Nicholas L. Miller, "Hegemony and Nuclear Proliferation," Ph.D. dissertation, MIT, 2014.

39. Report by the Committee on Nuclear Proliferation, January 21, 1965, *Foreign Relations of the United States, 1964–1968,* vol. 11, *Arms Control and Disarmament,* edited by Evans Gerakas, David S. Patterson, and Carolyn B. Yee (Washington, DC: Government Printing Office, 1997), Document 64, 173–82. For an early National Intelligence estimate dealing with the likelihood and consequences of new nuclear states, see "Nuclear Weapons Production in Fourth Countries: Likelihood and Consequences," June 18, 1957, National Intelligence Estimate 100-6-57, in *National Intelligence Estimates of the Nuclear Proliferation Problem: The First Ten Years, 1957–1967,* edited by William Burr, National Security Archive Electronic Brief Book (NSA EBB), Document 2, 155.

40. "Power-projecting states, states with the ability to project conventional military power over a particular target, have a lot to lose when that target state acquires nuclear weapons," which is why "power-projecting states fear nuclear proliferation to both allied and enemy states." Matthew Kroenig, *Exporting the Bomb: Technology Transfer and the Spread of Nuclear Weapons* (Cornell University Press 2010), 3.

41. Report by the Committee on Nuclear Proliferation, January 21, 1965.

42. Michael C. Horowitz, *The Diffusion of Military Power: Causes and Consequences for International Politics* (Princeton University Press, 2010), 106. As Richard Betts has pointed out, what may be good for the "system"—stability—may not be what the United States prefers. "If nuclear spread enhances stability, this is not entirely good news for the United States, since it has been accustomed to attacking small countries with impunity when it felt justified and provoked." Richard K. Betts, "Universal Deterrence or Conceptual Collapse? Liberal Pessimism and Utopian Realism," in *The Coming Crisis: Nuclear Proliferation, U.S. Interests, and World Order* (MIT Press, 2000), 65.

43. Trachtenberg, *A Constructed Peace,* 321.

44. For the argument that nuclear weapons embolden states, see Mark S. Bell, "Beyond Emboldenment: The Effects of Nuclear Weapons on State Foreign Policy," *International Security* 40, no. 1 (2015), 87–119; S. Paul Kapur, "India and Pakistan's Unstable Peace: Why Nuclear South Asia Is Not Like Cold War Europe," *International Security* 30, no. 2 (2005), 127–52; S. Paul Kapur, *Dangerous Deterrent* (Stanford University Press, 2007) and S. Paul Kapur, "Ten Years of Instability in a Nuclear South Asia," *International Security* 33, no. 2 (2008), 71–94. New nuclear states may act more aggressively in the immediate aftermath of acquiring nuclear weapons. See Michael Horowitz, "The Spread of Nuclear Weapons and International Conflict: Does Experience Matter?," *Journal of Conflict Resolution* 53, no. 2 (2009), 234–57.

45. For the argument that nuclear weapons place a great premium on resolve, on risk-taking, and perhaps ultimately on recklessness, see Marc Trachtenberg,

"Walzing to Armageddon?," *National Interest*, September 1, 2002 (http://nationalinterest.org/article/waltzing-to-armageddon-281).

46. Memorandum of Conversation, Dulles to Gromyko, October 5, 1957. For fears of how the People's Republic of China would be emboldened by acquiring nuclear weapons, see Francis J. Gavin, "Blasts from the Past: Proliferation Lessons from the 1960s," *International Security* 29, no. 3 (2004/2005), 100–135.

47. To see suggestions for what would be expensive measures to contain a nuclear Iran, see Colin H. Kahl, Raj Pattani, and Jacob Stokes, "If All Else Fails: The Challenges of Containing a Nuclear-Armed Iran," May 13, 2013, Center for a New American Security.

48. "Report on Strategic Developments over the Next Decade," October 12, 1962, 54.

49. For an excellent assessment of this concern, see Peter D. Feaver, "Command and Control in Emerging Nuclear Nations," *International Security* 17, no. 3 (1992/1993), 160–87. The United States, which spent far more than any other nuclear state on nuclear safety and command and control, was plagued by accidents and near misses. The classic work on this is Scott D. Sagan, *The Limits of Safety: Organizations, Accidents, and Nuclear Safety* (Princeton University Press, 1993). See also Eric Schlosser, *Command and Control: Nuclear Weapons, the Damascus Accident, and the Illusion of Safety* (New York: Penguin, 2013).

50. Joshua R. Itzkowitz Shifrinson, "Managing the Collapse of a Nuclear State: Problems and Prospects," paper prepared for the American Political Science Association annual meeting, August 28–September 4, 2014, Washington, DC; Joshua R. Itzkowitz Shifrinson, "The Second Face of Existential Deterrence: Nuclear Collapse and Regime Survival," Texas A&M University, 2014.

51. Paul K. Kerr and Mary Beth Nikitin, "Pakistan's Nuclear Weapons: Proliferation and Security Issues," Report to Congress, March 19, 2013 (Washington, DC: Congressional Research Service), 1.

52. George H. W. Bush and Brent Scowcroft, *A World Transformed* (New York: Knopf, 1998), 543–44. The U.S. intelligence community worried that South African Prime Minister John Vorster pursued nuclear weapons to induce the United States to provide more political support to the apartheid regime:

> We believe his price for formally agreeing to relinquish the nuclear option would come high. . . . He is aware that the US government attaches great importance to halting the spread of nuclear weapons. . . . What he wants most is a general softening of US policy towards South Africa. His position may well be put something like this: if you want us to renounce the acquisition of nuclear weapons, you must make it easier for us (white South Africans) to survive as a nation.

See Director of Central Intelligence, Interagency Intelligence Memorandum, South Africa's Nuclear Options and Decisionmaking Structures (circa July 1978), in *Proliferation Watch: U.S. Intelligence Assessments of Potential Nuclear Powers, 1977–2001*, edited by William Burr and Jeffrey T. Richelson, NSA EBB 451, Document 2.

53. Some tools—such as the George W. Bush administration's Proliferation Security Initiative—have elements of all three categories of the strategies of inhibition.

54. This may have been the case even earlier, as the 1943 Quebec agreement with Great Britain contained nonproliferation clauses and was a U.S. attempt to gain control over global supplies of fissile materials. See Susanna Schrafstetter and Stephen Twigge, *Avoiding Armageddon: Europe, the United States, and the Struggle for Nuclear Nonproliferation, 1945–1970* (Westport, CT: Praeger, 2004).

55. Even in a world of total disarmament, the United States has the knowledge, infrastructure, and resources to reconstitute its nuclear weapons more quickly than any other state, while possessing superiority in most forms of nonnuclear state power.

56. For the explicit nonproliferation focus of the 1963 partial test-ban treaty, see Marc Trachtenberg, *A Constructed Peace*.

57. Maria Rost Rublee, *Nonproliferation Norms: Why States Choose Nuclear Restraint* (University of Georgia Press, 2009), 217.

58. Nina Tannenwald, *The Nuclear Taboo: The United States and the Non-Use of Nuclear Weapons since 1945* (Cambridge University Press, 2007), 390.

59. T. V. Paul, *The Tradition of the Non-Use of Nuclear Weapons* (Stanford University Press, 2009), 190.

60. For an excellent analysis of the debates over the lines between nuclear nonproliferation and disarmament, see Jeffrey W. Knopf, "Nuclear Disarmament and Nonproliferation: Examining the Linkage Argument," *International Security* 37, no. 3 (2012/2013), 92–132.

61. For an excellent overview of such controls (and the difficulty of enforcing them), see R. Scott Kemp, "The Nonproliferation Emperor Has No Clothes: The Gas Centrifuge, Supply-Side Controls, and the Future of Nuclear Proliferation," *International Security* 38, no. 4 (2014), 39–78. For examples of the Eisenhower administration's efforts to limit the spread of gas centrifuge technology, see William Burr, "The Gas Centrifuge Secret: Origins of a U.S. Policy of Nuclear Denial, 1954–1960," National Security Archive (http://nsarchive.gwu.edu/nukevault/ebb518-the-gas-centrifuge-secret-origins-of-US-policy-of-nuclear-denial-1954-1960/index.html). For the history of nuclear secrecy, see Alex Wellerstein, "Knowledge and the Bomb," Ph.D. dissertation, Harvard University,

2010. For earlier and extensive attempts by the U.S. government to secure global supplies of nuclear materials, located largely in the colonies of European states, see *Foreign Relations of the United States, 1947*, vol. 1, *General; The United Nations*, edited by Ralph E. Goodwin, Neal H. Petersen, Marvin W. Kranz, and William Slany (Washington, DC: GPO, 1947), 803–906.

62. Shane J. Maddock, *Nuclear Apartheid: The Quest for American Atomic Supremacy from World War II to the Present* (University of North Carolina Press, 2014), 2.

63. Joint Chiefs of Staff, "Statement of Effect of Atomic Weapons on National Security and Military Organization," January 21, 1946, document NP00018, Nuclear Non-Proliferation collection, Digital National Security Archive.

64. There is obviously a controversy over whether and to what extent the 2003 U.S. attack on Iraq was driven by a desire to destroy its nuclear program and other weapons of mass destruction.

65. For preventive military action against nascent nuclear programs, see Trachtenberg, "Preventive War and U.S. Foreign Policy"; and Gavin and Rapp-Hooper, "The Copenhagen Temptation." See also Alexandre Debs and Nuno P. Monteiro, "Known Unknowns: Power Shifts, Uncertainty, and War," *International Organization* 68, no. 1 (2014), 1–31; Matthew Fuhrmann and Sarah E. Kreps, "Targeting Nuclear Programs in War and Peace: A Quantitative Empirical Analysis, 1941–2000," *Journal of Conflict Resolution* 54, no. 6 (2010), 831–59; and Lyle J. Goldstein, *Preventive Attack and Weapons of Mass Destruction: A Comparative Historical Analysis* (Stanford University Press, 2006). There is a large body of literature on preventive war; for an excellent overview, see Jack S. Levy, "Preventive War: Concept and Propositions," *International Interactions* 37, no. 1 (2011), 87–96.

66. Gavin and Rapp-Hooper, "The Copenhagen Temptation"; Sarah E. Kreps and Matthew Fuhrmann, "Attacking the Atom: Does Bombing Nuclear Facilities Affect Proliferation?," *Journal of Strategic Studies* 34, no. 2 (2011), 161–87.

67. Gavin and Rapp-Hooper, "The Copenhagen Tradition."

68. "Report on Strategic Developments over the Next Decade," October 12, 1962, 54.

69. Lorenz M. Luthi, *The Sino-Soviet Split: Cold War in the Communist World* (Princeton University Press, 2008); Sergy Radchenko, *Two Suns in the Heavens: The Sino-Soviet Struggle for Supremacy, 1962–1967* (Washington, DC: Woodrow Wilson Center Press, 2009); and Odd Arne Westad, ed., *Brothers in Arms: The Rise and Fall of the Sino-Soviet Alliance* (Washington, DC: Woodrow Wilson Center Press, 1998).

70. For U.S. efforts to convince the Soviet Union to join it in a preventive strike, see William Burr and Jeffrey T. Richelson, "Whether to 'Strangle the

Baby in the Cradle': The United States and the Chinese Nuclear Program, 1960–64," *International Security* 25, no. 3 (2000/2001), 54–99.

71. See Gerzhoy, "Coercive Nonproliferation"; and Miller, "The Secret Success of Nonproliferation Sanctions."

72. David James Gill, *Britain and the Bomb: Nuclear Diplomacy, 1964–1970* (Stanford University Press, 2014).

73. It also explains why most potential proliferators developed their nuclear programs secretly. See Jeffrey T. Richelson, *Spying on the Bomb: American Nuclear Intelligence from Nazi Germany to Iran and North Korea* (New York: W. W. Norton, 2006). This was true even for countries that were not adversaries of the United States, such as Israel and India. See Avner Cohen, *Israel and the Bomb* (Columbia University, 1999), and Gaurav Kampani, "New Delhi's Long Nuclear Journey: How Secrecy and Institutional Roadblocks Delayed India's Weaponization," *International Security* 38, no. 4 (2014), 79–114.

74. For an excellent account of the United States' extraordinary global intelligence effort to assess which states were interested in or capable of (or both) developing nuclear weapons, see Richelson, *Spying on the Bomb*. For the U.S. effort to use conventional arms sales to inhibit proliferation, see Bonny Yang Lin, "Arms, Alliances, and the Bomb: Using Conventional Arms Transfers to Prevent Nuclear Proliferation," Ph.D. dissertation, Yale University, 2012. Lin demonstrates that conventional arms sales may have caused Israel and Pakistan to delay their nuclear programs and helped induce South Korea to forgo its program.

75. The earliest versions of containment, in the 1945–1950 period, focused on economic aid, not forward military deployments and deep, entangling alliances; the United States rapidly demobilized its military and massively decreased its defense expenditures after World War II. The Soviet detonation of an atomic device in August 1949, combined with the communist ascension to power in the People's Republic of China in October 1949, inspired a rethinking of American strategy, laid out in the document penned largely by Paul Nitze, "A Report to the National Security Council—NSC 68," April 12, 1950, President's Secretary's file, Truman Papers, Harry S. Truman Library, Independence, MO.

76. For details of how this alliance was constructed to deal with the interlocking issues of the defense of Western Europe, the German question, and nuclear weapons, see Trachtenberg, *A Constructed Peace*, especially 95–145. Although the United States was reluctant to forwardly deploy large forces in Europe, there was no other way to both contain the Soviet Union and prevent Germany from becoming "too strong and too independent" and acquiring its own independent nuclear capabilities (ibid., 119).

77. Bruno Tertrais, "Security Guarantees and Nuclear Nonproliferation,"

Notes de la Fondation pour la Recherche Strategique 14 (2011) (https://www
.frstrategie.org/en/publications/notes/security-guarantees-and-nuclear-non-
proliferation-14-2011).

78. Jeffrey W. Knopf, "Security Assurances: Initial Hypotheses," in *Security Assurances and Nuclear Nonproliferation*, edited by Knopf, 13. See also Stephen Palley, "Analyzing U.S. Extended Nuclear Deterrence as a Non-Proliferation Tool," master's thesis, University of Chicago, 2007.

79. On security assurance provided by the United States to Sweden, see Thomas Jonter, "The United States and Swedish Plans to Build the Bomb, 1945–68," in *Security Assurances and Nuclear Nonproliferation*, edited by Knopf, 219–45. On U.S. security assurances keeping Japan non-nuclear, see Yuki Tatsumi, "Maintaining Japan's Non-Nuclear Identity: The Role of U.S. Security Assurances," in *Security Assurances and Nuclear Nonproliferation*, edited by Knopf, 137–61. For Australia, see Christine M. Leah, *Australia and the Bomb* (London: Palgrave Macmillan, 2014). On the role of the United States in keeping West Germany non-nuclear, see Francis J. Gavin, *Nuclear Statecraft: History and Strategy in America's Atomic Age* (Cornell University Press, 2012); and Lahti, "Security Cooperation as a Way to Stop the Spread of Nuclear Weapons?"

80. Mark Kramer suggests that Poland, Hungary, and Czechoslovakia eschewed developing or acquiring their own nuclear weapons, in contrast to what neorealism would have predicted, and focused instead on entering the NATO. The United States actively supported their entry. See Mark Kramer, "Neorealism, Nuclear Proliferation, and East Central European Strategies," in *Unipolar Politics: Realism and State Strategies after the Cold War,* edited by Ethan B. Kapstein and Michael Mastanduno (Columbia University Press, 1998), 385–463, 429.

81. For excellent analyses of the more suppressive aspects, see Gerzhoy, "Coercive Nonproliferation"; and Lanoszka, "Protection States Trust." For an incisive exploration of the unique characteristics of nuclear security guarantees, see Mira Rapp-Hooper, "Absolute Alliances: Signaling Security Guarantees in International Politics," paper prepared for the Nuclear Studies Research Initiative, Austin, Texas, October 2013. For alliances constructed for reasons other than capabilities aggregation, see Christopher Gelpi, "Alliances as Instruments of Intra-Allied Control," in *Imperfect Unions: Security Institutions over Time and Space,* edited by Helga Haftendorn, Robert O. Keohane, and Celeste A. Wallander (Oxford University Press, 1999), 107–39.

82. For early efforts to achieve nuclear primacy, see David Alan Rosenberg, "The Origins of Overkill: Nuclear Weapons and American Strategy, 1945–1960," *International Security* 7, no. 4 (1983), 20–21. Marc Trachtenberg argues that U.S. nuclear primacy—defined as the situation in which a pre-emptive nu-

clear strike against the Soviets might be the "least worst" option—lasted until 1963. See Trachtenberg, *A Constructed Peace*, 293–97. For the first-strike plan developed by the John F. Kennedy administration during the Berlin crisis, see Fred Kaplan, "JFK's First Strike Plan," *Atlantic Monthly* October 2001. See also *First Strike Options and the Berlin Crisis, September 1961*, edited by William Burr, National Security Archive, Electronic Briefing Book 56. Of course, even after the United States lost nuclear primacy over the Soviet Union, it still retained it vis-à-vis every other nuclear weapons state.

83. Robert Jervis, *The Meaning of the Nuclear Revolution: Statecraft and the Prospect of Armageddon* (Cornell University Press, 1989), 8. See also Jervis, *The Illogic of American Nuclear Strategy*.

84. Keir A. Lieber and Daryl G. Press, "The New Era of Nuclear Weapons, Deterrence, and Conflict," *Strategic Studies Quarterly* 7, no. 1 (2013), 3–14.

85. Long and Green, "Stalking the Secure Second Strike." For evidence that the Warsaw Pact countries viewed U.S. counterforce acquisitions and strategies in these terms, see Benjamin B. Fischer, "CANOPY WING: The U.S. War Plan That Gave the East Germans Goose Bumps," *International Journal of Intelligence and Counter-Intelligence* 27, no. 3 (2014), 431–64. For the best analysis of U.S. antisubmarine warfare capabilities, see Owen R. Coté Jr., *The Third Battle: Innovation in the Navy's Silent Cold War Struggle with Soviet Submarines*, Newport Paper 16 (Newport, RI: U.S. Naval War College Press, 2003).

86. Brendan Rittenhouse Green and Austin Long, "Striving for Checkmate without War: Soviet Reactions to U.S. Counterforce Capabilities, 1969–1989," paper prepared for the Nuclear Studies Research Initiative, Warrenton, Virginia, May 1, 2015.

87. Lieber and Press, "The End of MAD?"

88. With Atoms for Peace, the Eisenhower administration offered the economic and technological promise of civilian nuclear energy to states that eschewed nuclear weapons. With the Multilateral Force proposal, it was hoped that Western European states that might otherwise acquire their own, independent nuclear weapons, would have those needs satiated by participating in a shared, multilateral nuclear endeavor. Both policies, originally motivated by the inhibition mission, were dropped, in part, because of fears they encouraged proliferation.

89. For an excellent analysis of how both experts and intelligence officials consistently overestimated the number of states that would develop nuclear weapons, see Moeed Yusuf, "Predicting Proliferation: The History of the Future of Nuclear Weapons," Brookings Foreign Policy Paper 11 (Washington, DC: Brookings Institution, January 2009).

90. On Reagan, see Paul Lettow, *Ronald Reagan and His Quest to Abolish Nuclear Weapons* (New York: Random House, 2005).

91. The pathbreaking work on Eisenhower and nuclear sharing can be found in Trachtenberg, *A Constructed Peace*, especially 146–200. There is no doubt that Eisenhower was the least enthusiastic president when it came to inhibition. Even he, however, was loath to see independent national nuclear forces. For Eisenhower, a "whole series of independent and uncoordinated national programs would be unconscionably wasteful" (155).

92. Gavin, *Nuclear Statecraft*, 117.

93. Consider the issues surrounding the Dwight D. Eisenhower administration's proposal for an atomic stockpile for NATO: "We feel that a prompt U.S. initiative is required because of threat of national nuclear weapons production in Europe. . . . The primary purpose of action proposed below is to try to head off these pressures and prevent emergence of national programs which would certainly be contrary to basic U.S. interests." Telegram from Perkins to U.S. Secretary of State, Subject: Threat of National Nuclear Weapon Production Programs in Europe, document NH01056, Digital National Security Archive. I thank Nicholas Miller for alerting him to this document.

94. This assessment reflects a shift from my earlier views of Nixon; see Gavin, *Nuclear Statecraft*, 117–18.

95. National Security Study Memorandum 202: U.S. Non-Proliferation Policy, May 23, 1974, National Security Council Institutional files, Study Memorandum (1969–1974), box H-205, Richard Nixon Presidential Library, Yorba Linda.

96. William Burr, "A Scheme of 'Control': The United States and the Origins of the Nuclear Suppliers' Group, 1974–1976," *International History Review* 36, no. 2 (2014), 252–76. See also Or Rabinowitz and Nicholas L, Miller, "Keeping the Bombs in the Basement: U.S. Nonproliferation Policy toward Israel, South Africa, and Pakistan," *International Security* 40, no. 1 (2015), 47–86.

97. This appears particularly true in the Nixon administration, where despite Nixon's fulminations against the Nuclear Nonprofileration Treaty, the U.S. government continued to emphasize nuclear nonproliferation in its foreign relations.

98. As Trachtenberg highlights, Eisenhower loathed the restrictions placed on him by the McMahon Act. Trachtenberg, *A Constructed Peace*, 178, 197. See also Steve Weber, "Shaping the Postwar Balance of Power: Multilateralism in NATO," in John Gerald Ruggie, *Multilateralism Matters: The Theory and Praxis of an Institutional Form* (Columbia University Press, 1993), esp. 225–62.

99. "Minutes of Discussion," January 7–8, 1965.

100. For U.S. policies, see James Edward Doyle, "Nuclear Rollback: A New Direction for United States Nonproliferation Policy?" Ph.D. dissertation, University of Virginia, 1997; and Ariel E. Levite, "Never Say Never Again: Nuclear Reversal Revisited," *International Security* 27, no. 3 (2002/2003), 59–88.

101. Or Rabinowitz, *Bargaining on Nuclear Tests: Washington and Its Cold War Deals* (Oxford University Press, 2014), 207.

102. By the time Nixon met with Golda Meir in September 1969, Israel had already developed atomic weapons, and the inhibition strategies pursued by the Kennedy and Johnson administrations had failed. The Nixon administration moved to the next best option—mitigating the consequences. Rabinowitz argues that the conventional wisdom on U.S. policy toward Israel's nuclear program—that Israel was "an exception" to U.S. nonproliferation policies—is untrue. See Rabinowitz, *Bargaining on Nuclear Tests*, 1–2. Furthermore, she demonstrates that the deal with Israel was mirrored in similar arrangements with Pakistan and South Africa.

103. For this shift, see Brands, "Non-Proliferation and the Dynamics of the Middle Cold War"; and Gavin, "Blasts from the Past."

104. As Melvyn P. Leffler points out in an important article about postwar military planning, U.S. officials recognized that, regardless of which state presented the threat, the United States' national security circumstances had changed. "Defense in depth was especially important in light of the Pearl Harbor experience, the advance of technology, and the development of the atomic bomb." Leffler, "The American Conception of National Security and the Beginnings of the Cold War, 1945–48," *American Historical Review* 89, no. 2 (1984), 350.

105. For example, the most dangerous crisis of the Cold War—the 1958–1962 standoff between the Soviet Union and the United States—saw a conflation of the containment and inhibition missions. The Soviet Union initiated the crisis in 1958 largely over concerns about West Germany's nuclear ambitions, and the crisis was resolved by 1963, when the United States agreed that West Germany had to remain non-nuclear. This paved the way toward the superpowers' working to further their inhibition goals, first through the partial test ban treaty and ultimately through the NPT. See Trachtenberg, *A Constructed Peace*, esp. 251–56, 352–406; and Gavin, *Nuclear Statecraft*, 57–74.

106. Francis J. Gavin and James B. Steinberg, "Mind the Gap: Why Policymakers and Scholars Ignore Each Other, and What Can Be Done about It?" *Carnegie Reporter*, Spring 2012 (http://carnegie.org/publications/carnegie-reporter/single/view/article/item/308/).

107. Matthew Kroenig, "The History of Proliferation Optimism: Does It Have a Future?" *Journal of Strategic Studies* 38, nos. 1–2 (2015), 98–125.

108. Peter D. Feaver, "Nuclear Command and Control in Crisis: Old Lessons from New History," in *Nuclear Weapons in Security Crises: What Does History Teach?*, edited by Henry D. Sokolski and Bruno Tertrais (Carlisle, PA: Strategic Studies Institute and U.S. Army War College Press, 2013), 205–25; and Peter

Feaver, "What Do Policymakers Want from Academic Experts on Nuclear Proliferation?" *Monkey Cage* blog, *Washington Post*, July 8, 2014 (www. washingtonpost.com/blogs/monkey-cage/wp/2014/07/08/what-do-policy makers-want-from-academic-experts-on-nuclear-proliferation/).

109. As Colin Kahl notes,

> When it comes to catastrophic threats, policymakers are simply not comforted by claims that proliferation will not lead to nuclear terrorism or nuclear cascades or nuclear escalation *the vast majority of the time*. Instead, they tend to see even miniscule risks of extraordinarily bad outcomes as compelling reasons to prevent additional nuclear proliferation. . . . Because Iran is a second- or third-tier power, Realists tend to not take the Islamic Republic very seriously. They do not see a nuclear-armed Iran as a game changer in the Middle East or a direct threat to the United States. Waltz even suggests that a nuclear-armed Iran would be a net positive for international stability by serving as a check against Israeli and American militarism and intervention. Yet it is precisely because of the potential constraint on American (and Israeli) 'freedom of action' in the Middle East that U.S. policymakers so heavily weight some of the ills associated with a nuclear-armed Iran.

Colin Kahl, "Proliferation Optimism versus Proliferation Pessimism: The Case of Iran," paper prepared for the Nuclear Studies Research Initiative, Austin, Texas, October 2013, 28.

110. The classic work on military technology, its diffusion, and its influence on power is William H. McNeill, *The Pursuit of Power: Technology, Armed Force, and Society since A.D. 1000* (University of Chicago Press, 1982). Note Michael Horowitz's important insight that many factors contribute to whether and how well a state exploits and adapts military technology into its strategy. See Horowitz, *The Diffusion of Military Power*.

111. International relations scholars have long been puzzled by the United States' failure to translate its enormous economic power into peacetime military power before 1950. Fareed Zakaria, *From Wealth to Power: The Unusual Origins of America's World Role* (Princeton University Press, 1999). For an excellent historical account, see Walter McDougall, *Promised Land, Crusader State: The American Encounter with the World since 1776* (New York: Houghton Mifflin, 1997).

112. This is a major theme in Gavin, *Nuclear Statecraft*.

113. Schrafstetter and Twigge, *Avoiding Armageddon*.

114. For an excellent summary of the academic literature on proliferation and nonproliferation, see Jacques E. C. Hymans, "Nuclear Proliferation and Non-Proliferation," in *The International Studies Encyclopedia*, edited by Robert A.

Denemark (London: Blackwell, 2010), 5447–466. For a recent article on security considerations, see Nuno P. Monteiro and Alexandre Debs, "The Strategic Logic of Nuclear Proliferation," *International Security* 39, no. 2 (2014), 7–51. For the best supply-side explanations, see Matthew Fuhrmann, *Atomic Assistance: How "Atoms for Peace" Programs Cause Nuclear Insecurity* (Cornell University Press, 2012), and Kroenig, *Exporting the Bomb.*

115. Scott D. Sagan and Kenneth N. Waltz, *The Spread of Nuclear Weapons: A Debate Renewed,* 2nd ed. (New York: W. W. Norton, 2003), 38.

116. Jacques E. C. Hymans. "Veto Players, Nuclear Energy, and Nonproliferation: Domestic Institutional Barriers to a Japanese Bomb," *International Security* 36, no. 2 (2011), 154.

117. *The Absolute Weapon: Atomic Power and World Order,* edited by Bernard Brodie (New York: Harcourt, Brace and Company, 1946); Stephen Van Evera, *Causes of War: Power and the Roots of Conflict.* (Cornell University Press, 1999).

118. "The best way for a state to achieve nuclear superiority is by arming itself with nuclear weapons while making sure no other state has them. A state with a nuclear monopoly, by definition, does not have to worry about retaliation in kind if it unleashes its nuclear weapons." John J. Mearsheimer, *The Tragedy of Great Power Politics* (New York: W. W. Norton, 2001), 129.

119. The nuclear revolution may have decreased the value of imperial territory to great powers. Although it may be a coincidence, France and Great Britain put great efforts into developing nuclear weapons at the same time they were losing their colonies. The author is grateful to Alexander Lanoszka for this observation.

120. During the 1945–1949 period, when the United States possessed a nuclear monopoly, it demobilized its military and demonstrated little interest in projecting its military power abroad. It was only after the Soviet Union detonated an atomic device—far earlier than expected—combined with the communist victory in China and what was seen as Soviet-supported aggression on the Korean peninsula, that the United States began a massive military buildup that ultimately included deploying its forces abroad and developing a forward-leaning, damage-limitation nuclear strategy.

121. Mearsheimer, *The Tragedy of Great Power Politics,* 44. The author is grateful to Alexander Lanoszka for this insight.

122. Is inhibition a product of American exceptionalism or rather a leading power phenomenon that would be embraced by any country possessing the United States' geopolitical position? One obvious test would be to more closely examine the attitudes of the Soviet Union when it was a superpower. Although we know that the Soviets often cooperated with the United States during the Cold War on nuclear nonproliferation, we know far less about their motives or

whether they would have pursued inhibition without U.S. encouragement. For an intriguing look into the Soviet case, see Eliza Gheorghe, "Frenemies, Nuclear Sharing, and Proliferation: The Eastern Bloc, 1965–1969," paper prepared for the Nuclear Studies Research Initiative Workshop, May 1, 2015.

CHAPTER FIVE

1. The best version of this conventional wisdom can be found throughout John Lewis Gaddis, *Strategies of Containment: A Critical Appraisal of American National Security Policy during the Cold War* (Oxford University Press, 2005). See also Robert J. Art, *A Grand Strategy for America* (Cornell University Press, 2003), 214–16.

2. Much of this analysis is based on the pathbreaking work of Marc Trachtenberg. See especially "The Nuclearization of NATO and U.S.–West European Relations" and "The Berlin Crisis," in *History and Strategy* (Princeton University Press, 1991), 153–68 and 169–234, respectively; and *A Constructed Peace: The Making of the European Settlement, 1945–1963* (Princeton University Press, 1997), especially 95–145.

3. Russell F. Weigley, *The American Way of War: A History of United States Military Strategy and Policy* (Indiana University Press, 1960).

4. Robert Wampler, "Ambiguous Legacy: The United States, Great Britain, and the Formulation of NATO Strategy, 1948–1957," Ph.D. dissertation, Harvard University, 1991; David Alan Rosenberg, " 'A Smoking Radiating Ruin at the End of Two Hours': Documents on American Plans for Nuclear War with the Soviet Union, 1954–1955," *International Security* 6, no. 3 (1981/1982), 3–38; David Alan Rosenberg, "The Origins of Overkill: Nuclear Weapons and American Strategy, 1945–1960," *International Security* 7, no. 4 (1983), 3–71; "The Nuclearization of NATO and U.S.–West European Relations," in *History and Strategy*, by Marc Trachtenberg (Princeton University Press, 1991).

5. Gregory W. Pedlow, ed., "NATO Strategy Documents, 1949–1969," NATO Archives (www.nato.int/archives/strategy.htm).

6. Trachtenberg, "The Nuclearization of NATO."

7. Francis J. Gavin, "The Myth of Flexible Response: United States Strategy in Europe during the 1960s," *The International History Review*, 23, no. 4 (December 2001), 847–75.

8. Francis J. Gavin, *Nuclear Statecraft: History and Strategy in America's Atomic Age* (Cornell University Press, 2012), 30–56.

9. Austin Long and Brendan Rittenhouse Green, "Stalking the Secure Second Strike: Intelligence, Counterforce, and Nuclear Strategy," *Journal of Strategic Studies* 38, nos. 1–2 (2015), 38–73.

10. Robert Jervis, *The Illogic of American Nuclear Strategy* (Cornell University Press, 1984).

11. Trachtenberg, "The Nuclearization of NATO."

12. Francis J. Gavin, "Blasts from the Past: Proliferation Lessons from the 1960s," *International Security* 29, no. 3, 100–135. See also Shane J. Maddock, *Nuclear Apartheid: The Quest for American Atomic Supremacy from World War II to the Present* (University of North Carolina Press, 2010).

13. Nicholas L. Miller, "The Secret Success of Nonproliferation Sanctions," *International Organization* 68, no. 4 (2018), 913–44.

14. Susanna Schrafstetter and Stephen Twigge, *Avoiding Armageddon: Europe, the United States, and the Struggle for Nuclear Nonproliferation, 1945–1970* (Westport, CT: Praeger Press, 2004).

15. Many analysts overstated Soviet superiority in conventional capabilities throughout the Cold War and suggested that from the early 1960s on, NATO forces could most likely have withstood a Soviet invasion of Western Europe without immediate recourse to nuclear weapons. John J. Mearsheimer, "Why the Soviets Can't Win Quickly in Central Europe," *International Security* 7, no. 1 (1982), 3–39.

16. A Google search of "NATO" and "crisis" yields 26 million hits.

17. Francis J. Gavin, *Gold, Dollars, and Power: The Politics of International Monetary Relations, 1958–1971* (University of North Carolina Press, 2004).

18. These stories can be found in Gavin, *Gold, Dollars, and Power,* and Trachtenberg, *A Constructed Peace.*

19. On the Euromissile crisis, see the excellent edited volume, *The Euromissile Crisis and the End of the Cold War,* edited by Leopoldo Nuti, Frederic Bozo, Marie-Pierre Rey, and Bern Rother (Stanford University Press, 2015).

CHAPTER SIX

1. The literature on the nuclear strategy community is large. For the best overview, see Marc Trachtenberg, "Strategic Thought in America, 1952–1966," in *History and Strategy* (Princeton University Press, 1991), 3–46. For more general accounts of this intellectual community, see Gregg Herken, *Counsels of War* (New York: Alfred A. Knopf, 1985), and Fred Kaplan, *The Wizards of Armageddon* (Stanford University Press, 1983). For a convincing critique, both of the ideas and the influence of this community, see Bruce Kuklick, *Blind Oracles: Intellectuals and War from Kennan to Kissinger* (Princeton University Press, 2006), especially 49–71 and 95–151. For general histories of the nuclear age, see McGeorge Bundy, *Danger and Survival: Choices about the Bomb in the First Fifty Years* (New York: Random House, 1988), and John Newhouse, *War and Peace in the Nuclear Age* (New York: Vintage Books, 1988).

2. The most powerful statement of this view can be found in Robert Jervis, *The Meaning of the Nuclear Revolution: Statecraft and the Prospect of Armageddon* (Cornell University Press, 1989). This view can also be found in many of Kenneth Waltz's writings.

3. The literature on these issues is enormous. For one of the classics in the field, see Bernard Brodie, *Strategy in the Missile Age* (Princeton University Press, 1959). For two important recent studies, see Lawrence Freedman, *Deterrence* (Malden, MA: Polity Press, 2004), and Patrick M. Morgan, *Deterrence Now* (Cambridge University Press, 2003).

4. See Francis J. Gavin, *Nuclear Statecraft: History and Strategy in America's Atomic Age* (Cornell University Press, 2012), especially 57–74.

5. For the dangers of nuclear escalation in a conflict with China, see Joshua Rovner, "Two Kinds of Catastrophe: Nuclear Escalation and Protracted War in Asia," *Journal of Strategic Studies* 40, no. 5 (2017), 696–730; Caitlin Talmadge, "Would China Go Nuclear? Assessing the Risk of Chinese Nuclear Escalation in a Conventional War with the United States," *International Security* 4, no. 4 (2017), 50–92.

6. Jervis, *The Meaning of the Nuclear Revolution, passim*.

7. For a trenchant argument to this point, see Robert Jervis, *The Illogic of American Nuclear Strategy* (Cornell University Press, 1984).

8. See chapter 9, this volume, for my critique of the nuclear revolution theorists.

9. See, for example, John Mueller, *Retreat from Doomsday: The Obsolescence of Major War* (New York: Basic Books, 1989).

10. Austin Long and Brendan Rittenhouse Green, "Stalking the Secure Second Strike: Intelligence, Counterforce, and Nuclear Strategy," Journal of Strategic Studies 38, nos. 1-2 (2015), 38–73.

11. Francis J. Gavin, "Strategies of Inhibition: U.S. Grand Strategy, the Nuclear Revolution, and Nonproliferation," *International Security* 40, no. 1 (2015), 9–46.

12. Gavin, *Nuclear Statecraft*, 17–19.

13. Reid Pauly, "Stop or I'll Shoot, Comply and I Won't: The Dilemma of Coercive Assurance in International Politics," Ph.D. dissertation, MIT, 2019.

14. For the best account of the causes and relative reconciliation of the underlying geopolitical issues in Europe between the Soviet Union and the United States—namely, resolving Germany's political and military status—see Marc Trachtenberg, *A Constructed Peace: The Making of the European Settlement, 1945–1963* (Princeton University Press, 1999).

15. Paul Bracken, *The Second Nuclear Age: Strategy, Danger, and the New Power Politics* (New York: Henry Holt, 2012).

16. Etel Solingen, "The Political Economy of Nuclear Restraint," *International Security* 19, no. 2 (1994), 126–69; Tony Judt, *Postwar: A History of Europe since 1945* (New York: Penguin Press, 2005).

17. For a sample of these perspectives, see Niall Ferguson and others, eds., *The Shock of the Global: The 1970s in Perspective* (Harvard University Press, 2010); Francis J. Gavin and Mark Atwood Lawrence, eds., *Beyond the Cold War: Lyndon Johnson and the New Global Challenges of the 1960s* (Oxford University Press, 2014); and Daniel J. Sargent, *A Superpower Transformed: The Remaking of American Foreign Relations in the 1970s* (Oxford University Press, 2015).

18. Andrew J. Coe and Jane Vaynman, "Collusion and the Nuclear Nonproliferation Regime," *Journal of Politics* 77, no. 4 (2015), 983–97.

CHAPTER SEVEN

1. Francis J. Gavin, "History, Security Studies, and the July Crisis," *Journal of Strategic Studies* 37, no. 2 (2014), 319–31.

2. For the best explanation of how the empirical and conceptual should interact in historical work, see Marc Trachtenberg, *The Craft of International History: A Guide to Method* (Princeton University Press, 2006).

3. For one of the more sophisticated discussions of the differences between political scientists and historians of international relations, see Robert Jervis, "International Politics and Diplomatic History: Fruitful Differences," *H-Diplo/ISSF Essays*, no. 1 (March 12, 2010). See also Colin Elman and Miriam Fendius Elman, eds., *Bridges and Boundaries: Historians, Political Scientists, and the Study of International Relations* (MIT Press, 2001).

4. Bernard Brodie, ed., *The Absolute Weapon* (New York: Harcourt, Brace, 1946), 76.

5. Two useful expositions that lay out the ideas and influence of the strategists are Lawrence Freedman, *The Evolution of Nuclear Strategy*, 3rd ed. (New York: Palgrave Macmillan, 2003), and Fred Kaplan, *The Wizards of Armageddon* (Stanford University Press, 1983).

6. Bruce Kuklick suggests that the nuclear strategists were far less influential in the making of nuclear policy than they or conventional wisdom believed. See Bruce Kuklick, *Blind Oracles: Intellectuals and War from Kennan to Kissinger* (Princeton University Press, 2006), especially, 49–151.

7. Francis J. Gavin, "History and Policy," *International Journal* 63, no. 1 (2008/2009), 162–77.

8. The discussion that follows over the next four paragraphs is based on Francis J. Gavin, *Gold, Dollars, and Power: The Politics of International Monetary Relations, 1958–1971* (University of North Carolina Press, 2004).

9. Interview with General Lemnitzer, Supreme Allied Commander in Europe (1963–1969), February 11, 1970, by Dr. David Nunnerley, Oral History Collection, John F. Kennedy Presidential Library, 6–7.

10. Quoted in Leonard Wainstein and others, "The Evolution of U.S. Strategic Command and Control and Warning, 1945–1972," Institute for Defense Analyses, June 1975, DOD-FOIA, 287.

11. Francis J. Gavin, *Nuclear Statecraft: History and Strategy in America's Atomic Age* (Ithaca, NY: Cornell University Press, 2012), 30–56.

12. For the origins of the bureaucratic politics paradigm as it relates to nuclear issues, see the discussion in Trachtenberg, *History and Strategy*, 27–31.

13. For a withering, and to my mind convincing, critique of the bureaucratic politics paradigm, especially as developed by the so-called May Group composed of Harvard faculty and led by Professor Ernest May at the Kennedy School of Government, see Kuklick, *Blind Oracles*, 152–67.

14. The best explanation of this geopolitical logic can be found in Marc Trachtenberg, *A Constructed Peace: The Making of the European Settlement, 1945–1963* (Princeton University Press, 1999).

15. Gavin, *Nuclear Statecraft*, 75–103.

16. Hal Brands, "Rethinking Nonproliferation: LBJ, the Gilpatric Committee, and U.S. National Security Policy," *Journal of Cold War Studies* 8, no. 2 (2006), 83–113.

17. For Waltz's views, see Kenneth Waltz, "The Spread of Nuclear Weapons: More May Be Better," *Adelphi Papers*, no. 171 (London: International Institute for Strategic Studies, 1981). For a more nuanced but still defensive realist view, see Robert Jervis, *The Meaning of the Nuclear Revolution: Statecraft and the Prospects for Armageddon* (Cornell University Press, 1989).

18. Gavin, *Nuclear Statecraft*, 134–56.

19. Marc Trachtenberg, "Preventive War and U.S. Foreign Policy," *Security Studies* 16, no. 1 (2007), 1–31.

20. Francis J. Gavin and Mira Rapp-Hooper, "The Copenhagen Tradition: Rethinking Prevention and Proliferation in the Age of Deterrence Dominance," Tobin National Security Project (www.tobinproject.org/sites/tobinproject.org/files/assets/Gavin%26Rapp-Hooper_US_Preventive_War_Thinking.pdf).

21. Thomas C. Schelling, *Arms and Influence* (Yale University Press, 1966), 69–91. I am grateful to Marc Trachtenberg for his great insight on this issue.

22. Gavin, *Nuclear Statecraft*, 57–74.

23. Ibid.

24. See especially Justin Vaïsse, *Neoconservatism: The Biography of a Movement* (Harvard University Press, 2010).

25. Odd Arne Westad, "The Fall of Détente and the Turning Tides of His-

tory," in *The Fall of Détente: Soviet-American Relations during the Carter Years,* edited by Odd Arne Westad (Scandinavian University Press, 1997), 15. To see further details of the Soviet reaction and the theory that Brezhnev may have allowed the SS-20 deployment to placate a Soviet military angry over SALT I and SALT II negotiations, see David Holloway, "The Dynamics of the Euromissile Crisis, 1977–1983," in *The Euro Missile Crisis and the End of the Cold War,* edited by Leopoldo Nuti, Frédéric Bozo, Marie-Pierre Rey, and Bernd Rother (Washington, DC: Woodrow Wilson Center Press, 2015).

26. See especially Leopoldo Nuti, ed., *The Crisis of Détente in Europe: From Helsinki to Gorbachev, 1975–1985* (New York: Routledge, 2009). On documents relating to the Euromissile crisis, see Timothy McDowell, ed., "The Euromissiles Crisis and the End of the Cold War: 1977–1987," July 7, 2011, Nuclear Proliferation History Project, Wilson Center.

27. For the idea that obscure debates over nuclear strategies and deployments masked deeper differences in geopolitical outlooks, particularly in the United States, see Gavin, *Nuclear Statecraft,* 120–33.

28. Kenneth Waltz, "Why Iran Should Get the Bomb: Nuclear Balancing Would Mean Stability," *Foreign Affairs* 91, no. 4 (2012), 2–5.

29. John Keegan, *The Mask of Command: Alexander the Great, Wellington, Ulysses S. Grant, Hitler, and the Nature of Leadership* (New York: Penguin Books, 1988).

CHAPTER EIGHT

1. The nine states are the United States, Russia, Great Britain, France, China, Israel, India, Pakistan, and North Korea.

2. William Burr, "U.S. War Plans Would Kill an Estimated 108 Million Soviets, 104 Million Chinese, and 2.6 Million Poles: More Evidence on SIOP-62 and the Origins of Overkill," November 8, 2011, *Unredacted* (blog), National Security Archive (https://nsarchive.wordpress.com/2011/11/08/u-s-war-plans-would-kill-an-estimated-108-million-soviets-104-million-chinese-and-2-3-million-poles-more-evidence-on-siop-62-and-the-origins-of-overkill/).

3. "Nuclear Danger Today: Beyond the Cold War," Cuban Missile Crisis, Belfer Center for Science and International Affairs, Harvard, Kennedy School of Government.

4. Eric Schlosser, *Command and Control: Nuclear Weapons, the Damascus Incident, and the Illusion of Safety* (New York: Random House, 2014).

5. Julian Borger, "Nuclear Weapons Risk Greater Than in Cold War, Says Ex–Pentagon Chief," *The Guardian,* January 7, 2016 (www.theguardian.com/

world/2016/jan/07/nuclear-weapons-risk-greater-than-in-cold-war-says-ex-pentagon-chief).

6. President Wilson's Fourteen Points, Delivered in a Joint Session of the U.S. Congress, January 8, 1918 (https://wwi.lib.byu.edu/index.php/President_Wilson%27s_Fourteen_Points).

7. Remarks by President Barack Obama in Prague as Delivered, April 5, 2009, Office of the Press Secretary, White House.

8. Josh Rogin, "Obama Plans Major Nuclear Policy Changes in His Final Months," *Washington Post*, July 10, 2016.

9. United Nations General Assembly, "Taking Forward Multilateral Nuclear Disarmament Negotiations," First Committee, Seventy-First sess., Agenda Item 78 .

10. Kambiz Foroohar, "Nuclear-Armed Foes Unite against UN Call to Shed Their Bombs," October 27, 2016, Bloomberg Business (www.bloomberg.com/news/articles/2016-10-27/nuclear-armed-foes-unite-against-a-un-call-to-shed-their-weapons).

11. Quoted in Jeffrey A. Engel, ed., *The Four Freedoms: Franklin D. Roosevelt and the Evolution of an American Idea* (Oxford University Press, 2015), 18.

12. Marc Trachtenberg, "The Past and Future of Arms Control," *Daedalus* 120, no. 1, *Arms Control: Thirty Years On* (1991), 3.

13. Robert Jervis, "Cooperation under the Security Dilemma," *World Politics* 30, no. 2 (1978), 167.

14. See chapter 7, this volume.

15. John Lewis Gaddis, *The Long Peace: Inquiries into the History of the Cold War* (Oxford University Press, 1987).

16. Ibid., 231.

17. Quoted in Robert Jervis, *The Meaning of the Nuclear Revolution: Statecraft and the Prospect of Armageddon* (Cornell University Press, 1989), 4.

18. Paul Fussell, "Thank God for the Atom Bomb," *New Republic,* August 1981.

19. Ward Wilson, "The Myth of Nuclear Deterrence," *Nonproliferation Review* 15, no. 3 (2008), 421–39.

20. Ward Wilson, "The Myth of Nuclear Necessity," *New York Times*, January 13, 2013.

21. George Schultz and others, "A World Free of Nuclear Weapons," *Wall Street Journal*, January 4, 2007.

22. See especially Schlosser, *Command and Control.*

23. Quote taken from Richard Betts, *Nuclear Blackmail and Nuclear Balance* (Washington, DC: Brookings Institution, 1987), 199–200.

24. Dwight Garner, "After Atom Bombs' Shock, the Real Horrors Began Unfolding," *New York Times,* January 19, 2010.

25. A story on Public Radio International's website includes a chart that provides a flavor of these favorable trends: "The World Is Actually Safer than Ever. And Here's the Data to Prove That," PRI, *The Takeaway* (www.pri.org/stories/2014-10-23/world-actually-safer-ever-and-heres-data-prove).

26. Inaugural Address of President John F. Kennedy, Washington, DC, January 20, 1961.

CHAPTER NINE

1. Hal Brands, *What Good Is Grand Strategy? Power and Purpose in American Statecraft from Harry S. Truman to George W. Bush* (Cornell University Press, 2014), 3.

2. Robert Jervis, *The Meaning of the Nuclear Revolution: Statecraft and the Prospect of Armageddon* (Cornell University Press, 1990), 8.

3. Lawrence Freedman, *The Evolution of Nuclear Strategy* (New York: Palgrave Macmillan, 2003), 458.

4. Stephen M. Walt, "Rethinking the 'Nuclear Revolution,'" *Foreign Policy,* August 3, 2010 (https://foreignpolicy.com/2010/08/03/rethinking-the-nuclear-revolution/).

5. Robert Jervis, *The Illogic of American Nuclear Statecraft* (Cornell University Press), 12.

6. Charles L. Glaser, *Analyzing Strategic Nuclear Policy* (Princeton University Press, 1990), 95.

7. Todd S. Sechser and Matthew Fuhrmann, *Nuclear Weapons and Coercive Diplomacy* (Cambridge University Press, 2017), 6. The classic work arguing that nuclear weapons are ineffective for coercion is by Richard K. Betts, *Nuclear Blackmail and Nuclear Balance* (Washington, DC: Brookings Institution Press, 1987).

8. Joshua Rovner, "Was There a Nuclear Revolution? Strategy, Grand Strategy, and the Ultimate Weapon," *War on the Rocks,* March 6, 2018 (https://warontherocks.com/2018/03/was-there-a-nuclear-revolution-strategy-grand-strategy-and-the-ultimate-weapon/).

9. Scott D. Sagan and Kenneth N. Waltz, *The Spread of Nuclear Weapons: An Enduring Debate* (New York: W. W. Norton, 2012), 37.

10. Kenneth N. Waltz, "The Emerging Structure of International Politics," *International Security* 18, no. 2 (1993), 73.

11. Kenneth N. Waltz, "Nuclear Myths and Political Realities," *American Political Science Review* 84, no. 3 (1990), 732.

12. Sagan and Waltz, *The Spread of Nuclear Weapons*, 21–22.

13. Charles L. Glaser and Chaim Kauffman, "What Is the Offense-Defense Balance and Can We Measure It?," *International Security* 22, no. 4 (1998), 5–6. Italics added.

14. Stephen Van Evera, *Causes of War: Power and the Roots of Conflict* (Cornell University Press), 178.

15. John J. Mearsheimer, *The Tragedy of Great Power Politics* (New York: W. W. Norton, 2001), 129.

16. John Lewis Gaddis, "The Long Peace: Elements of Stability in the Postwar International System," *International Security* 10, no. 4 (1986), 121.

17. Highlighting an irony: If the nuclear revolution was so obvious, powerful, and irresistible, why do analysts have to spend so much time telling policymakers to pursue the policy (or not fight against it), if it was the natural consequence of the revolution?

18. There were, of course, exceptions to this view. Among the original strategists, Albert Wohlstetter was often critical of the focus on mutual assured destruction, as was Herman Kahn. For an overview of the early debates, see Fred Kaplan, *The Wizards of Armageddon* (New York: Simon and Schuster, 1983). Later critics of this view include Colin Gray and Keith Payne. See especially Colin S. Gray and Keith Payne, "Victory Is Possible," *Foreign Policy*, no. 39 (1980), 14–27.

19. Rovner, "Was There a Nuclear Revolution?"

20. Stephen I. Schwartz, "The Hidden Costs of Our Nuclear Arsenal: Overview of Project Findings," Brookings Institution, June 30, 1998 (www.brookings.edu/the-hidden-costs-of-our-nuclear-arsenal-overview-of-project-findings/).

21. The Congressional Budget Office estimates the cost of operating and modernizing U.S. nuclear security forces at more than $1.2 trillion over the next thirty years. Congressional Budget Office, *Approaches for Managing the Costs of U.S. Nuclear Forces, 2017–2046*, October 2017, report.

22. On nuclear sharing, see Marc Trachtenberg, *A Constructed Peace: The Making of the European Settlement, 1949–1963* (Princeton University Press, 1999). The best work on predelegation remains Peter Feaver, *Guarding the Guardians: Civilian Control of Nuclear Weapons in the United States* (Cornell University Press, 1992).

23. See the important scholarship of Keir Lieber, Daryl Press, Brendan Green, Austin Long, Niccolo Petrelli, and Giordana Pulcini, among others, cited throughout this chapter. Two excellent forthcoming works will also provide comprehensive insight on this history: Brendan Green, "The Meaning of the Nuclear Counterrevolution: Arms Racing and Arms Control after MAD," unpublished paper; and Timothy McDonnell, "The Sources of US Nuclear Posture, 1945 to Present," Ph.D. dissertation, MIT, 2019.

24. David Alan Rosenberg, "The Origins of Overkill: Nuclear Weapons and American Strategy, 1945–1960," *International Security* 7, no. 4 (1983), 3–71.

25. James Cameron, *The Double Game: The Demise of America's First Missile Defense System and the Rise of Strategic Arms Limitation* (Oxford University Press, 2017), 5.

26. John D. Maurer, "The Forgotten Side of Arms Control: Enhancing U.S. Competitive Advantage, Offsetting Enemy Strengths," *War on the Rocks*, June 27, 2018 (https://warontherocks.com/2018/06/the-forgotten-side-of-arms-con trol-enhancing-u-s-competitive-advantage-offsetting-enemy-strengths/).

27. Niccolo Petrelli and Giordana Pulcini, "Nuclear Superiority in the Age of Parity: US Planning, Intelligence Analysis, Weapons Innovation, and the Search for a Qualitative Edge, 1969–1976," *International History Review* 40, no. 5 (2018).

28. For excellent details on the characteristics of these systems and their influence on the strategic balance, see especially Austin Long and Brendan Rittenhouse Green, "Stalking the Secure Second Strike: Intelligence, Counterforce, and Nuclear Strategy," *Journal of Strategic Studies* 38, no. 1/2 (2015); Keir Lieber and Daryl Press, "How Much Is Enough? Testing Theories of Nuclear Deterrence," unpublished manuscript, cited with permission of the author; and Petrelli and Pulcini, "Nuclear Superiority in the Age of Parity." The best work on U.S. efforts on antisubmarine capabilities remains Owen R. Cote Jr., *The Third Battle: Innovation in the US Navy's Silent Cold War Struggle with Soviet Submarines* (Newport, RI: Naval War College, 2003).

29. Long and Green, "Stalking the Secure Second Strike," 41.

30. Brendan R. Green and Austin Long, "The MAD Who Wasn't There: Soviet Reactions to the Late Cold War Nuclear Balance," *Security Studies* 26, no. 4 (2017), 608.

31. Keir A. Lieber and Daryl G. Press, "The New Era of Counterforce: Technological Change and the Future of Nuclear Deterrence," *International Security* 41, no. 4 (2017).

32. Glenn Buchan and others, *Future Roles of U.S. Nuclear Forces: Implications for U.S. Strategy* (Santa Monica, CA: RAND, 2003), 92. Italics in original.

33. For a thorough exploration and ultimate rejection of the argument that an overly aggressive nuclear strategy was driven by "Pentagon bureaucrats and military officers pursuing organizational or service agendas, rather than national interest"—or what he calls "'pathological posture' theory"—see Timothy McDonnell, "The Sources of US Nuclear Posture, 1945 to Present," Ph.D. dissertation, MIT, 2019.

34. Brendan Rittenhouse Green and Austin Long, "The Geopolitical Origins

of US Hard-Target-Kill Counterforce Capabilities and MIRVS," in *The Lure and Pitfalls of MIRVs: From the First to the Second Nuclear Age*, edited by Michael Krepon, Travis Wheeler, and Shane Mason (Washington, DC: Stimson Center, 2016); and Petrelli and Pulcini, "Nuclear Superiority in the Age of Parity."

35. Green and Long, "The Geopolitical Origins of US Hard-Target-Kill Counterforce Capabilities and MIRVs," 21.

36. Glenn A. Kent and David E. Thaler, *First Strike Stability: A Methodology for Evaluating Strategic Forces* (Santa Monica, CA: RAND, 1989), 5.

37. Earl C. Ravenal, "Counterforce and Alliance: The Ultimate Connection," *International Security* 6, no. 4 (1982), 26–43.

38. Henry L. Trewhitt, *McNamara: His Ordeal in the Pentagon* (New York: Harper and Row, 1971), 115.

39. For insight on how American policymakers explored and assessed preemptive nuclear options, see Francis J. Gavin and Mira Rapp-Hooper, "The Copenhagen Temptation: Rethinking Prevention and Proliferation in the Age of Deterrence Dominance," unpublished paper.

40. Francis J. Gavin, "Beyond Deterrence: U.S. Nuclear Statecraft since 1945," in Linton Brooks, Francis J. Gavin, and Alexei Arbatov, *Meeting the Challenges of the New Nuclear Age: U.S. and Russian Nuclear Concepts, Past and Present* (Cambridge, MA: American Academy of Arts and Sciences, 2018), 6–20.

41. Kent and Thaler, *First Strike Stability*, 5. See also Brendan Rittenhouse Green and Austin Long, "Correspondence: The Limits of Damage Limitation," *International Security* 42, no. 1 (2017).

42. Francis J. Gavin, "Strategies of Inhibition: U.S. Grand Strategy, the Nuclear Revolution, and Nonproliferation," *International Security* 40, no. 1 (2015): 9–46.

43. Andrew J. Coe and Jane Vaynman, "Collusion and the Nuclear Nonproliferation Regime," *Journal of Politics* 77, no. 4 (2015), 983–97.

44. For excellent insight on the challenges this new environment presented to traditional constitutional practices in U.S. national security decisionmaking, see Matthew Waxman, "NATO and War Powers: Remembering the 'Great Debate' of the 1950s," *Lawfare,* July 11, 2018; Matthew C. Waxman, "The Power to Threaten War," *Yale Law Journal* 123, no. 6 (2014), 1626–91.

45. Exemplary works in this category include McGeorge Bundy, *Danger and Survival: Choices about the Bomb in the First Fifty Years* (New York: Random House, 1988); George Bunn, *Arms Control by Committee: Managing Negotiations with the Russians* (Stanford University Press, 1992); Gregg Herken, *Counsels of War* (New York: Knopf, 1985); Kaplan, *The Wizards of Armageddon*; Richard Rhodes, *Arsenals of Folly: The Making of the Nuclear Arms Race*

(New York: Alfred A. Knopf, 2007). Specialists in security studies and strategic studies demonstrate great appreciation for history, though they rarely pursue exhaustive, multiarchival work on their own and do not claim to do scholarly history. The best works in this tradition include the following: Richard Betts, *Nuclear Blackmail and Nuclear Balance* (Washington, DC: Brookings Institution Press, 1987); Lawrence Freedman, *Evolution of Nuclear Strategy,* 4th ed. (London: Palgrave Macmillan, 2019); Charles Glaser, *Analyzing Strategic Nuclear Policy* (Princeton University Press, 1990); Robert Jervis, *The Meaning of the Nuclear Revolution* (Cornell University Press, 1989); Scott Sagan, *Moving Targets: Nuclear Strategy and National Security* (Princeton University Press, 1990). It is no overstatement to say that those in security and strategic studies would be thrilled if the scholarly history profession in the United States would devote more intellectual resources to mining the extraordinary increases in archival materials made available in recent years. That said, some of the best work with primary materials has been done by scholars in this field, including Brendan Green, Keir Lieber, Austin Long, and Daryl Press.

46. What follows is just a sample of this excellent new work on national nuclear programs, much of it supported by the pathbreaking Nuclear Proliferation International History Project (NPIHP) (www.wilsoncenter.org/program/nuclear-proliferation-international-history-project). On Australia, see Christine M. Leah, *Australia and the Bomb* (New York: Palgrave Macmillan, 2014); on Brazil, see Carlo Patti, "Origins and Evolution of the Brazilian Nuclear Program (1947–2011)," NPIHP, November 15, 2012; Avner Cohen, *The Worst-Kept Secret: Israel's Bargain with the Bomb* (Columbia University Press, 2010); on Italy, see Leopoldo Nuti, "Italy's Nuclear Choices," *UNISCI Discussion Papers,* no. 25 (2011), 167–81; on Japan, see Fintan Hoey Sato, *America and the Cold War: U.S.–Japanese Relations, 1964–72* (London: Palgrave Macmillan, 2015); on Pakistan, see Feroz Khan, *Eating Grass: The Making of the Pakistani Bomb* (Stanford University Press, 2012); on Romania, see Eliza Gheorghe, "Atomic Maverick: Romania's Negotiations for Nuclear Technology, 1964–1970," *Cold War History* 13, no. 3 (2013), 373–92; on South Korea, see Se Young Jang, "Dealing with Allies' Nuclear Ambitions: U.S. Nuclear Non-Proliferation Policy toward South Korea and Taiwan, 1969–1981," Ph.D. dissertation, Graduate Institute of International and Development Studies, 2015; on Sweden, see Thomas Jonter, "The Swedish Plans to Acquire Nuclear Weapons, 1945–1968: An Analysis of the Technical Preparations," *Science and Global Security,* no. 18 (2010): 61–86; on West Germany, see Andreas Lutsch, "The Persistent Legacy: Germany's Place in the Nuclear Order," Woodrow Wilson International Center for Scholars, NPIHP Working Paper 5, May 19, 2015.

47. To give three examples: For an excellent history of U.S. arms-control policy during the Nixon presidency, see Cameron, *The Double Game*; for an excellent study of America's early nuclear strategies, see Edward Kaplan, *American Strategy in the Air-Atomic Age and the Rise of Mutually Assured Destruction* (Cornell University Press, 2015); for an excellent history of U.S. nuclear nonproliferation policies, see Shane Maddock, *Nuclear Apartheid: The Quest for American Atomic Supremacy from World War II to the Present* (University of North Carolina Press, 2010).

48. Hal Brands, "The Triumph and Tragedy of Diplomatic History," *Texas National Security Review* 1, no. 1 (2017), 132–43. Even when there are diplomatic historians, there is almost no incentive for them to work on U.S. nuclear weapons policy. "Yet the turn toward diplomatic history as cultural, social, or gender history often pulled the field in a very different direction, one that dramatically deemphasized matters of foreign policy as it was traditionally understood." See also Hal Brands and Francis J. Gavin, "The Historical Profession Is Committing Slow-Motion Suicide," *War on the Rocks*, December 10, 2018 (https://warontherocks.com/2018/12/the-historical-profession-is-com mitting-slow-motion-suicide/).

49. Francis J. Gavin, "What We Talk about When We Talk about Nuclear Weapons: A Review Essay," paper prepared for H-Diplo/ISSF Forum, "What We Talk about When We Talk about Nuclear Weapons," June 15, 2014. The entire forum is available at http://issforum.org/ISSF/PDF/ISSF-Forum-2.pdf.

50. The exception is Marc Trachtenberg's pathbreaking account of the first decades of the Cold War, which brilliantly integrates nuclear strategy into an understanding of U.S. grand strategy. Marc Trachtenberg, *A Constructed Peace: The Making of the European Settlement, 1949–1963* (Princeton University Press, 1999).

51. Gavin, "Strategies of Inhibition."

52. For one excellent example that reveals the deep interconnections between Cold War geopolitics, imperialism, and decolonization, international economics and globalization, and nationalism and regional rivalries, see Philip Zelikow and Ernest May, *Suez Deconstructed: An Interactive Study in Crisis, War, and Peacemaking* (Washington, DC: Brookings Institution Press, 2018).

53. Trachtenberg, *History and Strategy*, 46.

54. Bruce Kuklick, *Blind Oracles: Intellectuals and War from Kennan to Kissinger* (Princeton University Press, 2006), 15–16. "Yet my philosophers in government knew and understood little, and had little influence qua intellectuals, except to perform feats of ventriloquy."

55. For an excellent analysis, see Janne Nolan, *Guardians of the Arsenal: The Politics of Nuclear Strategy* (New York: Basic Books, 1989).

56. John Foster Dulles, "The Strategy of Massive Retaliation," speech before the Council on Foreign Relations, January 12, 1954; Robert McNamara, "No Cities," commencement address, University of Michigan, Ann Arbor, July 9, 1962; Robert McNamara, speech on anti-China missile defense and U.S. nuclear strategy, September 19, 1967 (www.nytimes.com/1967/09/19/archives/text-of-mcnamara-speech-on-antichina-missile-defense-and-us-nuclear.html); "Nixon's Nuclear Doctrine," *New York Times*, January 15, 1974; "The Carter Transformation of Our Strategic Doctrine," memo from National Security Adviser Zbigniew Brzezinski to President Jimmy Carter, August 26, 1980.

57. For an excellent synthesis of how policymakers wrestle with domestic politics in nuclear decisionmaking, see Elizabeth N. Saunders, "The Domestic Politics of Nuclear Choices: What Have We Learned?" (forthcoming).

58. Cameron, *The Double Game*, 7.

59. Francis J. Gavin, *Nuclear Statecraft: History and Strategy in America's Atomic Age* (Cornell University Press, 2012), 31.

60. David Alan Rosenberg, "Reality and Responsibility: Power and Process in the Making of United States Nuclear Strategy, 1945–68," *Journal of Strategic Studies* 9, no. 1 (1986), 35.

61. For a recent overview, with recommendations for how these procedures should be changed, see Richard K. Betts and Matthew C. Waxman, "The President and the Bomb: Reforming the Nuclear Launch Process, *Foreign Affairs* 97, no. 2 (2018), 119–28.

62. As Timothy McDonnell argues, "Presidents, defense secretaries and other members of the president's civilian executive team drive US nuclear posture, making posture decisions that they believe will advance American interests. At the same time, nuclear policy is a tough business, fraught with uncertainty and existential risk." Timothy McDonnell, "The Sources of US Nuclear Posture, 1945 to Present," Ph.D. dissertation, MIT, 2019.

63. For an excellent effort to make sense of the often contradictory policies and rhetoric of President Dwight D. Eisenhower on nuclear weapons, see Andrew P. N. Erdmann, "'War No Longer Has Any Logic Whatever': Eisenhower and the Thermonuclear Revolution," in *Cold War Statesmen Confront the Bomb*, edited by John Lewis Gaddis (Oxford University Press, 1999), 87–119.

64. Rosenberg, "Reality and Responsibility," 48. McNamara's view is obviously in slight tension with Rosenberg's argument.

65. Carol Cohn, "Sex and Death in the Rational World of Defense Intellectuals," *Signs* 12, no. 4 (1987), 490.

66. Michael Quinlan, "Thinking about Nuclear Weapons," Royal United Services Institute, Whitehall Paper 41, online edition 2005 (http://fisherp

.scripts.mit.edu/wordpress/wp-content/uploads/2017/03/Thinking-about-Nuclear-Weapons-RUSI-WHP41_QUINLAN1.pdf).

67. Tannenwald, *The Nuclear Taboo: The United States and the Non-Use of Nuclear Weapons* (Cambridge University Press, 2007), ix.

68. Reid Pauly, "Stop or I'll Shoot, Comply and I Won't: The Dilemma of Coercive Assurance in International Politics," Ph.D. dissertation, MIT, 2019.

69. Rebecca K. C. Hersman, Clark Murdock, and Shanelle Van, *The Evolving U.S. Nuclear Narrative: Communicating the Rationale for the Role and Value of U.S. Nuclear Weapons*, Center for Strategic and International Studies, October 2016.

70. See, for example, Patrick Malone, "Repeated Safety Lapses Hobble Los Alamos National Laboratory's Work on the Cores of U.S. Nuclear Warheads," Center for Public Integrity, June 18, 2017; "What the Air Force Can Learn from the Nuclear Cheating Scandal," *Washington Post*, editorial, April 6, 2014.

71. Robert Jervis, "Politics and Political Science," *Annual Review of Political Science*, no. 21 (2018), 10–11. "This intention matters because it led me to deemphasize the question of why, if the nuclear balance was so stable, the policy of multiple options was dangerous (as well as unnecessary). Relatedly, I said little about what was clear from my work on perceptions: If leaders on either side believed that nuclear superiority mattered, that belief would affect their behavior. These are nasty problems, and I think that had the political stakes not been as great, I would have delved into them more deeply."

72. Gaddis, "The Long Peace," 100.

73. Francis J. Gavin, "History, Security Studies, and the July Crisis," *Journal of Strategic Studies* 37, no. 2 (2014), 319–33.

74. "Even propositions about the achievement of nuclear weapons in deterrence lack hard evidence, since such propositions are essentially about alternative history—about what would have happened had matters been other than they were." Quinlan, "Thinking about Nuclear Weapons," 5.

75. The nuclear revolution framework would have predicted that these states would acquire nuclear weapons. Some excellent work exists on states that decided not to go nuclear. On Sweden, for example, see Thomas Jonter, *The Key to Nuclear Restraint: The Swedish Plans to Acquire Nuclear Weapons during the Cold War* (London: Palgrave Macmillan, 2016). On Australia, for example, see Christine M. Leah, *Australia and the Bomb* (New York: Palgrave Macmillan, 2014).

76. Philip Zelikow, "Review," *H-Diplo Roundtable Reviews* 15, no. 1 (2013), 29.

77. Quinlan, "Thinking about Nuclear Weapons," 5.

78. Richard Haas, "The Age of Nonpolarity," *Foreign Affairs* 87, no. 3 (2008), 44–56.

79. The Trump administration focused on the return of great-power geopolitical competition in both its national security strategy and its national defense strategy: *National Security Strategy of the United States* (Washington, DC: White House, 2017); *Summary of the 2018 National Defense Strategy of the United States of America* (Washington, DC: Department of Defense, 2018).

80. Lieber and Press, "The New Era of Counterforce," 9.

81. Michael Horowitz, "How Surprising Is North Korea's Nuclear Success? Picking Up Where Proliferation Theories Leave Off," *War on the Rocks,* September 6, 2017 (https://warontherocks.com/2017/09/how-surprising-is-north-koreas-nuclear-success-picking-up-where-proliferation-theories-leave-off/).

82. Lieber and Press, "The New Era of Counterforce," 10.

83. Ian Traynor, "Barack Obama Launches Doctrine for Nuclear-Free World," *Guardian,* April 5, 2009.

84. Edward Geist and Andrew J. Lohn, *How Might Artificial Intelligence Affect the Risk of Nuclear War?* (Santa Monica, CA: RAND, 2018), 1.

85. Beyza Unal and Patricia Lewis, *Cybersecurity of Nuclear Weapons Systems Threats, Vulnerabilities, and Consequences*, Chatham House, January 11, 2018.

86. Joshua Rovner, "Two Kinds of Catastrophe: Nuclear Escalation and Protracted War in Asia," *Journal of Strategic Studies* 40, no. 5 (2017), 702.

87. Caitlin Talmadge, "Would China Go Nuclear? Assessing the Risk of Chinese Nuclear Escalation in a Conventional War with the United States," *International Security* 40, no. 4 (2017), 90.

88. Michael Kofman, "Searching for Strategy in Washington's Competition with Russia," *War on the Rocks*, January 30, 2018 (https://warontherocks.com/2018/01/searching-strategy-washingtons-competition-russia/).

89. Andrew F. Krepinevich Jr., "The Eroding Balance of Terror: The Decline of Deterrence," *Foreign Affairs* 98, no. 1 (2019), 66.

90. Michael C. Horowitz, Paul Scharre, and Alex Velez-Green, "A Stable Nuclear Future? The Impact of Automation, Autonomy, and Artificial Intelligence," National Threat Initiative seminar with Michael C. Horowitz, University of Pennsylvania, 2017.

91. James M. Acton, "Technology, Doctrine, and the Risk of Nuclear War," research paper, American Academic of Arts and Sciences, 2018.

92. Tannenwald, *The Nuclear Taboo*, 19.

93. Heather Williams, Patricia Lewis, and Sasan Aghlani, "The Humanitarian Impacts of Nuclear Weapons Initiative: The 'Big Tent' in Disarmament," Chatham House, March 2015, 17.

94. Quoted ibid., 13.

95. Tannenwald, *The Nuclear Taboo*, 49.

96. Ibid., 370.

97. General (Ret.) James Cartwright, "Modernizing U.S. Nuclear Strategy, Force Structure and Posture," Global Zero U.S. Nuclear Policy Report, May 2012, 2.

98. Daryl G. Press, Scott D. Sagan, and Benjamin A. Valentino, "Atomic Aversion: Experimental Evidence on Taboos, Traditions, and the Non-Use of Nuclear Weapons," *American Political Science Review* 107, no. 1 (2013), 188–206.

99. Reid Pauly, "Elite Aversion to the Use of Nuclear Weapons: Evidence from Wargames," *International Security* 43, no. 2 (2018), 151–92.

100. For a summary of this critique of grand strategy, see Francis J. Gavin, "Review," *H-Diplo Roundtable Reviews* 7, no. 2 (2014).

101. Walter A. McDougall, "Can the United States Do Grand Strategy," *Telegram*, Foreign Policy Research Institute, April 13, 2010.

102. Francis J. Gavin and James B. Steinberg, "Mind the Gap: Why Policymakers and Scholars Ignore Each Other, and What Should Be Done about It?," *Carnegie Reporter* 6, no. 4 (2012).

103. Steve Coll, "Table Talk," Comment, *New Yorker*, February 6, 2012, 19–20.

104. Matthew Kroenig argues that nuclear states seek freedom of action in *Exporting the Bomb: Technology Transfers and the Spread of Nuclear Weapons* (Cornell University Press, 2010). For an excellent overview of how U.S. grand strategy has, since the earliest days of the republic, unilaterally gone on the offensive in an effort to eliminate vulnerability, see John Lewis Gaddis, *Surprise, Security, and the American Experience* (Harvard University Press, 2005).

105. As Richard K. Betts has pointed out, what may be good for the "system"—stability—may not be what the United States prefers. "If nuclear spread enhances stability, this is not entirely good news for the United States, since it has been accustomed to attacking small countries with impunity when it felt justified and provoked." See Betts, "Universal Deterrence or Conceptual Collapse? Liberal Pessimism and Utopian Realism," in *The Coming Crisis: Nuclear Proliferation, U.S. Interests, and World Order*, edited by Victor A. Utgoff (MIT Press, 2000), 65.

106. "The Acheson-Lilienthal and Baruch Plans, 1946," Department of State, Office of the Historian.

107. "If we were ruthlessly realistic, we would not permit any foreign power with which we are not firmly allied, and in which we do not have absolute confidence, to make or possess atomic weapons. If such a country started to make atomic weapons we would destroy its capacity to make them before it

had progressed far enough to threaten us." Memo from General Leslie Groves, wartime commander of the Manhattan Project, in January 1946, cited in Marc Trachtenberg, "A Wasting Asset: American Strategy and the Shifting Nuclear Balance, 1949–1954," *International Security* 3, no. 3 (1988/1989), 5.

108. Robert Jervis, foreword to *Global Nuclear Disarmament: Strategic, Political, and Regional Perspectives*, edited by Nik Hynek and Michal Smetana (London: Routledge, 2016), xix.

109. For the importance of counterfactuals for hypothesis testing, see James D. Fearon, "Counterfactuals and Hypothesis Testing in Political Science," *World Politics* 43, no. 2 (1991), 169–95; Francis J. Gavin, "What If? The Historian and the Counterfactual," *Security Studies* 24, no. 3 (2015), 425–30.

110. The most convincing version of this argument was made by John Mueller, in *Retreat from Doomsday: The Obsolescence of Major War* (New York: Basic Books, 1989).

111. I explore these possibilities in *Nuclear Statecraft*, 57–74.

112. Gideon Rose, introduction to "Do Nuclear Weapons Really Matter?," *Foreign Affairs* 97, no. 6 (2018), 8.

113. Quoted in Joshua Keating, "The 'Toxic Masculinity' of Nuclear Weapons: An Interview with Beatrice Fihn," *Slate,* November 12, 2018.

INDEX

Index

Index

Index

Obama, Barack, 6, 173, 189, 220
Occupation. *See* Conquest and occupation
Offensive realism, 106
Offensive strategies, 19–20. *See also* Counterforce strategies
Openness mission, 76, 79–80, 90–91, 100–01, 104
Operational history, 192, 209–10
Opportunity costs, 68
Optimum instability, 203

Pakistan: curtailment of nuclear weapons acquisition, 38, 81, 91, 99; modernization of weapons, 173; nuclear strategies of, 34–35, 85, 87; nuclear weapons program of, 184
Partial Test Ban Treaties, 37, 89, 124, 179
Paul, T. V., 90
Pauly, Reid, 133, 213
Perry, William, 172, 183
Petrelli, Niccolo, 200
Poland, NATO expansion and, 124–25
Policymaking: grand strategic approach to, 224–25; historical scholarship and, 149–50, 168; international relations scholars' understanding of, 102; Iran's nuclear efforts, challenges for, 45–46, 74, 166; language of nuclear strategy and, 214; norms and ideas regarding nuclear weapons and, 18–20; nuclear studies and, 1–2; presidential history and, 211; rhetorical history and, 210; rogue and nonstate actors, 161; safety of nuclear weapons and, 47; secrecy of nuclear policy, 17; statistical analysis of militarized threats and, 54; for strategic stability efforts, 14. *See also* Academic influence on policymaking
Politics in light of international relations, 28–36, 102
Posen, Barry, 78
Post–Cold War era: containment and openness strategies during, 79–80; disarmament and, 172, 183–84; inhibition strategies during, 77; nuclear age and, 145; nuclear environment, stability of, 136–37; U.S. nuclear strategy, 143–44
Preemptive strategies, 19–20, 43, 76, 116–17, 119–20
Press, Daryl, 95, 219–20

Preventive attacks, 25, 80, 91–92, 161. *See also* Counterforce strategies
Primary documents, 54, 206–07. *See also* Declassified documents
Project Solarium, 115, 157
Proliferation Security Initiative, 37
Public mindedness, 149
Public opinion, 222–23, 224, 230
Pulcini, Giordana, 200

Quadripartite Agreement on Berlin (1971), 33
Quinlan, Michael, 213, 217–18

Rabinowitz, Or, 99
RAND, 201–02, 220–21
Rapp-Hopper, Mira, 161
Rational deterrence theory, 67
Ravenal, Earl, 202–03
Reagan, Ronald, 171
Resolve: challenges in measuring, 64, 71, 207, 212; nuclear superiority and, 51–53; policymaking challenges and, 47; statistical analysis of, 55, 57–58, 68
Retaliation capabilities, 25, 58
Rhetorical evaporation, 133, 213
Rhetorical history, 192, 209–11
Rogue states, 82, 136, 160
Rosenberg, David Alan, 20, 112, 211
Rovner, Joshua, 195–96, 197–98, 221
Rublee, Maria Rost, 89
Rusk, Dean, 37, 72, 84, 157
Russet, Bruce, 67, 68
Russia: geopolitical assertiveness of, 219; modernization of weapons, 173, 219; NATO relations, 110; as U.S. rival, 172. *See also* Soviet Union

Sagan, Scott, 23–28, 46–48, 76
SALT I and SALT II. *See* Strategic Arms Limitations Treaties
Sargent, Daniel, 18
Schelling, Thomas: academic influence on policymaking and, 19; intellectual history of nuclear age, 209; on nuclear deterrence, 28, 29, 53, 63, 163
Schlesinger, James, 60, 153–54, 210
Schlosser, Eric, 9, 171
Schultz, George, 183
Scowcroft, Brent, 87
Sechser, Todd S., 51–55, 57, 62, 73, 195